Femininities in the Field

Full details of all our other publications can be found on http://www.channelviewpublications.com, or by writing to Channel View Publications, St Nicholas House, 31–34 High Street, Bristol BS1 2AW, UK.

Femininities in the Field

Tourism and Transdisciplinary Research

Edited by
**Brooke A. Porter and
Heike A. Schänzel**

CHANNEL VIEW PUBLICATIONS
Bristol • Blue Ridge Summit

DOI https://doi.org/10.21832/PORTER6508

Library of Congress Cataloging in Publication Data
A catalog record for this book is available from the Library of Congress.

Library of Congress Control Number: 2017044014

British Library Cataloguing in Publication Data
A catalogue entry for this book is available from the British Library.

ISBN-13: 978-1-84541-650-8 (hbk)
ISBN-13: 978-1-84541-649-2 (pbk)

Channel View Publications
UK: St Nicholas House, 31–34 High Street, Bristol BS1 2AW, UK.
USA: NBN, Blue Ridge Summit, PA, USA.

Website: www.channelviewpublications.com
Twitter: Channel_View
Facebook: https://www.facebook.com/channelviewpublications
Blog: www.channelviewpublications.wordpress.com

Copyright © 2018 Brooke A. Porter, Heike A. Schänzel and the authors of individual chapters.

All rights reserved. No part of this work may be reproduced in any form or by any means without permission in writing from the publisher.

The policy of Multilingual Matters/Channel View Publications is to use papers that are natural, renewable and recyclable products, made from wood grown in sustainable forests. In the manufacturing process of our books, and to further support our policy, preference is given to printers that have FSC and PEFC Chain of Custody certification. The FSC and/or PEFC logos will appear on those books where full certification has been granted to the printer concerned.

Typeset by Nova Techset Private Limited, Bengaluru and Chennai, India.

Contents

Foreword		ix
	Annette Pritchard and Nigel Morgan	
Preface		xiii
	Brooke A. Porter	
Introduction – Issues in the Field: A Female Perspective		1
	Brooke A. Porter and Heike A. Schänzel	
1	Safety First: The Biases of Gender and Precaution in Fieldwork	10
	Jill Hamilton and Russell Fielding	
2	Negotiating Machismo as a Female Researcher and Volunteer Tourist in Cusco, Peru	23
	Jane Godfrey and Stephen Wearing	
3	The Married Life (as a Marine Tourism Researcher)	37
	Shannon Switzer Swanson	
4	'Dale Chica!': A Surfer Chick's Reflections on Field Research in Central America	53
	Lindsay E. Usher	
5	Early Motherhood and Research: From Bump to Baby in the Field	68
	Brooke A. Porter	
6	'Mummy, When Are We Getting to the Fields?' Doing Fieldwork with Three Children	84
	Antonia Canosa	
7	The Dissemination of the Feminine: An In-depth Analysis of Independent Travel	96
	Gisele Carvalho	
8	Gender Bias and Marine Mammal Tourism Research	109
	Emmanuelle Martinez and Catherine Peters	
9	The Effect of Motherhood on Tourism Fieldwork with Young Children: An Autoethnographic Approach	126
	Catheryn Khoo-Lattimore	

10	Subjectivities Implode: When 'The Lone Male' Ethnographer is Actually a Nursing Mother … *Lisa Cooke*	140
11	Icebreaker: Experiences of Conducting Fieldwork in Arctic Canada with my Infant Son *Emma J. Stewart*	154
12	Researching in a Men's Paradise: The Emotional Negotiations of Drunken Tourism Fieldwork *Ana María Munar*	170
13	Motherhood within Family Tourism Research: Case Studies in New Zealand and Samoa *Heike A. Schänzel*	185
	Conclusion – Gender: A Variable and a Practice *Brooke A. Porter and Heike A. Schänzel*	200
	Index	209

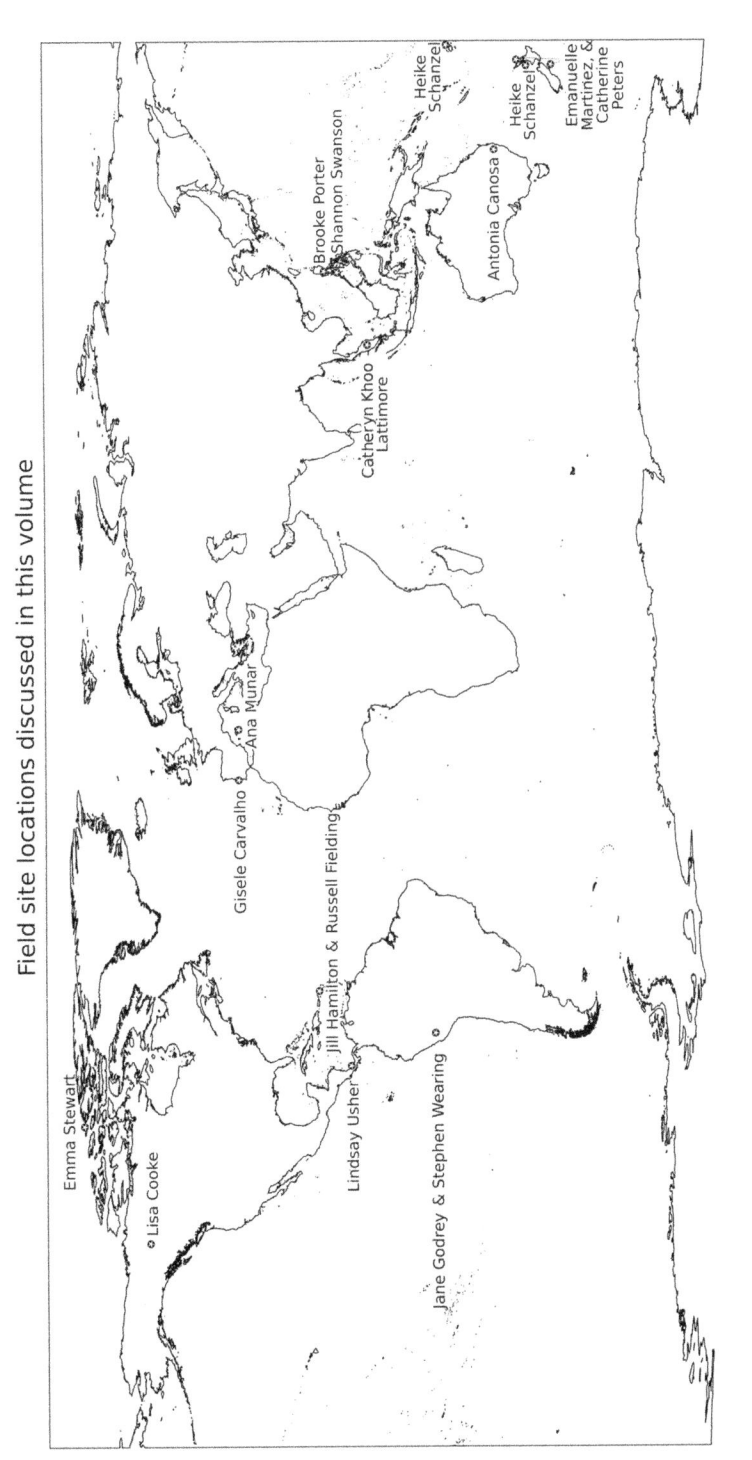

Field site locations discussed in this volume

Foreword

This is a genuinely grounding-breaking book, which creates a platform for new directions in tourism enquiry and in social science research methodologies. It is indeed a testament to the foresightedness of its editors Brooke and Heike and to the significance of its contributions that, now it has been published, it is hard to believe it took this long for a book of this type to materialise in the first place. In our opinion, it is one of the most important books in tourism studies, as it foregrounds and discusses how the researcher's positionality and especially gender shapes the research process from inception to writing. The book should be mandatory reading for every doctoral student, supervisor and ethics committee chair. It is compelling enough to hold one's attention from cover to cover but will also quickly become an invaluable aide memoire to be dipped into and consulted as researchers need guidance, a sense-check or reference point throughout their careers.

Together, the chapters of this collection provide a shared perspective about femininities as performed by female bodies, explore the factors and influences that impact on the female researcher in the field, scrutinise the ways in which we construct knowledge in the male-dominated worlds of academia, and lay down a baseline for comparisons for future tourism research experiences. The chapters draw on self-reflective analyses based on the authors' previous field experiences and span a variety of cultural and geographical contexts across Europe, Asia, Australia, Oceania, and North, Central and South America. Written in the first person, the cases are presented by the primary authors' ages beginning with the youngest and the experiences represent researchers in their twenties to fifties. The cases themselves are imbued with passion and deeply-felt sensibilities as well as practical reflections, raw emotions and candid contemplations, which rarely see the light of day in our sterile, formulaic academic writings. By revealing such transparency and recognising bias through ongoing reflection and re-examination, in this way alone, this book is hugely inspirational and transformational.

Gender continues to be a bias in the research process and arguably in the wider academic environment. Academia, so often perceived as a meritocracy and a driver of social change, remains a highly gendered sector exhibiting what some, such as Rosemary Deem, have described as a glacial pace of change towards gender equality. Men continue to dominate professional and senior research leadership roles and hugely outnumber women in the ranks of what we commonly refer to as the alpha scholars, a situation that has significant implications for the kinds of knowledge we create. While there is now much greater acknowledgement of the gender inequalities seen in individual disciplines and fields and measures are increasingly being taken to address them, high numbers of young female PhDs continue to leave academia – an outflow created at least in part by the lack of family-friendly work practices, expectations and demands, and perceptions that it is difficult to build a successful academic career and maintain family life. Women do not solely face these challenges, but women's working lives are more likely to be complicated by their domestic responsibilities and by societal perceptions of motherhood, which explicitly and implicitly challenge their suitability for promotion.

This book particularly focuses on how gendered practices, expectations and demands shape and impact the collection of field data, an area in which there is a literature, but one that is fragmented and largely written from a viewpoint that regards femininities as weaknesses. While the book's contributors do not discount that gender, either male, female or non-binary, may weaken or strengthen the research process, they explore the role of female researchers in the context of field access and experience. As the number and proportion of women continues to grow across all academic fields, so too does the number of women who combine reproductive and caregiving responsibilities with academia. This is a theme which runs throughout the collection and is foregrounded in several chapters. Brooke Porter examines early motherhood and research, Antonia Canosa discusses motherhood and fieldwork, Cateryn Khoo-Lattimore considers motherhood and access in her research with young children, Lisa Cooke reflects on her transformation from woman to mother during her fieldwork in far Northwest Canada, Emma Stewart describes how her infant son's presence enabled her to gain acceptance into Inuit communities and Heike Schänzel considers how motherhood influenced different aspects of her research career from scheduling to access and accompanied research in multiple field experiences. Many of their experiences of being 'in the field' as a mother are highly moving and make for emotional reading – itself something often seen as a 'contaminant' instead of an integral element in the research process.

A second theme within the collection is the sexism and sexual harassment several of the women experienced as researchers, particularly during their fieldwork. Surveys and studies report high rates of sexual harassment worldwide as our places of work, study and leisure (especially our streets and public transport), become harassment hotspots. This demands serious attention and yet the tourism voice has rarely registered in these debates, beyond some excellent work with hospitality workers. Not only are the spaces of the visitor economy precarious, sexualised spaces for both employees and guests, but there also remains an urgent need to scope, scrutinise and offer solutions for this pernicious problem within our own academic and student collectives. Recognising how fieldwork involves gendered issues of access and safety (Jill Hamilton and Russell Fielding; Ana María Munar), petty crimes and sexual harassment (Jane Godfrey and Stephen Wearing), sexual politics (Shannon Swanson) and confrontations of machismo (Lindsay Usher), this book reveals how gender influences not only researcher actions and participant reactions but also the very data itself.

In this and other regards, each of the following chapters explore different experiences and situations (both positive and negative) and while not generalisable, all those who conduct and supervise research (not just women) will likely find something in the book that resonates with them or makes them stop and think. Certainly, the focus on tourism studies does not limit the transferability of the cases presented and hopefully this collection will be followed by similar writings. Gender is neither a homogenous nor a binary concept and we need to know more about gender fluidity and the fieldwork experiences of differently sexed bodies and those who construct their genders in non-conforming ways. There is also an urgent need to consider how gender, race, ethnicity, class, age, sexuality and dis/ability combine to impact on research processes, practices and experiences. It is time to bring our humanity and its emotions and sensibilities closer to the centre of what we do as researchers; they can no longer remain marginalised in tourism (or social science) research and in the future perhaps we will regard this book as a key waymark on that journey.

Professors Annette Pritchard and Nigel Morgan
Cardiff, Wales
November 2017

Preface

Brooke A. Porter

This book began as an email reminder to myself a week prior to graduation, which also corresponded with the arrival of my second child, to consider a publication on the effects of infant 'research assistants' in the field. The idea remained dormant for nearly a year. It was at a conference in late 2015 that Heike Schänzel and I enjoyed a few in-depth conversations about women's access to research sites and participants. There, we informally agreed to co-author a research note on the subject. These conversations led to more conversations with other conference participants, many of whom are now esteemed contributors to this book. It became obvious that influential experiences in the field were being deliberately omitted by women not only from their doctoral theses but also from the academic tourism literature. From accessing participants and unsolicited marriage proposals, to increased research costs due to safety concerns and accompanied travel, gender has a significant influence on the field experience, or what Frohlick (2002) refers to as 'embodied entanglements that play out between our selves or subjectivities and our research sites, both before and while we are in the field' (2002: 50).

Together, Heike and I decided that the topic warranted an entire edited book rather than a brief research note. For me, this book is the guide I was looking for when my supervisory team 'nudged' me into the research field. Until recently, I have not labelled myself a feminist, though I have been challenging gender roles as long as I can remember. This avoidance of feminism has actually been an unwillingness to accept the issues surrounding gender, specifically the challenges faced by many women. Since the confirmation of this project, my focus on the subject of gender has been acute. Moving on from a gender blindness, I recognise gender influences everywhere. I came to realise 'that neither a gender-blind approach nor "add women and stir" was a satisfactory solution' (Bell, 1993b: 30), but what is needed is a 'feminist paradigm' leading to true gender scholarship also inclusive of the male voice (Schänzel & Smith, 2011) and gender diverse voices. I now share these observations and comments openly with others. Only through active engagement and open discussion can we bring light to the issues and find a way forward. For Heike, this is the book that she can pass on to her female research students and her supervising colleagues, as we all need to become more acutely aware of gendered field experiences. For her, it also means acknowledging potential biases in family tourism research and that accompanied research with children can bring real benefits for the researcher and the research outcomes. In short, we want this book to be a useful tool for all genders engaging in field research during all stages of their careers.

Introduction – Issues in the Field: A Female Perspective

Brooke A. Porter and Heike A. Schänzel

Dr Brooke Porter is an early career researcher in the human dimensions of fisheries and coastal environments. Her work explores tourism as a development and conservation strategy in lesser-developed regions, with emphasis on surf and adventure tourism. She is focused on developing simple and effective development and conservation strategies for coastal communities. Her choice to combine motherhood and doctoral studies meant that, to date, the majority of her fieldwork experiences have been accompanied. Previously overlooking these influences, she has now learned the importance of exploring and contextualising the effects of accompanied fieldwork. She has worked in various capacities with NGOs, international aid agencies and educational institutions on Maui, New Zealand, the Philippines and in Africa. She is a postdoctoral research fellow at AUT university and serves as a Scientific Adviser to The Coral Triangle Conservancy.

Dr Heike Schänzel is a Senior Lecturer and programme leader postgraduate in International Tourism Management at Auckland University of Technology in New Zealand. It had taken her 20 years in between having three children to finish studying and enter academia. She considers herself as a mid-career researcher with a particular focus on families, children and adolescents in tourism who draws on her own experiences as a mother travelling and researching. Her other research interests include: tourist behaviour and experiences; sociality in tourism; femininities and paternal masculinities in tourism research; innovative and qualitative research methodologies; and critical theory development in tourism. She is passionate about better understanding family fun (along with the avoidance of conflict) and the facilitation of sociality and meaningful experiences from the perspectives of diverse families within the context of leisure, tourism and hospitality.

Why Study Femininity in Tourism Field Research?

Femininity is defined as the quality of being female. The label 'female' is commonly accepted as one of two overarching gender categories, with the opposing category defined as male. There is, however, increasing recognition of gender diversity and a gender revolution (see *National Geographic*, January 2017) which sees gender as a spectrum, arguing for inclusion of transgender and non-binary, a gender identity that is neither male nor female. Gender is, itself, full of complexities. As Golde (1986) describes, 'even the perception of biological gender is not isolable but is intertwined with age, marital status, and other attributes' (1986: 88). Likewise, Turnbull (1986) describes these changings of self (often intertwined with sexuality) as a type of mobility through gender role ascription, but he also notes the potential for fluidity in gender roles even in a single field experience. As an example of role mobility, Nader (1986), in explaining her ethnographic work in Mexico, described the villagers' unrest at her short hair, button-down shirts and sneakers. Unable to categorise her by gender, the villagers decided that she could shift between genders. Nader used this to her advantage and as a result 'gained the greatest freedom of movement among both men and women' (1986: 104) as an androgynous or non-binary person. Complex or not, gender issues and gender influences on fieldwork are deserving of our attention. While this book compilation is focused on women, there is scope to expand the gender debate further in the future beyond binary categorisations. For the purpose here, and simplified to a biological context, a female possesses the organs necessary to bear offspring or produce eggs. However, noting the fluidity within (and perhaps between) gender identification, this book compilation explores temporal, spatial and social factors that affect and influence field research as an association of the female gender.

The word 'femininity' carries echoes of the feminist movements. We accept feminism as a call for equality. This book, though, was not born of feminist defence, nor is it meant to further postmodern critique (Bell, 1993b). Our call for equality is in recognising that gender issues in fieldwork are deserving of our attention. In doing so, we acknowledge that viewing the field as a masculine space is defunct. Therefore, this book aims to draw attention to the subject of gender bias from the female perspective by exploring and framing the female field experience within modern societal constructs. The cases explored in this text are discrete, self-reflective analysis of individual field research experiences that are communicated in the first person. The subjectivities of these experiences are intended to enhance reflexivity for future researchers who find themselves in similar field experiences or find their data have been subject to similar biases. This book compilation investigates gendered field experiences specific to tourism research and in doing so continues the traditions established by anthropologists and ethnographers. The foundations of gender issues in field research as laid by Golde (1986), Whitehead and Conaway (1986), Warren (1988) and others in the 1980s, are continued here and brought into the 2010s as the focus of inquiry into human interactions increasingly shifted to tourism. The intention of focus on tourism studies is not meant to limit the transferability of the cases presented, but rather it is meant to balance the tourism discourse in a manner similar to what Bell (1993b) describes as a feminist ethnography.

Tourism studies are, by nature, cross-cultural and cross-disciplinary. Given the diversity of the tourism field, it is likely that the researcher will, time and again, be expected to navigate a new field experience, be it conducting research in an unfamiliar culture, in a foreign language, or within a setting of foreign societal constructs. Despite the diversity of tourism studies, there has been little attention given to the issues surrounding the effects of gender on fieldwork other than an acknowledgement that reflection on gender identities are necessary for tourism researchers (see Phillimore & Goodson, 2004). In particular, there is a need to advance tourism discourse to the point where outward biases, such as gender, are an expected part of the literature. Despite the academy's general oversight or lack of attention to gender biases, the influence of gender is obvious in many fieldwork situations. As Golde (1986) explained, her experiences led her to a general conclusion that:

> sex role operated as a determinant of the topics of information I could discuss with each sex, the abundance of information provided, the difficulty in using direct questioning (inappropriate for a girl) as a means to collect data, and most important, the quality of interaction with members of different age and sex groups in the culture. More succinctly, being a female influenced in some degree who could freely talk to me, what they said, where interaction could take place, and why they were motivated to behave as they did. (1986: 89)

Perhaps we have placed gender as a fringe component of the research process, as extraneous to the data, or as potentially impeding to the career of the female social scientist.

As (social) scientists, the need to validate our data remains of the utmost importance. Why then, do we gloss over the effects of a bias as obvious as gender? Acknowledging, exploring, and evaluating the role of gender on fieldwork could serve the social sciences greatly by increasing overall transparency and validity within tourism studies. Gender, despite being an outward and identifying characteristic of a researcher, has maintained an androgynous role in print. Landes (1986), in her account of women's attempts for equality in anthropology, chose fieldwork over domesticity and a marriage proposal, stating, 'My Ph.D. had unsexed me' (1986: 122). Similarly, Macintyre (1993) noted that 'some women anthropologists assumed or were given the role of an "honorary male"' (1993: 47) as if that was aspirational for women. Androgyny has been a goal for many researchers in the field

(Landes, 1986) when socially and legally it is only debated now in Western societies. For example, an accomplished trans woman professor noted the difficulties of getting manuscripts and grant proposals accepted following transition to the female gender (which included adopting a feminine given/ first name; Alter, 2016). This more recent example of gender transformation along with academically enforced androgyny highlights gender inequalities but also denigrates fundamental markers of identity.

Biases are a fixed component of research. Yet, despite the ostensible importance of addressing gender as an outward bias, gender remains a liminal construct in the literature. The issues and effects of gender, instead, are disseminated more commonly as field myths (Warren, 1988). Gender issues in field studies have been recognised in the anthropological literature with an acute focus seen in texts from the 1980s and 90s (e.g. Bell *et al*., 1993; Flinn *et al*., 1998; Golde, 1986; Warren, 1988; Whitehead & Conaway, 1986). Yet, the literature discussing the effects of gender biases in tourism research methods remains fragmented, with an acknowledged female perspective remaining largely absent in research outputs. Multiple anthropologists argue that the accepted gender-inflection in the literature authorship continues to be masculine (Bell, 1993a; Frohlick, 2002; Karim, 1993; Keller, 1985; Macintyre, 1993), with those pieces addressing the feminine perspective viewed as 'special cases' (Bell, 1993a: 3). This observation also holds true for the tourism literature and tourism research which has been described as gender-blind (see Figueroa-Domecq *et al*., 2015). This compilation of chapters by international female tourism researchers acknowledges gender as an undeniable variable in the research process, particularly fieldwork. This focused attention to and identification of gender as a source of bias is not meant to divide the sexes. Rather, it is meant to suggest that gender, as a most outward, identifiable and influential variable, receives the same attention as any other potential bias (e.g. temporal, spatial).

Previous researchers have argued that women excel in fieldwork due to being more 'person-oriented; it is also said that participant observation is more consistent with the traditional role of women' (Nader, 1986: 114). Likewise, Mead (1986) presumed that women are more competent at fieldwork due to their inherent ability to relate to people, and tourism is inherently all about people. Warren (1988), reflecting on the social place of women, states that women's role 'in Western society has been to stand behind men, out of their sight: as mothers, wives, secretaries, and servants' (1988: 18). Traditionally, women have played a significant role in the household decisions 'taking care of the family's education, health and dietary needs' (Bennett, 2005: 451). When these 'traditional' gender roles transfer to the modern-day female academic experience, they may have considerable effect on the research, as constraints that apply at home are added to the field situation. Traditional roles of women also mean that female researchers might gain easier access when it comes to other women and their families and by extension their communities. The female field experience and resulting gender biases (both positive and negative) clearly influence research outcomes. Warren (1988) describes the embodied characteristics of fieldwork as a function of gender in 'size, shape, hair and skin, clothing and movement, sexual invitation or untouchability' (1988: 24–25). Similarly, Bell (1993b) adds to these characteristics: 'class, educational background, ethnicity, age, marital status and sexual preference', noting that 'woman' is anything but a unitary category (1993b: 33). Some characteristics can be easily altered, others less so.

The experiences of the contributors to this volume reflect not only issues of feminine visibility and invisibility or androgyny in the field, but also explore the negotiation between fieldwork responsibilities and the fulfilment of traditional gender roles (e.g. spouse, mother). These cases allow us to go below the surface of the female experience and gain deeper insights into what it means to be a female tourism researcher out in the field. Through these cases, we bring critical attention to important gender biases in fieldwork practices. The case analyses from around the world that are presented here raise awareness of the influence and bias that gender brings to tourism research. The individual experiences challenge the default gender-inflection currently accepted in the literature. The self-reflective cases presented in this text are meant to offer the reader insights into specific field experiences that can then be extrapolated to other research sites. This information has multiple applications to the research process. First, the attention to potential biases will assist the researcher in fieldwork preparation through the identification of potential gender-related issues. Second, the cases presented as self-reflective analyses of research experiences dissect fieldwork expeditions and offer suggestions on how gender issues and biases affected these field experiences. The results seek to improve the researcher's awareness of gender-related influences and biases affecting fieldwork and field observations, as well as potentially framing the data analyses. Finally, the contributors' experiences provide a baseline for comparison and reflection by researchers, improving transparency in the final evaluation of their data.

Intentions and Structure of the Book

The chapters that follow are experiential. The field experiences span different geographical locations covering Europe, Asia, Australia, Oceania, and North, Central and South America. Despite the lack of contributions about field experiences in African countries, the following case studies address the gap in the literature regarding responses to gender-specific treatments in the field in tourism. The contributions are based on self-reflective analyses of the authors' previous field experiences. These cases are infused with passions and sensibilities as well as practical considerations. As Kouritzin (2002) acknowledged, field notes are far from sterile. Yet the raw emotions and honest reflections jotted in our field notes are seldom reflected in published manuscripts. The intentional perceptive and emotive focus associated with a self-reflective analysis answer Kouritzin's (2002) call to introduce transparency and recognise prejudice through ongoing reflection and re-examination. In being reflexive, the contributors become bricoleurs who understand that research is an interactive process between themselves, the research environment and the participants requiring a process of 'getting entangled' in different forces and constraints (Ateljevic et al., 2005). The cases presented in this volume address many fieldwork myths (refer to Warren, 1988) that are persisting today, and transform these experiences from mythological and liminal into semiotic works. The descriptive accounts of gender biases aim to provide future researchers with the awareness needed to anticipate and respond to gendered issues in the field.

Through critical self-reflections, these case studies address subjectivities associated with, and those that supersede, gender. While the majority of experiences are uniquely 'female', it is our goal that the stories and self-reflected analyses presented in this book compilation will be of benefit to all sexes in every role within research (e.g. the researcher at any level, supervisors, instructors, ethics committees) in recognising the importance of addressing gender as an outward bias in fieldwork. In fact, two chapters are co-authored by male supervisors or colleagues providing an insightful contrast of gendered perspectives and pointing toward a more inclusive gender scholarship.

After a few failed attempts at grouping the contributions, we opted to organise the cases in this book by the primary authors' ages, beginning with the youngest. The experiences represent researchers in their twenties to fifties. The labels so commonly assigned to females (e.g. single, married, spinster, mother, grandmother) are not necessarily a linear progression, and these labels can, and often do, change as a result of circumstances. The chapters that follow are self-reflective case studies using first person narratives that analyse the role of gender in previous fieldwork tourism research by a collection of individuals each at different stages in their life and research journeys. Many of the contributions in this book stemmed from qualitative fieldwork in which people, groups or communities were the focus of the research.

The first chapter begins with accounts from the Caribbean Island of Nevis. Jill Hamilton and Russell Fielding bring forth gendered issues of access and safety as they compare their field experiences. The second chapter, co-authored by Jane Godfrey and Stephen Wearing, again delves into safety issues including petty crimes and sexual harassment from field experiences in Peru. Chapter 3, authored by Shannon Swanson, describes how being married positively influenced the sexual politics of her field experiences in the Philippines. The fourth chapter, written by Lindsay Usher, explores how gendered influences were revealed in the data and even in her own actions while surfing in Central America. Chapter 5 returns to the Philippines where Brooke Porter reflects upon being pregnant and later with her baby during field excursions. In Chapter 6, Antonia Canosa looks at how her role as a mother influenced where, when and how her fieldwork was conducted. Chapter 7 revisits research that explored gendered influences on travel in Brazilian women; author, Gisele Carvahlo, reflects on how her gender afforded her greater access to participants. In Chapter 8, co-authors Emmanuelle Martinez and Catherine Peters describe gender biases that stemmed from issues of social stereotypes (e.g. women skippering vessels) during their New Zealand field studies on interactions between tour vessels and marine mammals. Catheryn Khoo-Lattimore, in Chapter 9, looks at how her position as a mother influenced her research approach and access during research with young children in Malaysia. In Chapter 10, Lisa Cooke explores how her transformation from woman to mother during her fieldwork in remote Northwest Canada was a far cry from the characteristics of the usual lone male ethnographer. Emma Stewart describes the influence of her infant son's presence in gaining acceptance into and building trust with Inuit communities in Chapter 11. In Chapter 12, Ana María Munar revisits the role of her husband during an accompanied fieldwork experience on drunken tourism in Mallorca, Spain. In Chapter 13, Heike Schänzel considers how motherhood influenced different aspects of her research career, from scheduling to access and accompanied research in multiple field experiences in New Zealand and Samoa. Despite the different contexts and discourses of these contributions, each case highlights the various influences gender can have on fieldwork. Although gender identification remains more or less unchanged, societal constructs continue to evolve, and, as a result, the female field experience is one of adaption. Consequently, there is a general need to continually revisit gender biases in fieldwork.

Summary

The collections presented in this book focus on the influences of gender in tourism studies fieldwork through international case studies. It is a much-needed compilation addressing the absence of femininities in the field and presenting a comprehensive, multidisciplinary, and global approach to understanding women researching tourism. Yet, there is more to be gained than simply the influence of gender on the research process in various situations. The contributions that follow offer detailed accounts of fieldwork as an exciting element in the research process. Many of the field experiences revealed by the women in this book are highly emotional and make for affecting reading. These stories are meant to be soul searching and moving. The feedback we got from most of our women authors was that their chapter in this book was the hardest but also the most rewarding writing they have done in their academic career. So why has it taken that long to hear about their insights in the field when some of these research cases lie years in the past? Maybe because the individual stories of these women display

Figure 0.1 Multitasking. Co-editor Brooke Porter, reviewing field notes with baby in tow (four months old)

their passionate feelings about field research as essential, when, traditionally, academic work should be considered as rational, methodological, and dispassionate. Maybe as Caplan (1993: 19) suggests, males are either in denial of the need for a more reflective approach to research as 'this is an area which men have yet to take on board, or that many of them find writing autobiographically more difficult than do women'. Maybe women have always felt more connected to their loved ones and tend to struggle when not being accompanied on their research (see Figure 0.1 on the pleasure of combining research with the comfort of maternal love).

Many questions still need answering. Yet, undeniably, much can be gained from embracing the emotional and subjective woman (and man or gender diverse) as a way forward to not only gender treatments and gender diversity but also a more progressive academia. We, as editors of this book compilation, along with the contributors hope to be part of a passionate and emotional rebellion in the academic world that can provide us with a more authentic academic voice. It makes our biases clear and, more than anything else, it makes our work more honest and meaningful. Instead of perceiving academia as a bastion removed from reality, it might just make us more relatable and relevant.

References

Alter, C. (2016) What trans men see that women don't. *TIME*. See http://time.com/transgender-men-sexism/

Ateljevic, I., Harris, C., Wilson, E. and Collins, F.L. (2005) Getting 'entangled': Reflexivity and the 'critical turn' in tourism studies. *Tourism Recreation Research* 30 (2), 9–21.

Bell, D. (1993a) Introduction 1: The context. In D. Bell, P. Caplan and W.J. Karim (eds) *Gendered Fields: Women, Men & Ethnography* (pp. 1–18). London: Routledge.

Bell, D. (1993b) Yes Virginia, there is a feminist ethnography. In D. Bell, P. Caplan and W.J. Karim (eds) *Gendered Fields: Women, Men & Ethnography* (pp. 28–43). London: Routledge.

Bell, D., Caplan, P. and Karim, W.J. (eds) (1993) *Gendered Fields: Women, Men & Ethnography*. London: Routledge.

Bennett, E. (2005) Gender, fisheries and development. *Marine Policy* 29 (5), 451–459. doi:10.1016/j.marpol.2004.07.003.

Caplan, P. (1993) Introduction 2: The volume. In D. Bell, P. Caplan and W.J. Karim (eds) *Gendered Fields: Women, Men & Ethnography* (pp. 19–27). London: Routledge.

Figueroa-Domecq, C., Pritchard, A., Sergovia-Pérez, M., Morgan, N. and Villacé-Molinero, T. (2015) Tourism gender research: A critical accounting. *Annals of Tourism Research* 52, 87–103.

Flinn, J., Marshall, L.B. and Armstrong, J. (eds) (1998) *Fieldwork and Families: Constructing New Models for Ethnographic Research*. Honolulu, HI: University of Hawaii Press.

Frohlick, S.E. (2002) 'You brought your baby to base camp?': Families and field sites. *The Great Lakes Geographer* 9, 49–58.

Goldberg, S. (ed.) (2017) The shifting landscape of gender. Gender Revolution [Special issue]. *National Geographic* 231 (1).

Golde, P. (1986) Odyssey of encounter. In P. Golde (ed.) *Women in the Field: Anthropological Experiences* (2nd edn, pp. 67–96). Los Angeles, CA: University of California Press.

Karim, W.J. (1993) With *moyang melur* in Carey Island: More endangered, more engendered. In D. Bell, P. Caplan and W.J. Karim (eds) *Gendered Fields: Women, Men & Ethnography* (pp. 78–92). London: Routledge.

Keller, E.F. (1985) *Reflections on Gender and Science*. New Haven, CT: Yale University Press.

Kouritzin, S. (2002) The 'half-baked' concept of 'raw' data in ethnographic observation. *Canadian Journal of Education* 27, 119–138.

Landes, R. (1986) A woman anthropologist in Brazil. In P. Golde (ed.) *Women in the Field: Anthropological Experiences* (2nd edn, pp. 117–139). Los Angeles, CA: University of California Press.

Macintyre, M. (1993) Fictive kinship or mistaken identity?: Fieldwork on Tubetube Island, Papua New Guinea. In D. Bell, P. Caplan and W.J. Karim (eds) *Gendered Fields: Women, Men & Ethnography* (pp. 44–62). London: Routledge.

Mead, M. (1986) Field work in Pacific Islands, 1925–1967. In P. Golde (ed.) *Women in the Field: Anthropological Experiences* (2nd edn, pp. 292–331). Los Angeles, CA: University of California Press.

Nader, L. (1986) From anguish to exultation. In P. Golde (ed.) *Women in the Field: Anthropological Experiences* (2nd edn, pp. 67–96). Los Angeles, CA: University of California Press.

Phillimore, J. and Goodson, L. (eds) (2004) *Qualitative Research in Tourism: Ontologies, Epistemologies and Methodologies*. London: Routledge.

Schänzel, H.A. and Smith, K.A. (2011) The absence of fatherhood: Achieving true gender scholarship in family tourism research. *Annals of Leisure Research* 14, 143–154.

Turnbull, C.M. (1986) Sex and gender: The role of subjectivity in field research. In T.L Whitehead and M.E. Conaway (eds) *Self, Sex, and Gender in Cross-cultural Fieldwork*, (pp. 17–27). Urbana: University of Illinois Press.

Warren, C.A.B. (1988) *Gender Issues in Field Research* (Qualitative research methods series 9). Newbury Park, CA: Sage Publications.

Whitehead, T.L. and Conaway, M.E. (eds) (1986) *Self, Sex, and Gender in Cross-cultural Fieldwork*. Urbana: University of Illinois Press.

1 Safety First: The Biases of Gender and Precaution in Fieldwork

Jill Hamilton and Russell Fielding

Jill Hamilton is a Master of Environmental Management candidate at Duke University, focusing on coastal fisheries and marine conservation. From her earliest experiences travelling and conducting qualitative research in the Caribbean, she has felt the often-conflicting desire to learn and explore fearlessly, while also keeping her personal safety in mind. More recently, she has begun to consider how being young and female can both help and hinder one's ability to build trust, access information and balance opportunity and risk while in the field. As an undergraduate at the University of Denver, she examined the environmental and cultural aspects of marine management and tourism in the Caribbean islands of Nevis and Bonaire, and recently worked with Environmental Defense Fund to help develop conservation and management strategies for Cuban fisheries. At Duke, she explores community- and ecosystem-based approaches to marine management, and contributes to small-scale fisheries research at the Nicholas Institute for Environmental Policy Solutions.

Russell Fielding is an assistant professor in the Department of Earth and Environmental Systems at the University of the South in Sewanee, Tennessee. He conducts research on the sustainability of – and interactions between – food and energy systems in the Caribbean. He earned a PhD in geography at Louisiana State University in 2010. In the context of a small, undergraduate-only, liberal arts college, Fielding emphasises the value of providing research experiences for students through collaboration with Sewanee faculty as well as local NGOs, universities, and government institutions. His spouse and two small children often accompany him to field sites which allows for both the joy and challenge of combining fieldwork and family time.

When conducting fieldwork as a young woman, especially internationally or in an unfamiliar location, safety is often a concern. As a female, one is taught gendered lessons of personal safety, awareness and precaution from a young age (Superle, 2013), teachings which may subconsciously contribute to research bias, such as selecting interview and data collection sites based on personal safety, or choosing study participants based on perceived reputation or personality. A researcher's gender may also contribute to gaining varied levels of trust and openness from interviewees. This reflective case study explores the experiences of a young female student on the Caribbean island of Nevis, contrasts these experiences to that of a male researcher, and considers the biases that may stem from gender and precaution in the field.

In the summer of 2014, I found myself in the back of a colourful taxi van, flying down the winding roads of St. Kitts on my way to Nevis (Figure 1.1), the island where another student and I would be conducting research for our undergraduate thesis projects. She had come to look at the island's hydroponic farms, and I to study the area's marine tourism industry and marine conservation efforts, searching for ways that Nevis, and other small Caribbean islands, could sustainably manage their coasts and waters.

The driver, speaking in a strong Caribbean accent, was giving us a crash course in the islands' local dialect, a type of creole spoken in a small area of the Lesser Antilles.

'*Wa gwaan?*' he had us repeat, a huge smile spread across his face, failing to contain his laughter at our struggled attempts to copy the simple phrase. 'It means, "What's going on, what's up!"'

Figure 1.1 The winding roads of St. Kitts with Nevis in the background, its summit covered in clouds (Photo: Hamilton)

He dropped us off on a secluded sandy beach, and a speedboat soon arrived at the small wooden dock. 'You are Jill and Dani!' the two men aboard waved and called, wide smiles similarly spread across their faces. We smiled back as they pulled us aboard, handed us two local beers and sped off towards the lush, green island in the distance. 'Welcome to Nevis.'

Oualie: Land of Beautiful Waters

Nevis, like numerous other islands in the Caribbean, is experiencing a decline in the health of its coral reefs (Bruckner & Williams, 2011), a phenomenon that could threaten not only the area's tourism industry, but the livelihoods of local residents as well, many of whom depend on reef fishing for sustenance and income (Whittingham *et al.*, 2013). During my time on Nevis, I conducted formal and field-based interviews with stakeholders in the marine tourism, fishing and conservation sectors, gathering stories of Nevisians' relationship with the marine environment and seeking insight into culturally feasible ways in which the island's coasts and waters could be sustainably managed.

I had first learned about Nevis from my professor at the University of Denver, Russell Fielding, who had conducted research on the island several years prior. He had told us of the local Nevisian norms and the welcoming, hospitable culture we would experience, having us jot down the 'must see' restaurants and bars on the island and introducing us electronically to the few people he knew there. Through our professor's connections, we contacted a local SCUBA instructor, who kindly offered to let us stay with her free of charge during our time on the island – an accommodation that allowed us to afford travelling to Nevis on our tight research stipend, and to stay with an individual that our connections trusted.

Stepping off the boat onto Nevis' Oualie Beach, we were welcomed by a group of smiling strangers, all of whom already knew our names. 'The island is small, and you'll make connections quickly', I remembered our professor saying, similarly assuring me that my planned method of conducting interviews, a combination of snowball sampling and intercept interviews in the field, would be an easy feat in the small island community.

During my first few days on the island, I focused on meeting locals and learning who I should talk to about reef health, the islands fisheries and the history of marine management efforts. Many of these conversations happened organically, and people were willing and eager to share their knowledge and point me in the right direction. A list of repeated names began to emerge, and I was able to set up a first round of interviews from the suggestions I received.

Along with these beneficial connections and recommendations, however, came a different type of knowledge as well. A group of American scientists were conducting an annual assessment of the area's coral reefs, and having conducted research on Nevis in the past, had a good understanding of the island's local geography, culture and people. A few times after having conversations with various local men, I was pulled aside by female scientists and told to 'Watch out for him', or 'Stay away from him'. From conversations with these scientists, I inferred that I needed to be somewhat cautious of who I interviewed and where I travelled while on the island, and concluded that most of my interviews would be more safely conducted with Dani present, rather than by myself.

As a young woman travelling with another young female, both of us having limited knowledge about the community we were temporarily a part of, I viewed any precautionary information provided to me as a form of valuable knowledge meant to keep us safe. I took note of the good-natured advice I received, using it as an extra reminder that even among the welcoming, hospitable culture and the beautiful island views, I still needed to be aware of my personal safety.

A Gendered View of Safety and Precaution

The type of thoughts and interactions I had during my first few days on Nevis – casual conversations regarding safety and precaution – were not new or unusual to me. Starting at a young age, women, myself included, are continually encouraged to think about personal safety and employ precautionary techniques to reduce risk in public spaces (Superle, 2013). Frequent reminders from family, friends, universities and the media for women to be aware of their surroundings, take precautionary actions whenever possible and to avoid situations that may put themselves at increased risk result in daily, often subconscious, strategies that are used to stay safe (Silva & Wright, 2009).

Perceived risk, and the subconscious or conscious actions that women take to mitigate these risks, is a gendered phenomenon that may contribute to bias in fieldwork. From selecting interview and data collection sites to choosing study participants, female researchers may be more aware of possible safety concerns than their male counterparts, resulting in possibly biased approaches to data collection. Furthermore, as experienced through the aforementioned conversations with female scientists on the island, 'Women are more likely to be protected by their host communities, which in some cases ... can result in less rather than more access to information' (Warren, 1988: 45). Being more aware of possible risks may influence the level of precaution that a female takes in the field, compared to men.

Searching for a Local View of the Sea

Keeping the advice I had received in mind about safety on the island, I began my research. According to Warren (1988), 'Living within a society, or visiting one as a fieldworker, presupposes a gendered interaction, a gendered conversation, and a gendered interpretation' (1988: 10) – ideas that rang particularly true while conducting interviews on Nevis.

My mornings on Nevis were spent down at local docks and beaches, conducting intercept interviews with fishers as they prepared their boats for the day (Figure 1.2). In areas I knew well, or that had restaurants, hotels or SCUBA shops nearby, such as Oualie Beach, I conducted interviews alone, armed with a small notepad, a recording device and a stack of business cards showing my affiliation with my university. In more secluded areas, Dani joined me, helping to take notes or ask a few simple questions.

Approaching and talking to fishers, all of whom were male, never proved to be a significant challenge. I was often greeted with a smile and a wave, and a simple 'hello' was all it took to initiate a conversation. While flirtation from interviewees was something I experienced on several occasions, I found that as soon as I turned on my recorder and began the formal interview process, nearly all participants adopted a more serious tone, their view of me seeming to shift towards the task at hand and away from my gender, age or perhaps my whiteness – traits that may have influenced their initial willingness to participate.

While my concern for safety and the precautionary advice I had received may have limited my site selection and choice of interviewees, I found that the role of my gender shifted once I began actually interviewing individuals. When speaking with fishers, I felt that my gender and appearance – a friendly-faced, young female – was advantageous. I was

Figure 1.2 Fishing boats line Nevis' Oualie Beach, ready to be taken to the island's nearby reefs (Photo: Hamilton)

not perceived as a threat, nuisance or figure of authority, but merely an interested individual, passionate about conservation and coral reefs. As argued by Warren (1988), women fieldworkers are often viewed as 'more accessible and less threatening' (1988: 45) than men, resulting in increased access to the information sought. The information I was able to obtain from the interviewees was plentiful and easily accessible. Nearly all fishers were willing to share their personal stories of how the reef and the number of fish they caught had changed over time. We discussed the challenges facing Nevisian fishers, the knowledge they had surrounding fish population cycles and the biology of the ecosystem, and solutions that they believed could help the reef stay healthy and resilient.

As I had learned from background research and my initial interviews with individuals on the island, illegal fishing was widespread and problematic off Nevisian coasts, and posed one of the biggest threats to the area's reef health. Identified as a problem associated not only with the lack of enforcement of local fishing laws, but with cultural traditions, economic barriers and a general lack of education surrounding the consequences of overfishing, illegal fishing was a subject I knew I had to cover in my conversations with fishers. Transitioning from the flowing, easy conversations that defined the start of each of my interviews, I would eventually breach the topic of illegal fishing.

'What are the local fishing laws? Do most people follow them?' I would ask interviewees. The friendly, helpful answers that had previously been given to me would often stop abruptly. As interviews shifted towards more controversial subjects, any perceived advantages gained through my gender, age or appearance became less noticeable. Questions regarding laws and the legality of fishing practices on the island were almost always followed by a glance over the shoulder, an exchanged look of worry with a crewmate and a sharp change in the interviewee's stance and tone. On some occasions, interviewees spoke openly and candidly about how few people followed these laws, sometimes even admitting that they themselves rarely followed regulations. But on most occasions, these questions marked a turning point in the interview.

'Turn off your recorder', I was sometimes told, followed quickly by another inquiry to confirm that the interviews would be kept completely anonymous. Many interviewees glanced down at the business card I had handed them, ensuring that I was 'just a student', as opposed to a local authority or enforcement figure from the area's Department of Marine Resources. Many fishers stopped the interview completely, walking away before I had the chance to remind them that their answers were optional, and would be kept anonymous and non-identifiable. During one interview with a group of young Nevisian men diving for conch, interview questions were met with such aggressive verbal attacks that Dani and I, startled by the abrupt reactions from the interviewees, quickly left the beach, unwilling to put ourselves in danger by trying to diffuse the situation.

I often left interviews in the field, whether controversial topics such as illegal fishing were touched upon or not, feeling shaken and unsettled, wishing that I had been 'tougher' or 'more resilient' in the face of my male interviewees. While the openness and willingness to talk that marked the start of my interviews seemed likely a result of my gender or age, I often wondered how my interviewees would have reacted if I were male. If I had appeared less vulnerable and more able to defend myself against possible verbal or physical altercations, would they have answered questions differently, reacted less suddenly, or been less likely to end interviews early? Being female, should I have avoided controversial topics completely in order to avoid any confrontation? If I had not grown up with constant reminders of the need for personal safety, messages implying female vulnerability and the need to employ precautionary safety techniques, would I have been more willing to put myself at possible risk?

In his paper exploring illegal fishing in the Philippines, Fabinyi (2007) discussed the conversations he had with fishers during *tagay* sessions – casual drinking nights during which individuals would often openly discuss their illegal fishing behaviours. While I am unsure if equivalent gatherings exist on Nevis, it is hard to imagine a situation where a female researcher would be welcome at this sort of event. Twice on Nevis, when informally interviewing male restaurant owners or SCUBA operators over a beer at night, the conversation quickly became uncomfortable; the interviewee's comments and physical actions – touching my arm, back or winking – heightening my awareness of my personal safety and taking away from the focus of the interview. While I often wished to gain the type of insightful knowledge defined by the casual settings that Fabinyi (2007) described, I often chose to avoid situations of this nature, due to my gender and my awareness of increased risk.

Exploring Fishing and Tourism in a Formal Setting

As the tourism sector on Nevis continues to grow, an increasing number of hotels and restaurants are providing a greater market for local fishers to sell their catch (Nevis Statistics and Economic Planning, 2008). When interviewing hotel and restaurant owners, study participants reported that local restaurants do not enforce fishing regulations when buying from local fishers. Rather, they buy undersized lobster and immature conch, strengthening the market for illegally caught fish and contributing to an increasing decline in vital stocks.

In contrast to the challenges that interviews with fishers posed, the interviews I conducted with people in a pre-arranged, formal setting, such as offices, restaurants, hotels or departmental headquarters, lacked the safety concerns that were often prevalent in the field. Similar to my perceived experiences during interviews with fishers, I found that my age and gender put people at ease when I showed up to their offices. My status as a student gave me an 'in' on many occasions, and most people, including present and former directors of the Department of Marine Resources, the major of the St. Kitts and Nevis Coast Guard, and the directors of environmental non-profits, were extremely willing to share their knowledge in return for my eagerness and interest on the subjects at hand.

My interviewees from the tourism and conservation sectors opened up to me easily and without hesitation, several of them divulging their somewhat controversial opinions to me. A former director of an agency confided in me his negative opinions of how laws and regulations were currently being enforced; another non-profit leader chastised the government and political climate on the island. 'If you share this, just don't include my name', most would add after the fact, quickly jumping back to wherever they had left off in the interview, willing and eager to continue sharing their honest thoughts on anything I wished to discuss.

A Male Perspective of Nevisian Hospitality and Fieldwork

Russell Fielding, Assistant Professor at the University of the South in Sewanee, Tennessee, shares his experiences conducting fieldwork on Nevis as a graduate student in 2008.

'Drive on the left, this is British territory!' I remind myself as I steer the rented Suzuki 4×4 along the narrow, potholed road of Nevis' northern shore. Out one window I catch views of the Caribbean Sea – so blue it doesn't look real. On the other side, the land slopes upward and disappears into the clouds. About 3,000 feet up, through the thick jungle, past the abandoned sugar plantations and boutique resorts, is the top of Nevis Peak, the highest point on this tiny island.

I slow down and pull off the main road into the Oualie Beach resort area. The door to the SCUBA shop is open, as is the large shutter window, and I can hear laughter and a conversation spoken in that sweet Caribbean lilt coming from within. I walk inside and shake hands with Ellis A. Chaderton, owner of Scuba Safaris, the oldest and most respected SCUBA outfitter on the island. 'Everyt'ing good, mon?' he asks, 'what you want to know?' I've come to interview Ellis.

'You've been diving here for a long time?' I ask Ellis, a large man with a shaved head and wide smile.

Ellis tells me that he was born on Nevis and that he has been diving these waters since his teens. I ask him if he has seen a lot of changes in that time. I ask about the fish, about the lobster and conch, about the water quality. I ask about environmental protection and government policy. Ellis answers all of my questions while simultaneously handing out rental masks and wetsuits to the tourists who have signed up for his afternoon dive charter. Then I ask a question that really gets his attention: 'What about coral bleaching? Do you see any of that around here?'

'Coral bleaching? Yes, mon', Ellis says, 'we got plenty bleaching here.' I start asking him specific questions about the bleaching – which I learned in class can be related to climate change and is an indicator of the general state of the ocean's health. Ellis cuts me off: 'Mon, we can talk about the coral but why don't you just go see it for yourself?' He tosses a mask and snorkel my way and introduces me to Elvan, the dive master for the afternoon charter.

I protest: 'I'm not here on vacation, Ellis. I'm just a grad student. I can't afford to go diving.'

'No problem, mon. It's on the house. You need to see this', Ellis answers, and with that I join Elvan on the dive boat, along with a group of about eight tourists.

The dives are amazing. Yes, some of the coral shows signs of bleaching and I'm sure that the reef is not nearly as healthy, nor the water as clear or the marine life as abundant, as when Ellis started diving here years ago. But what colours! What variety of fish! What adventure! Since SCUBA is a sport that you never do alone, I swim with Elvan, the dive master, as we are the only two who came on board without dive partners. At a depth of about twenty-five feet I am sure I can hear Elvan, swimming just behind me, laughing and whooping with joy. I turn back and see that he is holding a thin piece of sea grass, around which a tiny seahorse has curled its tail. Behind his regulator I can see the corners of Elvan's mouth drawn up in a huge grin. Back on the boat, Elvan tells me that this was the first time he had seen a seahorse in the wild. It was mine too.

The dive trip is the most memorable of my many experiences of Nevisian hospitality that summer. The overall aim of my research on Nevis was to understand the state of local food production on the island (Fielding & Mathewson, 2012), and toward this end, in addition to viewing the reefs and the farms, my fieldwork involved talking with as many fishers and farmers as possible. Time and again I was welcomed onto porches and into courtyards, living rooms, and agricultural fields. A big problem in Nevisian agriculture is the presence of green vervet monkeys (*Chlorocebus aethiops*), an invasive species that the early European colonists first brought from Africa as pets. The monkeys now outnumber humans on Nevis and can easily destroy a season's worth of produce with a short session of snacking.

Perhaps it was my inquisitiveness, my whiteness, my gender, or my official-looking Moleskine notebook that allowed the local farmers and fishers to open up to me about their livelihoods and the challenges they experienced. In professional meetings I was, without exception, treated with equal parts hospitality and respect. Personally too. During that summer on Nevis I met and befriended many locals – some Nevisian, others American or British – and spent most evenings socializing at private homes, in beach bars, or even aboard a yacht.

But this was not always the way my fieldwork in the Caribbean went. For every day of free SCUBA diving, there was a night spent on the beach. I mean on the beach, as in, lying directly on the sand and trying to sleep there because I couldn't afford proper lodging. This was my method on several Caribbean islands including Puerto Rico, St. Barthélemy, and Isla Mujeres off the coast of Mexico's Yucatan peninsula. On St. Kitts I slept for free not on the beach but on the deck of a borrowed sailboat. On Cuba it was the open terrace of a train station.

A night spent outdoors naturally feels exposed. This feeling is at the root of both the lure and the vulnerability of sleeping out. To fall asleep to the sound of lapping waves, lying on a mattress of soft sand covered by a sarong is an idyllic postcard image. At the same time though, its reality requires an attitude of 'not a target' – or perhaps 'nothing to lose' – with regard to your possessions and even your own body. On St. Barts I awoke at dawn to the gradual realization that there were people standing nearby, talking softly in French. Turning slightly so as to appear still asleep I saw the black boots and long guns of the gendarmes – the military police force, which always look out of place on the beaches of France's many tropical colonies. Worried that I would be cited – or possibly arrested – for camping, which according to the sign was interdit (not allowed), I began collecting my things quickly to move on. Glancing back at the officers I caught the eye of one young, uniformed man who laughed as he called out to me, '*Bonjour!*' Then noticing my nervous hurry, he gestured toward my makeshift bed and added, 'Pas de problème!' Not a problem.

Before shifting my major research focus to the Caribbean I spent several seasons conducting research in the Faroe Islands of the North Atlantic. The back page of my Faroese field notebook is taken up with large block letters spelling, 'TÓRSHAVN,' my usual first destination after arriving at the airport. Rarely having enough research funds to justify the expensive bus ride from the airport to the capital (never mind a taxi!) I got into the habit of walking straight from baggage claim to the road outside the airport and holding up the notebook and a thumb. I was always picked up quickly and once my driver even passed the bus on its way into Tórshavn. Every experience with Faroese hitchhiking ended with me being dropped off in front of the

> door of the research station where I lodged with nothing more than a wish for '*Góða eydnu*,' or good luck, from the driver.
>
> When I reflect on the level of exposure necessitated by the simultaneous need to conduct overseas fieldwork and lack of financial resources, I'm surprised by the level of security I felt, given the situations. In locations with no prior contacts, limited language skills, tightly stretched budgets, and sometimes even a lack of lodging or transportation arrangements, I felt remarkably safe.
>
> Whether hitchhiking to my field site, sleeping on the beach, being welcomed into a farmhouse, or SCUBA diving with strangers, academic fieldwork has overwhelmingly exposed me to the welcoming, hospitable, and altruistic side of humanity. The occasional interaction with uncooperative government officials, potential interviewees who would rather not talk, pushy touts, hopeful drug dealers and pimps, or hearsay robberies – never experienced personally – turns my otherwise naïve view of 'the field' onto a closer path toward reality. I acknowledge the position of privilege that affords me this easy travel. My whiteness, maleness, and – at least during my years as a graduate student researcher – obvious lack of wealth must contribute to the overall sense that this person is 'not a target.'

The Biases of Gender and Precaution in the Field

Precautionary methods to reduce personal risk, such as continually being alert and aware of one's surroundings, avoiding isolated places and being wary of strangers – especially men – are a few of the many techniques that women use to stay safe in public (Superle, 2013). Often in the form of subconscious decisions or split-second reactions, an increased sense of fear among women and an increased focus on keeping oneself safe may stem from gendered lessons of safety taught from a young age (Superle, 2013), or perhaps the overall sense, to reflect upon Fielding's words, that women are considered 'a target'.

The effects of gender in the field, and the subsequent use of precaution, can be seen in many forms and in both a positive and negative light. The chance encounters often experienced in fieldwork, such as an invitation to go diving with local men or to spend time getting to know locals in their homes, may be less capitalised upon by female researchers than by men, as these opportunities may be accompanied by a greater level of risk. Additionally, informal interview settings, especially casual gatherings involving alcohol, may be less accessible to females conducting research alone. Methods to reduce the burdens of research cost, such as hitchhiking, spending a night in a stranger's home or sleeping out on a beach, would be similarly difficult to justify for a young woman. By employing precautionary techniques, female researchers may be limited in the breadth and depth of local knowledge they obtain, missing opportunities to expand their local connections in favour of safety. These factors may be heightened when the group of interest is predominantly male.

Conversely, being female may provide an increased level of access to information while conducting research, both in formal settings and in the field. While difficult to separate from the influence of age, student-status, friendliness or inquisitiveness, being female may increase one's ability to evoke trust and openness from male interview participants. In particular, male participants may be more willing to initially engage in conversation if the researcher is female, due to either increased trust or the influence of flirtation.

Although it is impossible to know if my experiences conducting research would have differed if I were male, my decisions on Nevis, from who to interview, where to conduct interviews and when to stop an interview, were undoubtedly influenced by my gender and my awareness of my personal safety. My heightened sense of risk, stemming from the inherent nature of conducting research in an unfamiliar location, conversations with female scientists in the community and the gendered lessons of personal safety I have grown up with, were sources of bias in my work.

It is important to note that the study of gender is not my area of expertise, and the perspective has been used in this chapter to reflect back upon personal experiences, raising ideas that may be relatable to others conducting fieldwork. Other young, female researchers may wish to consider the ways in which gender affects site selection, participant selection and interactions with participants in their studies, especially when fieldwork is being conducted in an unfamiliar location, unfamiliar culture, or alone. Cost-reduction strategies, such as hitchhiking or camping, are often not viable options for women, and additional funding from their universities should be considered in instances where female researchers may be burdened by the need to keep themselves safe. Universities may wish to provide additional training opportunities for young women conducting fieldwork, including ways in which safe, unbiased practices can be incorporated into research design.

Finally, while I was aware of risk and my personal safety, it is important to note that I was never hurt or harmed while conducting research on Nevis. My time was predominantly defined by the welcoming, kindhearted and hospitable people I met.

Since my time on the island, St. Kitts and Nevis has created its first marine managed area, including the designation of two marine reserves (Nevis Historical and Conservation Society, 2017). While it's still too early to tell if the country's marine management plans will be successful, I am hopeful and excited to follow the story of the islands that welcomed me with open arms, and left me transfixed, years before.

Qualitative research, including field-based interviews, is a powerful approach to finding answers to questions that may be missed through purely quantitative methods. While it is unreasonable to suggest that women put themselves at increased risk to reduce potential bias, it is important to consider the biases that gender and precaution may contribute to a study, acknowledging the positives and negatives of these biases and exploring the ways in which they could be managed in the future.

References

Bruckner, A. and Williams, A. (2011) *Assessment of the Community Structure, Status, Health and Resilience of Coral Reefs off St. Kitts and Nevis*. Landover, MD: Khaled bin Sultan Living Oceans Foundation.

Fabinyi, M. (2007) Illegal fishing and masculinity in the Philippines: A look at the Calamianes Islands in Palawan. *Philippine Studies* 55, 509–530.

Fielding, R. and Mathewson, K. (2012) Queen of the Caribbees: Farming and fishing foci on the island of Nevis. *Focus on Geography* 55, 132–139.

Nevis Historical and Conservation Society (2017) Marine Managed Areas. See http://www.nevisheritage.org/biodiversity-project/marine/marine-managed-areas/ (accessed 16 April 2017)

Nevis Statistics and Economic Planning (2008) Tourism. *Nevis Statistical Digest*.

Silva, L.C. and Wright, D.W. (2009) Safety rituals: How women cope with the fear of sexual violence. *The Qualitative Report* 14, 747–773.

Superle, T. (2013) 'I just really like walking, to tell you the truth': Gendered discourses of safety and danger in urban public spaces. Unpublished Doctoral dissertation, Carleton University, Canada.

Warren, C. (1988) *Gender Issues in Field Research*. Newbury Park, CA: Sage Publications.

Whittingham, E., Booker, F., Turner, R., Ford, R., Townsley, P., Cattermoul, B., Forster, J., Campbell, J., Morrish, N., March, J. (2013) *Reef Dependency and Change: St Kitts and Nevis Case Study* (Report prepared as part of the Future of Reefs in a Changing Environment Project). See http://www.force-project.eu/sites/default/files/WP2_St%20Kitts%20%26%20Nevis%20case%20study_IMMl.pdf

2 Negotiating Machismo as a Female Researcher and Volunteer Tourist in Cusco, Peru

Jane Godfrey and Stephen Wearing

Dr Jane Godfrey is an early career researcher and completed her PhD in Management at the University of Technology Sydney in 2016. She is a sociologist by training and her PhD focused on the commodification of volunteer tourism within neoliberal consumer culture using a qualitative case study from Peru. She completed a Master of Tourism at the University of Otago in 2011 exploring the motivations of backpackers travelling to New Zealand. Before this, she worked as an English language teacher in Germany. Jane is passionate about travel and has lived in five countries and travelled to nearly 30 more. She currently lives in Wellington where she works as a research analyst in New Zealand's public sector.

Stephen Wearing is a Conjoint Professor at the University of Newcastle (UoN). His research and projects are in the area of Leisure and Tourism Studies, with a PhD focused on sustainable forms of tourism. Stephen's early work was in the area of leisure and feminist theory with his mother Betsy Wearing. He has also made seminal contributions in other areas including ecotourism, and volunteer tourism and community development; the importance of community-based approaches in the leisure, recreation and tourism sector has formed the focus of his research. His practical experience as a town planner, environmental and park planner at local, state and international levels have provided him with real-world experiences that he brings to his teaching and research. He also co-founded and ran a volunteer tourism non-governmental organisation (NGO) which started in 1992 and has worked in nine countries on over 500 community-based projects, many of them with women's groups in small remote rural communities.

Introduction

There is a lack of research exploring the impact of the researcher's gender and sexuality on the research process (Clark & Grant, 2015; Kulick, 1995; Warren & Hackney, 2000). Data collection and fieldwork are embodied experiences: 'we present our own flesh to the other while we are engaged in the act of observation' (Warren & Hackney, 2000: 21) and therefore our gender has consequences for our research. Although often ignored in the literature, it is not uncommon for young female researchers to experience sexual harassment and objectification by local men while conducting data collection in developing countries (for example, Clark & Grant, 2015; Kloß, 2016; Miller, 2015). As Kloß (2016: 1) states, female researchers often describe these experiences of sexual harassment during data collection as 'rather common', yet the topic remains relatively unexamined within the methodological literature.

In this chapter, I explore my own embodied experiences of collecting data in Cusco, Peru. As the one who conducted the data collection, this chapter is written from the first author's viewpoint. In late 2012, I spent 15 weeks in Cusco conducting data collection for my doctoral thesis. My thesis focused on commodified volunteer tourism and consumer culture and I spent my time in Cusco conducting participant observation by becoming a volunteer tourist myself. I lived with other volunteer tourists and volunteered teaching English at a local community centre. I also conducted interviews with other volunteer tourists. This chapter describes my experiences of sexual harassment in Cusco and adds to the emerging literature focusing on raising awareness of the role of gender and sexual(ised) harassment during data collection and fieldwork. This chapter is based on my own personal experiences and observations in Cusco, and draws on in-depth qualitative interviews I conducted with 21 female volunteer tourists aged between 18 and 64 years. They are all referred to in this chapter by pseudonyms.

My Own Experiences of Sexual Harassment in Cusco

My first experience of sexual (or street) harassment in Peru occurred on my first day in Cusco. We had just finished orientation at the volunteer tourism organisation's office and I was part of a group of seven young, female, volunteer tourists walking to the community centre where I would be teaching English for the next four months (Figure 2.1). I was 27 years old and the oldest of the group, who were mainly in their early twenties. It was about 5:30pm and starting to get dark. I had been warned by both local Cusqueños and other tourists that the community centre was on a slightly 'dodgy' street; however, I felt confident the volunteer organisation would not place us at a site that was unsafe and assumed these warnings were somewhat exaggerated. Although away from the main tourist area, we were still less than a kilometre from Cusco's main square, Plaza de Armas, which is a popular tourism area.

Figure 2.1 Cusco streetscape

The street the community centre was on was only one-lane wide so we were walking single-file along the footpath. A man walked past in the opposite direction. As he passed behind me, he reached between my legs from behind, pushing his fingers in between the top of my legs with his palm facing upwards and his hand cupped so his fingertips poked into me between my legs over the seam of my jeans. While I have had my backside unexpectedly 'pinched' by men in the street in Europe in the past, normally this involves grabbing the fleshy part of the buttocks. In contrast, the man in Cusco grabbed right in between my legs, which I found much more intrusive.

This was my first experience in Cusco of this type of behaviour and I was somewhat stunned and unsure how to react. I turned around in confusion to look for whoever had touched me when another young female volunteer tourist who was in her late teens or early twenties and had been walking a few paces behind me suddenly started screaming and shouting at a man behind us; 'she burst into tears and said he had touched her in her "private place"' (Research diary, 7 August 2012). The volunteer programme coordinator telephoned the local police to lodge a complaint, although warned that she did not necessarily expect them to do anything. Many of the female volunteer tourists who were with me that day were put off by the experience and I was the only one who continued to volunteer at the community centre.

This was primarily because I wanted to teach English to adults and this was the only volunteer tourism project to allow me to do that.

While the experience described in the previous paragraph occurred on my first day in Cusco, fortunately this type of physical harassment turned out not to be a common occurrence. Instead, most of the street harassment I experienced in Cusco was verbal, including men making kissing and sucking noises and various sexual comments. I would often catch men of all ages staring openly at my chest. The female volunteer tourists and I experienced this type of street harassment on an almost daily basis. This behaviour rarely occurred in the main tourist areas, except perhaps late at night, but instead mostly occurred in the streets away from the main road where few foreigners went but where many of the volunteer tourism projects were located.

The streets around the community centre where I volunteered and our volunteer tourist house were acknowledged by both the volunteer tourism organisation and my local students to be slightly more dangerous than other parts of Cusco. Consequently, it is possible that perhaps I and the other female volunteer tourists staying at this house experienced more street harassment than those who stayed in other parts of Cusco. My local students, who were almost all male, often warned me about walking home alone after dark and would occasionally accompany me the 200 metres from the community centre to the volunteer tourist house where I was staying. Although no students ever did anything to cause me to doubt their intentions, in some cases when I did not know the student and we were the only two people on the dark street I felt more uncomfortable and at risk than if I had walked home alone.

Cusco is still a relatively traditional city and 'dress is generally fairly conservative and women rarely wear shorts, opting instead for long skirts' (McCarthy *et al.*, 2013: 541) (see Figure 2.2). Female volunteer tourists were warned at the orientation to avoid exposing their legs and upper arms and to never walk alone at night. I was careful to dress modestly, ensuring my arms, legs and chest were covered. In one interview, the interview participant and I were comparing our experiences of sexual harassment in Cusco. I told her about the one day I wore a skirt in Cusco:

> It was really hot and the skirt came to just below my knees, it was perfectly respectable … I was walking down the street and I could hear all these wolf-whistles but I couldn't tell where they were coming from and then finally I realised there was a truck going along beside me [slowed to walking speed] and it had like rubble in the back of the truck. It was like a proper truck filled with rubble and then there were like six construction guys sitting on top of the rubble just looking down at me checking me out.

This experience made me very uncomfortable and I went home to change into jeans. Like the other (male and female) volunteer tourists, I wore jeans, a t-shirt and sneakers most days in Cusco.

Figure 2.2 Typical dress of local women in Cusco (both Western and traditional styles)

The two examples of harassment described so far in this chapter can be referred to as street harassment and were relatively one-sided since I did not engage with the men or respond directly to their behaviour. However, there were other behaviours that highlighted the differences in attitudes towards women in Cusco compared to the post-feminist ideas that shape behaviour in the Western home countries of both myself and the other volunteer tourists. For example, we often visited local bars and nightclubs near the main square of Plaza de Armas (Figure 2.3) and became friendly with many of the local Cusqueños who worked at these bars and clubs. Some of these staff were employed to stand outside and encourage tourists into their club. These men, and they were always men, would often offer us drinks vouchers and we would often engage in playful negotiations to get more free drinks, pitting staff from the different bars and clubs against each other to see who would give us the most vouchers. The staff knew each other and these interactions were light-hearted since we were recognised as regular customers.

Often these men would put their arms around a woman's shoulders or waist in an attempt to 'steer' the woman towards their bar or club. One night, one of these men came up and started walking next to me, asking what our plans were for the night and whether we would be going to his nightclub. He put his hand on one of my buttocks and I twisted to shake him off. We were still walking and talking and he put his hand back on, and again I stepped away. The third time he put his hand back I laughed and physically removed his hand, telling him to 'Stop doing that!' although I kept this exchange light-hearted (see also Kloß, 2016). He seemed to find

Figure 2.3 Plaza de Armas (the main square of Cusco)

my objections funny, laughing and replying 'But I like it! It is a good thing!' with the implication being that I should find his unwanted touching a compliment. Whether or not this was sexual harassment or misplaced flirting is debatable. However, it was his bemusement that I was offended by this behaviour, and his refusal to stop even when I specifically asked him to, that highlights some of the cross-cultural differences in attitudes towards women and women's role in relation to men. The Latin American concept of 'machismo' is explored further in the following section.

While I have recounted three specific examples of my own experiences in Cusco, these experiences were common among all the female volunteer tourists I spoke with (although perhaps most common for those in their early to mid-twenties). The female volunteer tourists often compared stories of sexual harassment and negotiated plans with each other to avoid walking alone, especially after dark. Many of the female volunteer tourists also recounted their experiences of sexual or street harassment in their interviews. For example, a 36-year-old female volunteer tourist from Australia spoke of being assaulted by a taxi driver when going home one night alone:

> He offered to open the door and I was still fumbling around for money ... and next thing I know he's groping my boob and he's got my hands down his pants.

It is worth noting that this is one of the more extreme examples and that most of the sexual harassment the other volunteer tourists and I experienced on a day-to-day basis was not physical.

Machismo and Sexual Harassment in Cusco

These experiences of sexual harassment in Cusco are not unusual, with warnings issued to tourists in Peru that 'staring, whistling, hissing and catcalls in the street are run-of-the-mill' (McCarthy *et al.*, 2013: 541) and that sexual assault 'occurs frequently' (Australian Department of Foreign Affairs and Trade, 2015, para. 4). Dynamics between men and women in Peru differ somewhat from the volunteer tourists' home countries (Alyse, 2009) and this is particularly evident in Cusco and elsewhere in the more traditional Andean region (McCarthy *et al.*, 2013). Sexual harassment in Peru is not solely targeted towards foreign women, with one survey suggesting over half of women in Lima had experienced sexual harassment (Ojeda, 2015). Street sexual harassment can be defined as:

> Un conjunto de prácticas cotidianas, como frases, gestos, silbidos, sonidos de besos, tocamientos, masturbación pública, exhibicionismo, seguimientos (a pie o en auto), entre otras, con un manifiesto carácter sexual ... Las realizan hombres solos o en grupo. (Vallejo & Rivarola, 2013: 2)
>
> A combination of daily practices, like phrases, gestures, whistles, sounds of kissing, fondling, public masturbation, exhibitionism, pursuits (by foot or by car) amongst others, with a clear sexual character ... This is done by men alone or in groups. [my translation]

In 2014, Peru passed a law that made this type of street harassment illegal and it is now punishable by up to 12 years in jail (Ojeda, 2015).

As the guidebooks warn, 'machismo is alive and well in Latin America' (Lonely Planet, 2016, para. 1). This concept of machismo emphasises men's sexual appetites and women's role as objects to be used for (men's) sexual pleasure. As the mayor of Lima, Susana Villaran, has been quoted as saying: 'some men ... believe a short skirt or a low-cut neckline is an invitation to harassment'; this is connected to the idea of machismo and the belief that 'a woman's body is an object that can be appropriated' (Chase, 2014, para. 8). Rather than being driven by sexual desire, sexual harassment is a way for one group (that is, men) to assert their power and dominance over the 'other' (that is, women) (Kloß, 2016; Vallejo & Rivarola, 2013).

Although Peruvian women also experience sexual harassment in Peru (Ojeda, 2015), the harassment experienced by me and other foreign (white) women in Cusco is also likely because 'Peruvian men consider foreign women to have looser morals and be easier sexual conquests than Peruvian women' (Lonely Planet, 2016, para. 1; see also Brak-Lamy, 2012). While I do not attempt to excuse any forms of sexual harassment, from what I observed in Cusco female volunteer tourists often behaved in ways that could be deemed inappropriate by local standards as they conflicted with the traditional Catholic value system. For example, I often observed many female volunteer tourists (and young tourists more generally) heavily intoxicated and kissing their partners in public – both actions considered inappropriate by local standards. Many of the male and female volunteer tourists I observed in Cusco regularly engaged in casual sex with multiple partners (see also Bauer, 2007); these partners were most often other tourists, although many volunteer tourists also had sexual relationships with local men and women (Bauer, 2008).

These types of behaviour reinforce the locally held view that Western women are promiscuous and sexually available, and perhaps at least partly explains why local men objectified foreign women. The concept of machismo also applies since men are expected or encouraged to have a lot of sexual experiences, while women are expected to be virgins until marriage. Because local women are unavailable sexually, local Cusqueño men instead turn to foreign women. As one Cusqueño man is quoted as saying: you should 'have plenty of sex with tourists, then marry a good local girl' (Bauer, 2008: 621).

It is important to note here that sexual harassment from local men towards foreign women was not the only sexualised interaction between the two groups. Many tourists in Cusco have sexual relationships with local people and some local Cusqueño men report being 'hunted down' by female tourists who are attracted to their 'exoticism' (Bauer, 2008: 617). The concept of 'bricherismo' in Cusco refers to local men and women who make a living through developing sexual relationships with foreign tourists. Bauer (2008: 618) conducted research with 'bricheros' (local men who engage in bricherismo) in Cusco and found that these men believed that many female tourists (including volunteer tourists) were interested in sex with local men. Female tourists were largely unaware that going to a nightclub was interpreted by local men as advertising that they were 'available'.

More pertinent to this research project, Bauer (2008: 618) also writes that local men questioned the motives of longer-term volunteer tourists since they 'arrived for some supposedly beneficial project, yet, every night they were in the discos [nightclubs] picking up locals'. I spent many nights drinking at nightclubs in Cusco and although I flirted and danced with men, this was not a signal to all men in the room that I was 'available' for sex or that sex with local men was my reason for coming to Cusco – although based on Bauer's (2008) research it would appear that this was the message received by some. This would go some way towards explaining the reasons behind local men's sexualised behaviour towards me and other female volunteer tourists.

In addition to gender-based power differences based on concepts of machismo, Peru's colonial past has also resulted in a racial hierarchy reminiscent of that implemented by the Spanish 'conquistadors' where essentially the (white) Spanish were placed at the top of the hierarchy, followed by 'mestizos' or those of mixed Spanish-indigenous heritage, and finally 'indígenas' or indigenous Peruvians at the bottom (McCarthy *et al.*, 2013). Although no longer overt, in many ways this racial hierarchy still exists (Ñopo *et al.*, 2010), and is particularly prevalent in Cusco and throughout the Andean region. Sexual harassment by the mestizo/indígena Cusqueños towards the mostly white, female volunteer tourists could therefore be framed as a way in which the local men negate their supposed inferior status based on the racial hierarchy, and instead reclaim their gender-based dominance over the female volunteer tourists.

Experiences of sexual harassment against volunteer tourists are not unique to Cusco. For example, Vrasti (2013: viii) said she was 'repeatedly hassled, mocked, scammed, stared and shouted at' in Morocco, stating that she 'resented being treated like a walking dollar sign or a sex object'. Post-colonial theory suggests that tourists, including volunteer tourists, should respect the local cultural norms and values. However, difficulties arise when these cultural norms conflict with feminist theory which emphasises a woman's right to be free from harassment based on her gender. However, it should be explicitly noted that although sexual harassment against women is common in Cusco, that is not to say that it is condoned within Peruvian society (see also Buist, 2015). Paula, a 23-year-old Australian volunteer tourist, laughingly recounted how her friend had been grabbed in the street by a young Cusqueño man:

> [My friend] had some guy like touch her thigh, he was like a 20-year-old with his mum, and she [the friend] was like 'I'm not taking this' turned around and started shouting and him and told his mum, and his mum started shouting at him!

As noted earlier, street harassment is illegal in Peru. Any time I spoke about these types of experiences to local men I knew in Cusco, including my students and staff at the volunteer tourism organisation, they expressed horror and embarrassment that I had had such experiences in their city.

How these Experiences Affected the Research Process

The experiences researchers have while in the field, and the relationships they form with people they interact with, will shape and affect the way they perceive and interpret their experiences, and ultimately, how they interpret the data collected (Altork, 1995). My experiences in Cusco differ from many of the other examples of sexual harassment described in the literature, many of which come from the field of anthropology, since the people I was researching (the female volunteer tourists) were also recipients, rather than perpetrators, of the sexual harassment. Therefore, I was able to avoid issues other researchers have experienced when the sexual harassment is perpetrated by someone who is also a gatekeeper to the research process (see, for example, Kloß, 2016). Nonetheless, as explored in the following paragraphs, my experiences of sexual harassment in Cusco did impact the research process.

The volunteer tourists at the case study site largely operated within an enclave or bubble (Godfrey *et al.*, 2015), interacting mostly with other volunteer tourists and backpackers. The other volunteer tourists and I lived and socialised together and any interaction with local Cusqueños was largely limited to the volunteer tourism projects or occurred in public spaces such as the street or in shops. Therefore, my experiences of sexual harassment were largely confined to the context of the research, rather than directly impacting the data collection and analysis process. Due to the size of the city and its popularity as a tourist destination, people were not aware we were volunteers but rather assumed we were simply tourists and often treated us as such, expressing surprise that we had been in the city for more than a few days. This compares with other studies of volunteer tourism where the volunteer may be one of the few foreigners in a small village. Similarly, while local Cusqueños viewed the volunteer tourists as 'tourists', my role as researcher was also invisible (although the volunteer tourists, the volunteer tourism organisation, and my students at the community centre were all aware of my research project) and, therefore, I was also treated as 'just another tourist' (see also Garcia, 2015).

The most specific impact of the experiences described in this chapter on the data collection process was that I chose to leave Cusco a week early, thus reducing the period of participant observation from 16 to 15 weeks. Before arriving in Cusco, I had booked a tour from La Paz in Bolivia to Rio de Janeiro in Brazil following data collection. Originally, I intended to travel by myself from Cusco to La Paz, a distance of around 650 kilometres. However, ultimately, I chose to leave Cusco a few days early so I could travel with a male volunteer tourist who was travelling the same route. This decision was not solely because of the sexual harassment I experienced in Cusco, but also because of the level of petty crime.

Petty crime in Peru is 'rampant' and 'street crimes such as pickpocketing, bag-snatching and muggings are still common' (McCarthy *et al.*, 2013: 537). The Australian Department of Foreign Affairs and Trade (2015, para. 4) website cautions that 'armed robbery, muggings and car-jacking, occurs frequently in Peru'. During my time in Cusco my handbag was stolen and many of the other volunteer tourists were also victims of theft – some at knifepoint. One night, two local men slashed the strap on my handbag with a knife and ran away with it leaving me still wearing the handbag strap. One of my friends, a male tourist from Australia, ran after the thieves who responded by throwing a fist-sized rock, hitting my friend in the head. Taken together, these experiences of sexual harassment and petty crime made me hesitant about travelling to Bolivia by myself. I found the constant need for vigilance and awareness of my surroundings in response to both sexual harassment and petty crime to be emotionally and physically draining, noting at one point that 'the sexism in Cusco is getting to me a bit' since 'every time I go outside guys make sucking noises at you, whistle at you or just look you up & down' (Research diary, 19 October 2012).

Peru is a popular tourism destination and, like many other female tourists who visit the country each year, I had read the advice in guidebooks about what to wear and how to behave. Nonetheless, the possibility of the type of experiences recounted in this chapter did not occur to me when preparing my research ethics application from my university office in Sydney.

> Oddly enough, physical assault and sexual harassment weren't considered for the ethics approval but maybe they should have been! (Research diary, 7 August 2012)

While perhaps not common, other researchers have also reported safety concerns in the field as the result of becoming the object of (unwanted) sexual attention by local men; for example, being the subject of sexually explicit and threatening comments (Miller, 2015), being physically assaulted (Kloß, 2016), or even raped (Moreno, 1995). It is important to note here that while female researchers can be careful and behave in ways that reduce the chances of being harassed (for example, dressing modestly and not walking through dangerous areas alone at night), being the victim of sexual harassment is in no way a reflection of the researcher's ability to conduct data collection (Kloß, 2016).

Although I would hesitate to claim there are positive consequences to being sexual harassed and objectified, some of these experiences in Cusco arguably helped the volunteer tourists to develop closer friendships, although this may also have exacerbated the 'enclave' of volunteer tourists separated from the local community. The female volunteer tourists tended to avoid walking alone after dark if possible, and would often discuss and make plans to avoid having to do so; for example, leaving their volunteer project half an hour earlier than scheduled so they could walk as part of a group. This was in response to the risk of both sexual harassment as well as petty crime, although the male volunteer tourists did not seem to be as concerned and would often walk alone even in the early hours of the morning. As a result, the female volunteer tourists spent a lot of time together and also bonded over sharing stories of harassment.

These shared experiences allowed me access to the other female volunteer tourists in ways a male researcher may not necessarily have enjoyed. As well as my gender, my age meant that I had similar experiences to the other female volunteer tourists and these allowed me to better understand their reported (and observed) experiences of sexual harassment which, unsurprisingly, often negatively impacted their perceptions of the host community in ways the male volunteer tourists were not always aware of. As a result of safety concerns, I also spent more time with the male volunteer tourists than I would have otherwise. There was an implied agreement that when possible one of the male volunteer tourists would 'chaperone' the female volunteer tourists if walking at night. As a result, the volunteer tourists in our house developed a strong sense of camaraderie which further strengthened our bonds as a group. For example, in her interview, one 20-year-old American volunteer tourist referred to the other volunteer tourists in the house as 'like my family'. These experiences, and the sheer amount of time we spent together, helped me foster closer relationships with the other volunteer tourists which I believe resulted in a greater depth of data.

Final Reflections

I found this chapter very difficult to write for many reasons. Partly, this is because there is often an implied suggestion that having experienced sexual harassment or objectification in the field somehow diminishes my role as a researcher and therefore raises doubt about the quality of my research findings (see also Clark & Grant, 2015). While I write from a constructionist viewpoint which reflects my belief that knowledge is constructed as part of the research process, acknowledging that my research is influenced or affected by my gender could be framed as a weakness or shortcoming if viewed from the more traditional positivistic viewpoint that there is a 'truth' waiting to be 'discovered'. This hesitation has also been stated by other researchers – perhaps unsurprisingly, most of whom are also young and female. There is the suggestion or implication that these experiences of sexual harassment in the field would not have happened if I were a 'better' researcher (see also Kloß, 2016), although the fact that these experiences were common to all the female volunteer tourists in Cusco (except perhaps those who were much older) suggests there was little I could have done to avoid harassment.

Additionally, I hesitated to 'expose myself' by writing about these experiences and my reactions to them. In particular, I found it difficult to negotiate how much of my experience to share. In some cases, the harassment came from men I knew (and who were connected with the volunteer tourism organisation) and I have therefore chosen not to include these experiences to avoid identifying the people involved. I wanted to provide enough examples and details to describe my experiences in Cusco, while simultaneously withholding certain experiences that I felt uncomfortable sharing. More than four years since data collection, I have gained some distance from the experiences reported here; however, at times writing this chapter forced me to reflect on some rather unpleasant memories. I would like to emphasise that while this chapter focuses on the negative interactions I had with local Cusqueños, I also had many very positive experiences and, overall, thoroughly enjoyed my time in Cusco. I was very fond of my (mostly male) students at the community centre and still count many of the people I met in Cusco as good friends.

I also struggled at times with whether I was making a 'mountain out of a molehill', since other researchers have described more serious examples of sexual harassment. For example, one anthropologist (who wished to remain anonymous) wrote about being raped by her field assistant in Ethiopia in the 1980s (Moreno, 1995). While I have classified my experiences as sexual harassment, I acknowledge that my experiences with the nightclub staff member may have been related more to cross-cultural differences in understandings of appropriate touching rather than his attempt to 'assert his dominance' through sexual harassment or similar. What is considered appropriate, and what a woman interprets as harassment, may be culturally defined (Pryor *et al.*, 1997) and can vary from woman to woman.

It is important to note that this chapter is written from my own viewpoint and based on my own experiences, which, while perhaps common in Peru, do not represent how all Peruvian men behave. Some of what I found offensive and construed as sexual harassment may have in fact been the result of cross-cultural differences. However, in some ways the motivations of the behaviour are irrelevant since the focus of this chapter is how *my experiences* of these situations affected the research process. Rather than exploring the complexities of cross-cultural sexual harassment in Peru, this chapter instead serves as an example of the types of gendered experiences young female researchers may encounter during data collection and how these experiences may affect the research process.

When planning data collection overseas, researchers, especially young, female researchers conducting data collection in a male-dominated culture, should consider the possibility of sexual harassment/assault in the field, and have a plan in place both to ensure their safety and to deal with any potential 'traumatizing effects and challenging emotions' they may experience (Kloß, 2016: 5; see also Clark & Grant, 2015). While this chapter has focused on sexual harassment directed towards women, male researchers should similarly have a plan in place to protect their own physical safety and emotional wellbeing during extended periods of fieldwork overseas. More importantly, there should be an emphasis on avoiding 'victim blaming' and any physical or sexual harassment or assault while in the field, and any emotional reactions to these experiences, should not be framed as the reflection of poor research skills or ability.

References

Altork, K. (1995) Walking the fire line: The erotic dimension of the fieldwork experience. In D. Kulick and M. Willson (eds) *Taboo: Sex, Identity and Erotic Subjectivity in Anthropological Fieldwork* (pp. 107–139). London, England: Routledge.

Alyse (29 September 2009) Sexual politics and gender roles … make my head hurt. *Real Talk*. See http://gringarealtalk.blogspot.co.nz/2009/ 09/sexual-politics-and-gender-roles-make.html

Australian Department of Foreign Affairs and Trade (2015) Peru – Safety and security. See http://smartraveller.gov.au/countries/peru

Bauer, I. (2007) Understanding sexual relationships between tourist and locals in Cuzco, Peru. *Travel Medicine and Infectious Disease* 5, 287–294.

Bauer, I. (2008) 'They don't just come for Machu Picchu': Locals' views of tourist-local sexual relationships in Cuzco, Peru. *Culture, Health & Sexuality* 10, 611–624.

Brak-Lamy, G. (2012) Emotions during fieldwork in the anthropology of sexuality: From experience to epistemological reflexions. *Electronic Journal of Human Sexuality* 15 (18). See http://www.ejhs.org/volume15/Emotions.html

Buist, E. (30 January 2015) Men tricked into catcalling their own mothers: The video that went viral. *The Guardian*. See www.theguardian.com

Chase, R. (13 June 2014) Peru considers making sexual street harassment a crime. *Peru This Week*. See www.peruthisweek.com

Clark, I. and Grant, A. (2015) Sexuality and danger in the field: Starting an uncomfortable conversation. *Journal of the Anthropological Society of Oxford* 7, 15–24.

Garcia, P. (2015) In the name of the tourist: Landscape, heritage, and social change in Chinchero. Unpublished doctoral thesis. University of St Andrews, Fife, Scotland.

Godfrey, J., Wearing, S. and Schulenkorf, N (January 2015) Neo-colonialism and the volunteer tourist gaze: Commercial volunteer tourism in Cusco, Peru. Paper presented at the Council for Australasian Tourism and Hospitality Education (CAUTHE) Conference, Gold Coast, Australia.

Kloß, S.T. (6 April 2016) Sexual(ized) harassment and ethnographic fieldwork: A silenced aspect of social research. *Ethnography*. Advance online publication. doi: 10.1177/1466138116641958

Kulick, D. (1995) Introduction. In D. Kulick and M. Willson (eds) *Taboo: Sex, Identity and Erotic Subjectivity in Anthropological Fieldwork* (pp. 1–28). London: Routledge.

Lonely Planet (2016) *Peru – Women Travellers*. See www.lonelyplanet.com/peru/women-travellers

McCarthy, C., Miranda, C.A., Raub, K., Sainsbury, B. and Waterson, L. (2013) *Peru* (8th edn). Footscray, Australia: Lonely Planet Publications.

Miller, T. (2015) 'Listen to your mother': Negotiating gender-based safe spaces during fieldwork. *Journal of the Anthropological Society of Oxford* 7, 80–87.

Moreno, E. (1995) Rape in the field: Reflections from a survivor. In D. Kulick and M. Willson (eds) *Taboo: Sex, Identity and Erotic Subjectivity in Anthropological Fieldwork* (pp. 219–250). London, England: Routledge.

Ñopo, H., Chong, A. and Moro, A. (2010) What do we know about discrimination in Latin America? Very little! In H. Ñopo, A. Chong and A. Moro (eds) *Discrimination in Latin America: An Economic Perspective* (pp. 1–12). Washington: Inter-American Development Bank and The World Bank.

Ojeda, H. (23 April 2015) More than half of Lima's female population has experienced sexual assault. *Peru This Week*. See www.peruthisweek.com

Pryor, J.B., DeSouza, E.R., Fitness, J., Hutz, C., Kumpf, M., Lubbert, K. … Wang Erber, M. (1997) Gender differences in the interpretation of social-sexual behavior. *Journal of Cross-Cultural Psychology* 28, 509–534.

Vallejo, E. and Rivarola, M.P. (2013) *La violencia invisible: Acoso sexual callejero en Lima y Callao – Cuadernos de Investigación 4*. Lima, Peru: Instituto de Opinión Pública de la Pontificia Universidad Católica del Perú. See http://repositorio.pucp.edu.pe/index/bitstream/handle/123456789/34946/Cuadernos%20de%20investigaci%C3%B3n%204.pdf?sequence=1

Vrasti, W. (2013) *Volunteer Tourism in the Global South: Giving back in Neoliberal Times*. London: Routledge.

Warren, C.A.B. and Hackney, J.K. (2000) *Gender Issues in Ethnography* (Qualitative Research Methods Series 9, 2nd edn). Thousand Oaks, CA: Sage Publications.

3 The Married Life (as a Marine Tourism Researcher)

Shannon Switzer Swanson

Shannon Switzer Swanson is a published photojournalist, National Geographic Explorer and PhD student in the Emmett Interdisciplinary Program in Environment and Resources at Stanford University. Both her masters and current doctoral work focus on blending theory and practice from the fields of anthropology, psychology and ecology to address pressing marine conservation issues. Her work to date has been conducted as a newly married woman working without the accompaniment of her partner in the field and has focused on community-based management of marine resources in Southeast Asia and Oceania, primarily in the Philippines and Indonesia. She applies mixed qualitative and quantitative methods from both the social and natural sciences and explores new research methods using film and photography to engage community members as active participants in the research process and to further empower coastal communities to manage their resources in a way that sustains both prosperous livelihoods and a healthy environment.

Introduction

Mud oozes through my naked toes like molasses. Following the lead of the schoolchildren visiting from Korea, I have abandoned the cumbersome rubber boots that kept filling with muddy water and slowing me down. We navigate a tangled mass of mangrove trees, thicker in some places, thinner where local residents have harvested wood for charcoal leaving behind large swaths of treeless mudflats. We bob and weave under vines and over roots while being careful to keep our feet from sinking too deep into the mud, where a bed of sharp mussel shells lies. We push on in slow motion, hoping not to face-plant in the slippery mud, until we reach the designated planting area in this partially-restored mangrove forest.

At first, the kids hesitate, then a few of the boys begin digging. They wield their small shovels but quickly abandon them and use their hands. The girls flash peace signs at each other and snap photos on their cell phones. One of the girls decides the boys are having too much fun without her. She puts her cell phone away and begins digging too, bypassing the shovel, plunging both hands into the mud. Other girls follow suit. An onslaught of laughter and giggles rip through the forest. I snap images with my camera and jot notes but long to abandon these efforts and join the boisterous mess of planting. I feel out of place as a white, 30-year-old female, following this group of primary school students, acting as a paparazzo and note-taker – not an integral part of the scene but inserted like a fifth limb.

The planting continues, until I notice one of the girls lift a handful of mud into the air, cock back her arm, and fling the goo at her nearest friends. One of the boys fires back, and then all hell breaks loose. I try to protect my camera as the black mud flies in every direction. The mud is an equal opportunist and treats all of its targets the same way. I come out of the debacle covered head to toe; only my camera remains relatively unscathed. We all stand grinning at each other. We look ridiculous. Thanks to mud, the great equaliser, for a few moments I forget my foreignness, my age, my ethnicity, my gender. Likewise, the Korean visitors are consumed in the present moment and seem to have transcended their role as tourists to embrace the larger meaning of the mangrove forest – a communal ground. In this moment, I feel at home in the mangroves on the edge of a small fishing village enmeshed in the vast archipelago of the Philippines.

Feeling neither here nor there, neither fully part of one's own culture nor the culture of study, is as old as time, older than the furthest reaches of formal anthropology, when individuals from one clan wandered off into the bush to discover 'the other'. The famous French anthropologist, Claude Lévi-Strauss (1955), sums it up cogently:

> The conditions in which he lives and works cut him off physically from his group for long periods; through being exposed to such complete and

sudden changes of environment, he acquires a kind of chronic rootlessness; eventually, he comes to feel at home nowhere .... (1955: 55)

As a woman who studies marine tourism, among other topics, and employs ethnographic methods in my work, I identify with this quote while simultaneously acknowledging that it reveals how femininity has often been ignored in the field, with the male pronoun assumed as the norm.

Feminist and other scholars have argued that this transient experience can create relationships of unequal power in the field that are important to examine via thoughtful reflexivity (Peake & Trotz, 1999; Sultana, 2007). Equally critical is understanding this transient existence through the oft-ignored lens of femininity in order to conduct robust and candid scholarship. Such reflexivity requires a female researcher to understand her relationship with research participants, the integrity of her data collection methods and the details of her data analysis processes within the space of the position she occupies in the world. Reflexivity allows researchers to acknowledge the false hope of objectivity, clearing space to examine each of our implicit biases and recognise they are an inevitable and critical force that shapes our fieldwork.

It is in this spirit of honest research that I write this chapter on conducting fieldwork, as, not only a white, heterosexual, Caucasian woman, but as one who is married. Wedlock has its advantages as a researcher – first and foremost, in my experience it lends a cloak of neutrality. This 'cloak' has created a safe zone that has allowed me to interact with women of other cultures as a non-threatening female, and allowed me to develop platonic camaraderie with men. Yet, at the same time, I have found male research participants prone to sugar-coat their responses and be less direct with information to which they think I will be sensitive. In this chapter, I will discuss the unique research experience of working alone in the field as a married woman and the many nuanced effects of my positionality on the data I collect for marine tourism studies.

An Overview of My Married-Female Positionality

Although I am married, I have conducted all of my fieldwork, to date, on my own, without the company of my husband. Despite this, I have found that the symbolic act of wearing a wedding ring provides an invisible force field that communicates I am 'off limits' – that I am already committed to another person and I am proud to let everyone know about it, even though that person is not physically present. The simple act of wearing the ring (I wear a very plain and non-valuable one while in the field), in addition to telling stories and showing pictures of how my husband and I met, our wedding and our day-to-day lives, is often welcomed with great interest and excitement. Not only are people interested, but based on my experience in the field, my relationship status has provided an invisible barrier that sends the signal that I am a matriarchal figure and not a sexual object (e.g. Fluehr-Lobban & Lobban, 1986). The reality of my married status gives me comfort and confidence in the field. Much of the data I collect involves interviews and participant observation, and this positionality gives me a sense of autonomy and ease when interacting with research participants.

Because of the confidence it generates, I have found that my marital status provides a professional foundation for the relationships I form with a male, be he an interviewer, interviewee or informant in any capacity. Being married not only reduces any expectations that something romantic might arise from the relationship, but it has also placed me in a mentoring role. For example, male participants have asked me for help with their own relationships, because they see me as someone with marital experience (Fluehr-Lobban & Lobban, 1986). Perhaps I position myself as such due to growing up with parents who are marriage and family therapists. I was raised feeling comfortable talking about interpersonal issues and seem to unwittingly encourage this in others.

In addition to my married status providing an automatic layer of protection from unwanted male attention and objectification, in many of the countries where I have worked in Southeast Asia and the Pacific, being married is considered healthy for a young woman in that it complies with the social norm of women fulfilling the role of being a nurturing partner concerned with caring for material bodies (Nast, 1994). Because of this, when the topic of marriage arises, my status seems to put both men and women at ease, because they see this as right and good. Alternatively, I have been criticised for being away from my husband, and for not having children, as these are also predominantly seen as not 'normal' behaviours for a woman of my age at my field sites, and by being with the study participants instead of at home with my own family, I am breaching the field site's community norms (Fluehr-Lobban & Lobban, 1986). To illustrate many of these nuanced effects of my positionality on my research, I will look at a particular case study of research I conducted in a town in the Philippines known as Barangay Silonay, in the province of Oriental Mindoro. I worked with this community during the summer of 2014 and spring of 2015 to understand their perceptions of a mangrove restoration and alternative livelihood project, which included ecotourism components, implemented by Conservation International during the three prior years.

Case Study Background

Silonay, established in 1733, is thought to be the oldest barangay in Calapan City (Erasga, 2012) (see Figure 3.1). In 2012, Silonay was home to 1472 residents, 95% of whom were literate in the national language of

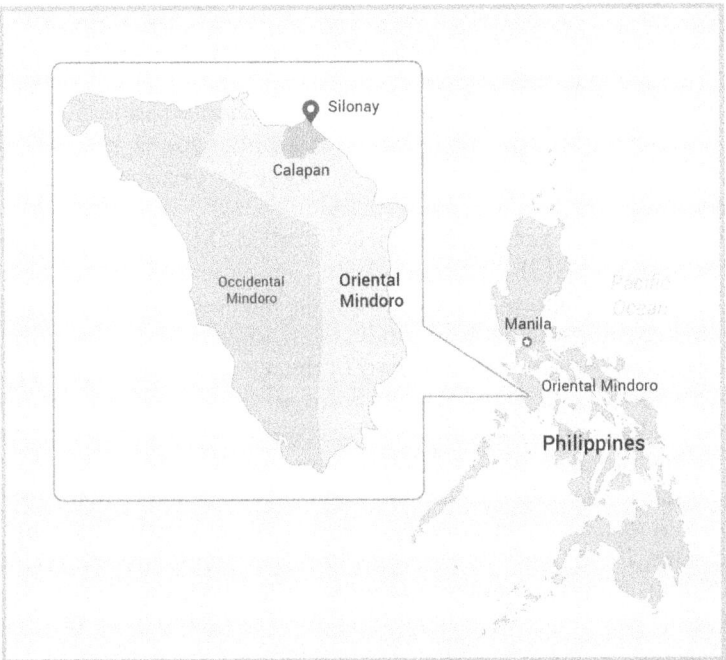

Figure 3.1 Map of Silonay. Map copyright Ben Swanson

Tagalog (Erasga, 2012). A socio-economic survey conducted by Conservation International looked at three categories of variables: socio-economic, governance and social vulnerability. The survey provided two particularly useful insights about the community. First, it found that about 70% of full-time fishermen reported a decrease in income compared to the three prior years; and, second, that 66% of respondents reported not earning enough income to cover their family's expenses (Erasga, 2012). Based on these results and others generated from a series of focus group discussions, key informant interviews, and group interviews, Conservation International concluded that both fishing and non-marine economic opportunities must be available in tandem in order to alleviate poverty and that these efforts must be decentralised and generated at the grassroots level (Erasga, 2012). This strategy of providing alternative livelihood opportunities to fishers, including earning income from ecotourism, aligns with other literature on the topic (see Pauly, 1997).

Accordingly, Conservation International began working with a community-led group called Sama-Samang Nagkakaisang Pamyanan ng Silonay (SNPS), training members of the organisation in mangrove restoration techniques, protected area monitoring, alternative livelihood ventures and the basics of climate change adaptation, including how mangrove restoration can increase protection from storm surges and sea level rise (Boquiren *et al.*, 2010). The members were then charged with spreading this knowledge and recruiting other Silonay residents into the group. In April of 2013, an official conservation agreement was established with SNPS obligating its members to oversee 25 hectares of mangrove reforestation with funds provided through Conservation International. Once that was completed, another 10 hectares of an abandoned fishpond were restored under a separate contract (A. Bool, personal communication, 8 August 2014).

As part of the agreement, officially called the 'Silonay Mangrove EcoPark Project' (SMEP), Conservation International provided training for alternative livelihood activities including opening and stocking a small shop and creating value-added products, in addition to paying members to plant mangrove propagules as part of the restoration effort. The intent of these efforts was to provide an incentive to stop felling mangrove trees for charcoal as well as to relieve fishing pressure by providing alternative income for fishermen (Pauly, 1997). Ecotourism was another component of the intersectoral income diversification to provide alternative income.

Interest in ecotourism as a conservation tool grew in the 1980s and 90s (see Young, 1999), but has received a backlash in more recent years (see Kiss, 2004). Today, ecotourism remains a common, though not always successful, conservation strategy (Oracion *et al.*, 2005). In the case of SMEP, ecotourism was introduced in two forms. First, in the form of visitors paying to plant mangrove propagules as SNPS leaders taught them about the importance of mangroves in general and to Silonay in particular. Second, in addition to this 'teaching forest' model, the community also built a boardwalk into the restored mangrove forest area that tourists can pay to enter and explore. Conservation International trained several younger members of the community as tour guides to lead visitors through the mangroves on the boardwalk or by kayak to draw attention to different species of birds and other fauna.

The first part of my study began in the summer of 2014, a year and a half after Conservation International initiated SMEP. In order to understand how residents of Silonay perceived the programme, I conducted 50 filmed interviews about their experiences with SMEP as part of a participatory research project. Prior to these interviews, I spent time in Manila at the Conservation International headquarters in order to conduct final preparations for the project. Here is where I will begin to unravel how my positionality as a married woman shaped my research.

Housing Options in the City

The positionality of being a woman, and a married one, affected each step of my research, before even reaching my field site to conduct the research itself. Although I had secured funding for my project, I was working within a tight budget. As a young woman, I was fortunate to be able to stay with the family friend of a colleague I had first met while living in Uganda. Maricel Santos (I have used pseudonyms throughout) lived in Teachers Village in Quezon City, which was very close to Conservation International Manila headquarters. While staying with her, I learned that Ate (pronounced Ah-tay, a title of respect meaning 'sister') Maricel was a single woman in her mid-50s, who often hosted young women at her home. At the time of my arrival, two women in their late 20s were also staying with Ate Maricel, and as we spent time discussing their work and career ambitions, I took comfort in their female camaraderie. Staying with Ate Maricel while in the Manila Metro area accommodated my limited budget and eased my traveling nerves before heading into the field. I would not have been able to stay with her had I been male. In this situation, being effectively 'single' in the field created space and time for this female camaraderie to develop.

Having this unexpected support and solidarity at the beginning and end of my research helped to punctuate my work in an unexpected way. As Golde (1970) highlights, the idea of needing to seek 'protection' as a women field researcher due to perceived vulnerability is an issue that arises 'even before the ethnographer takes up residence in a new community; it is first clearly seen in the reactions of the several worlds – academic, political, administrative – she passes through before arriving at her final destination' (1970: 5). Perhaps as a single or married male I would have found this via some other avenue, but the camaraderie I experienced at Ate Maricel's was unique, and something that arose serendipitously, based on my position as a lone female. This gave me more confidence as I moved to my field site and set a tone for the female relationships I was about to make in Barangay Silonay. I entered the site ready and open to meeting new people.

Relationship with Conservation International, Manila Office

Over the years, navigating interactions with male suitors who I worked with in various professional settings was a constant nuisance and something that distracted from and often degraded the value of my work. On numerous accounts, praise in various forms given by male colleagues about my appearance made me question the motives behind any praise I received, which should have stemmed purely from the merit of my work. In an attempt to thwart this unwanted attention, some women feel comfortable fabricating a partner. As an example, I observed this when I worked for several years as a restaurant server. My co-workers routinely wore fake wedding bands and had no qualms talking to guests about their fictitious husbands. I, on the other hand, was unconvincing at this game and cracked immediately. When I was single, I was open about my status when asked and fended off courters with other tactics. However, it was tiresome to be constantly on guard and aware of potential unwanted romantic intentions. This was true in many professional settings as both a researcher and during my time as a photojournalist prior to returning to research and scholarship.

At the same time as staying with Ate Maricel, I was working with staff at the Conservation International office in Quezon City. My first point of contact with Conservation International was the male office director, Kuya (a title of respect, meaning 'brother') Marvin. While being married is not an ironclad defence against potential suitors, the designation has seemed to give me more room to breathe in professional relationships with men. Men are less likely to wonder if our working relationship could turn into something romantic. Though not to say Kuya Marvin would have had anything but professional intentions were I single, being married gave me more confidence during interactions when working with him.

My married status afforded me confidence when I first connected with Kuya Marvin over Skype and continued after my arrival in Manila working with Conservation International staff coordinating research logistics for the field site in Oriental Mindoro. The rest of the staff I worked with were female, one in her early 30s with a young infant, one in her mid-40s and single, and one in her mid-20s and single. With each of these women, I felt that being married allowed me to relate to them in an empathetic way. I had been single for many years of my adult life, not having a serious relationship until I was 25, but now also could relate to the one staff person who was married. Even though she had a young child, I related to her – with a sense of awe in her ability to balance caring for her daughter and her work with Conservation International. Being able to relate to these women at different levels and meet them at their stage of life helped us accomplish our tasks, which included finalising the interview questions, translating documents, and arranging ground logistics at the field site, smoothly and with camaraderie.

Relationship with Interviewers

When we first arrived in Barangay Silonay, I was introduced to Grace Ramos, who was the treasurer of the community group, SNPS, and worked in a contract position with Conservation International on the mangrove restoration aspect of SMEP. Ate Grace was immediately warm and friendly, and, I would soon learn, a strong and hard-working single woman in her late 30s. Ate Grace was my main interviewer and gateway to the community. Both my age and my marital status made it easy to connect with Ate Grace and discuss relationship and family issues, as well as religious beliefs. Being able to have these candid discussions allowed me to be open with her when it came to conducting the interviews.

For example, I felt comfortable explaining to her how to be more flexible with the interview questions and to make sure that she did not speak over the interviewees, because it would ruin the audio on the footage. Our shared femininity facilitated rapport building, and made these interview arrangements easier to discuss and implement. This reflects what human geographer Sultana (2007) found in her fieldwork in rural Bangladesh: that though she did not share the same identity with her female research participants, her femininity enabled her 'to share affinities' giving her and her participants 'some common ground from which to speak' (2007: 378). Similarly, while power dynamics certainly existed between myself and Ate Grace, our common ground as females made them easier to navigate. Had I been a male researcher, the male-female power imbalance would have added an additional power differential creating important dynamics which male researchers have historically failed to account for in their research outcomes (Yeats & Prentice, 1996).

The other interviewer I worked with was Jay Andrada, who was a staff member with the Bureau of Fisheries and Aquatic Resources regional office based in Calapan City and contracted with Conservation International. We conducted interviews together during the weekends when Ate Grace had her days off. Kuya Jay was a few years younger than me and, because he had his own vehicle, was very helpful in showing me areas outside of the Barangay. Had I been a young single woman, I would have been less comfortable spending time with Kuya Jay, but I quickly learned about his long-term girlfriend and their relationship became one of the topics he most enjoyed discussing with me. This is similar to the experience of Fluehr-Lobban and Lobban (1986) who reported community members seeking their advice on relationship problems. Once again, being able to build this rapport with Kuya Jay translated to a working relationship when conducting the filmed interviews that was comfortable and easy. With the help of both Ate Grace and Kuya Jay, we were able to interview and film 50 interviews in two weeks – a feat I had been very concerned about completing prior to my arrival.

Relationship with other SNPS Women

In the Philippines in general, and Barangay Silonay specifically, within the first few exchanges after meeting someone, they would ask my age, my marital status, and whether or not I had children. This cultural forwardness about personal information meant these aspects of my positionality were immediately exposed. This was the case with the women who were closest to Ate Grace; they were also involved with SNPS and would spend time near the mangrove entrance on a daily basis.

Being married helped to position me as non-threatening to these women. It allowed me to interact with the men involved with SNPS without evident suspicion from the women about possible interests in their respective partners, something faced by women field researchers who have been perceived as sexual rivals by other women in the studied community (e.g. Cupples, 2002: 357). Women in the SNPS group once even asked me if I found Filipino men attractive. In general, I did not, but fearing that either an affirmative or negative response could be perceived as rude or suspect, I was able to answer that, as evidenced by my husband, who is 6'7", and of whom they had seen pictures, I preferred very tall men, and most Filipino men were not that tall. Everyone listening thoroughly enjoyed this answer. We laughed together, and at the same time I had been completely honest in my response. A comment about Filipino men being too short for my liking would likely have been perceived as an insult in the absence of reference to my physical husband.

Partially because of my inability to speak Tagalog, but also likely because of not having children myself, some of the women seemed to see me, at times, as a child. In fact, Joy Tomás, who worked with SNPS producing various value-added products among other tasks, would often order me around like one. Ate Joy was similar in age to me but had three younger children, the eldest of whom was 12. Each day I spent in Silonay, she would tell me to go take a photo of something or to come over and talk to this person. She even once told me directly that I was like a 'little child', because I always needed help, asked numerous questions, and only knew the most basic words in Tagalog. I think the fact that I had no children added to her perception of me as childlike, though she did not ever explicitly state that.

Ate Joy was also very attentive to my wardrobe. She would constantly comment on what I was wearing, sometimes saying things like, 'You are Pinoy, Shannon, you dress just like us'. This was when I was wearing elastic pants paired with a baggy t-shirt. One day, when I wore a more form-fitting t-shirt that was sheer with another spaghetti strap shirt underneath, she exclaimed that I was wearing 'a very sexy shirt' (see Figure 3.2). It was valuable to hear Ate Joy's uncensored comments, because her responses to my clothes provided a way to gauge whether or not what I was wearing was appropriate for the given context of Barangay Silonay. This scenario aligns with past observations that as women field researchers 'our bodies are inscribed, prohibited, or disciplined according to others' worldviews and interpretations of our bodies' (Falconer Al-Hindi & Kawabata, 2002: 113; see also Cupples, 2002; Nast, 1998). Attire and appearance are issues about which women fieldworkers must constantly make decisions, and, as documented by other female ethnographers, I have often attempted to downplay my femininity to appear as 'genderless' as possible in order to prevent unwanted attention (Cupples, 2002).

As women, clothing choice, whether we acknowledge it or not, sends messages to those with whom we work; especially men, who may not be as vocal as Ate Joy, but who may act on the message they think we are sending. Whether or not we choose to acknowledge our sexuality as women in the field, we inevitably become sexualised objects to members of the researched communities, and this objectification constrains our research in often unpredictable ways (Cupples, 2002; Morton, 1995). For me, avoiding this sexualisation has been a very tangible and ever-present concern.

Figure 3.2 Riding in the back of a tricycle in my 'sexy' shirt

This was true during my work in Silonay, in which I was constantly assessing how the community perceived me both intellectually and physically.

Because of Ate Joy's vocal opinion of my wardrobe, I knew where I stood on dress. If she did not seem to take notice of me, I knew that I was dressing within 'pinoy' norms. If she took notice of my attire, I knew not to wear the same item of clothing again. Ate Joy's comments were very useful in gauging whether or not what I was wearing might be a distraction, not just for the male interviewees and my male translator, but also for the women, who might be concerned about my revealing or 'sexy' dress.

Besides my dress, the women of the SNPS group were endlessly interested in my husband. What he did, what he sounded like, what I liked about him. They demanded he come visit, so they could meet him. This inquisition about my husband was a nice diversion from attention directly aimed at me. It was as if knowing that I had a husband back home who loved me, and that I was not wandering the world like a rootless soul, comforted them. Being married seemed to make me more relatable and less of an outsider, because it fit within the cultural views of the residents of Barangay Silonay. In other words, through sharing our values of family, we were able to share common ground based on overlapping affinities (Haraway, 1991; Nagar & Raju, 2003; Sultana, 2007).

Relationship with Interviewees

The interviews I conducted with the help of Ate Grace and Kuya Jay were semi-structured. A notable difference between my relationships with the SNPS women and those with the interviewees was that most of the interviewees did not ask about my marital status. This left these interviewees to make assumptions about my marital and familial status to which I would never be privvy. It is likely that both the knowledge of my status (for those who asked) and the unspoken assumptions about it affected the data. Researchers have gathered evidence through empirical work showing that the more visible attributes of sex, age and race can trigger different emotional and cultural biases affecting responses even during brief interview encounters (Herod, 1993; see Hyman *et al.*, 1954; Turner & Martin, 1984). In an attempt to neutralise potential gender response bias of interviewees, 25 women and 25 men were interviewed, thus providing a tool for comparison between the two groups.

Although I did not realise it at the time, looking back, I can say that my positionality as a female likely shaped the interview questions. I initially developed the interview questions on my own. Conservation International staff (who were all women, except for one) later reviewed the questions, yet provided minimal input. In revisiting the interview instrument, it is apparent that the questions were emotive and would have differed if developed by a male researcher. For example, each interview began with questions about what the interviewee liked about Silonay in general, what their hopes and wishes were for themselves and their family, and what they wished for Silonay. This relational line of questioning aligns with Nast's observations of the 'fundamental lived differences in the socio-spatial organisation of women's and men's lives' (Nast, 1994: 54); essentially, that my femininity shapes my approach to knowing, which in turn shapes how I approach qualitative data gathering. I believe this relational questioning revealed nuanced insights that may otherwise have been overlooked by a male researcher. For example, we learned that there was a common desire for Silonay to be well known for how well it cares for its nature – a sentiment that may have been difficult to determine from less emotive lines of questioning. At the time of the interviews, I recognised that these were 'non-traditional' interview questions in the sense that they did not seek to answer a specific question about the project but to provide context for how the interviewees perceived their home. However, when creating and asking these questions, I did not explicitly acknowledge that my positionality as a woman, nor my femininity, had inherently shaped these questions.

The next set of questions was fisheries-related. These included questions about how involved the interviewee was in fisheries activities, if he/she earned enough money from fishing, if he/she knew how the fishery was managed, and if he/she was familiar with fisheries-related laws. With this set of questions in particular, I believe that the male respondents might have engaged in more detailed and answered in more depth had I been a man (Aries, 1976; Herod, 1993), and especially another fisherman. When fisheries-related questions were posed to women, despite their direct involvement in the fishery (e.g. selling catch at market), many did not seem to feel they had the authority to speak on the subject. This was true both when women participants were in the presence of only women (myself and Ate Grace), and in cases where genders were mixed (myself and Kuya Jay) (refer to Figure 3.3).

We then moved to questions related to the ecotourism that the community had recently started in the mangrove area, which included youth groups from church organisations and classrooms paying to plant mangroves and other visitors touring the mangrove area by kayak or boardwalk. We asked how the interviewee felt about having visitors in their home, and how they felt ecotourism was impacting their barangay, city, and province. We also asked for any suggestions they might have for implementing new ecotourism activities in Silonay. Interviewees overwhelmingly responded positively to the tourism questions, stating that they loved to welcome and share their home with visitors. It is quite possible that my position as both an outsider and a female may have influenced these responses. The former, in that interviewees might have wanted to be polite and make me feel comfortable and the latter, in that they perceived me as a non-threat. Perhaps if I were a man, this response could have been less positive on the whole. However, it is important to recognise

Figure 3.3 Filming an interview with a female participant while Ate Grace asks the questions

that in this case gender may have played a minimal role in generating positive responses for our tourism questions, due to the well-documented cultural norm of Filipinos' saying 'yes', when they often mean 'no' in order to minimise conflict and to save face (Roces & Roces, 2009).

The final set of questions involved asking about climate change and climate adaptation. These included questions regarding how much respondents knew about climate change and what it meant to them, how they felt they had been affected by climate change, what they have done to address climate change, and if they thought the mangrove restoration project had changed their well-being and the well-being of their community. These questions elicited more in-depth responses, on the whole, from women, some of whom shared stories of emotional experiences they faced during typhoons including personal loss and physical destruction. Our male respondents did not talk about climate change in conjunction with this narrative of personal loss. As with the fisheries-related questions, had respondents been solely in the presence of men when they were asked these questions, it is possible that male respondents may have given lengthier and more in-depth responses. Overall, the main data collected for this project were in the form of these filmed interviews. Looking back, there are many ways that my femininity, as well as the positionality of my translators, could have been affected by both male and female participants.

Addressing the Biases

At the time of writing papers based on this research, it did not occur to me to include explicit statements about my positionality as a married woman and how this may have biased my results. However, in the write-ups I did state how the potential bias that my perceived affiliation with Conservation International and the affiliation of my translators with Conservation International may have hindered candid responses from the interviewees. Indeed, the fact that both translators were contract employees for Conservation International and one was heavily involved with SNPS may have skewed the interview data and resulting film. The interviewer affiliation with Conservation International may have caused interviewees to portray a more positive picture of the project than they otherwise might have. However, it is interesting to note that considering my femininity in this statement of positionality never crossed my mind. At the time of this research, I was not aware of the growing body of literature examining gender and how it influences data collection and analysis.

After reflecting on my femininity and how it likely shaped my research outcomes in Silonay, I have a new appreciation of the integral role my 'femaleness' plays in my work. Each layer of my femininity – being a woman, a married woman and a married woman working alone – shaped the data I collected in subtle ways and had both positive effects, such as eliciting more emotive and thorough responses from women, and drawbacks, including evoking stereotypes that affected male responses. The many facets of my femininity shape how I move through the world, and shaped how I moved through the various stages of this research project even prior to setting foot in the field.

One thing is certain and has been shown time and again: we all carry a particular positionality, of which femininity and masculinity is a part, that affects how we perceive information that we collect, as well as the perception of our research participants, and those very real conditions subtly affect the outcomes of our research (Emerson *et al.*, 2011). However, far from invalidating the research, these gender-related perceptions and biases give meaning to our outcomes and often reveal particular slices of context and nuance that another researcher with different positionality would never be able to access. As we continue to grapple with our femininity in the field, it is important to remember that 'gender relations are dynamic processes, not static categories, and the ways they shape the research process change over time and in space' (Herod, 1993: 313). Therefore, we, as women field researchers, must remain committed to constantly acknowledging and engaging with our femininity in order to continue conducting relevant research with meaningful outcomes.

References

Aries, E. (1976) Interaction patterns and themes of male, female, and mixed groups. *Small Group Behavior* 7 (1), 7–18.

Boquiren, R., Di Carlo, G. and Quibilan, M.C. (2010) *Climate Change Vulnerability Assessment of the Verde Island Passage, Philippines*. Arlington, VA: Conservation International.

Cupples, J. (2002) The field as a landscape of desire: Sex and sexuality in geographical fieldwork. *Area* 34, 382–390. doi: 10.1111/1475-4762.00095.

Emerson, R., Fretz, R. and Shaw, L. (2011) *Writing Ethnographic Fieldnotes*. Chicago, IL: The University of Chicago Press.

Erasga, D. (2012) *Socio-economic Baseline of Barangay Silonay*. Capalan City: Conservation International.

Falconer Al-Hindi, K. and Kawabata, H. (2002) Towards a more fully reflexive feminist geography. In P. Moss (ed.) *Feminist Geography in Practice: Research and Methods* (pp. 103–115). Oxford and Massachusetts: Blackwell.

Fluehr-Lobban, C. and Lobban, R. (1986) Families, gender, and methodologies in the Sudan. In A. Whitehead and M.E. Conaway (eds) *Self, Sex, and Gender in Cross-cultural Fieldwork* (pp. 182–196). Urbana: University of Illinois Press.

Golde, P. (1970) *Women in the Field: Anthropological Experiences*. Berkley, CA: University of California Press.

Haraway, D. (1991) *Simians, Cyborgs, and Women: The Reinvention of Nature*. New York, NY: Routledge.

Herod, A. (1993) Gender issues in the use of interviewing as a research method. *Professional Geographer* 45, 305–317.

Hyman, H.H., Cobb, W.J., Feldman, J.J., Hart, C.W. and Stember, C.H. (1954) *Interviewing in Social Research*. Chicago: Unveristy of Chicago Press.

Kiss, A. (2004) Is community-based ecotourism a good use of biodiversity conservation funds? *Trends in Ecology and Evolution* 19, 232–237. doi: 10.1016/j.tree.2004.03.010.

Lévi-Strauss, C. (1955) *Tristes Tropiques*. London: Penguin Books.

Morton, H. (1995) My chastity belt: Avoiding seduction in Tonga. In D. Kulick and M. Willson (eds) *Taboo: Sex, Identity and Erotic Subjectivity in Anthropological Fieldwork* (pp. 168–185). London: Routledge.

Nagar, R. and Raju, S. (2003) Women, NGOs and the contradictions of empowerment and disempowerment: A conversation. *Antipode* 35 (1), 1–13. doi: 10.1111/1467-8330.00298.

Nast, H.J. (1994) Opening remarks on 'Women in the field'. *Professional Geographer* 46 (1), 54–66.

Nast, H.J. (1998) The body as 'place': Reflexivity and field-work in Kano, Nigeria. In H.J. Nast and S. Pile (eds) *Places Through the Body* (pp. 93–116). London and New York: Routledge.

Oracion, E.G., Miller, M.L. and Christie, P. (2005) Marine protected areas for whom? Fisheries, tourism, and solidarity in a Philippine community. *Ocean and Coastal Management* 48, 393–410. doi: 10.1016/j.ocecoaman.2005.04.013.

Pauly, D. (1997, July) Small-scale fisheries in the tropics: Marginality, marginalization, and some implications for fisheries management. In *Global Trends: Fisheries Management. American Fisheries Society Symposium* (Vol. 20, pp. 40–49).

Peake, L. and Trotz, A. (1999) *Gender, Ethnicity and Place: Women and Identities in Guyana*. London, England: Routledge.

Roces, A. and Roces, G. (2009) *Culture Shock! Philippines: A Survival Guide to Customs and Etiquette*. Asia: Marshal Cavendish International.

Sultana, F. (2007) Reflexivity, positionality and participatory ethics: Negotiating fieldwork dilemmas in international research. *Acme* 6, 374–385. doi: 10.1016/j.ijedudev.2008.02.004.

Turner, C.F. and Martin, E. (1984) *Surveying Subjective Phenomenon*. New York: Russell Sage Foundation.

Yeats, R.S. and Prentice, C.S. (1996) Introduction to special section: Paleoseismology. *Journal of Geophysical Research-Solid Earth* 101, 5847–5853.

Young, E.H. (1999) Balancing conservation with development in small-scale fisheries: Is ecotourism an empty promise? *Human Ecology* 27, 581–620. doi: 10.1023/a:1018744011286.

4 *'Dale Chica!'*: A Surfer Chick's Reflections on Field Research in Central America

Lindsay E. Usher

Lindsay E. Usher is an early career researcher who is an assistant professor of Park, Recreation and Tourism Studies in the Human Movement Sciences Department at Old Dominion University in Virginia. Her research interests include surf culture and tourism, recreation conflict and the coastal communities' perspectives on adapting to climate change. Lindsay served as an Ecotourism Facilitator in the US Peace Corps in Guatemala from 2006–2008. She has co-led and organised university study abroad courses to New Zealand, Australia, Fiji and Nicaragua. When she's not working, Lindsay trains for triathlons and drives to the beach to surf. Her most recent adventure has consisted of getting married and becoming a stepmom. Her husband is also an academic.

Introduction

I do not do feminist research. I am a feminist and I am a researcher but much like Belinda Wheaton (2002) and others (Olive & Thorpe, 2011), I did not set out to conduct research which would primarily be on, about or for, the benefit of women. I wanted to research surfing. I wanted to do research on localism in a surf tourism destination. Localism is the territoriality of local surfers over a surf break: mild expressions of localism include locals violating surfing rules to show dominance or reminding visiting surfers of the rules; more severe expressions of localism include property damage and bodily harm being inflicted upon visiting surfers (Alessi, 2009; Nazer, 2004; Olivier, 2012; Preston-Whyte, 2002). Despite the prevalence of the phenomenon of localism in the surfing literature, few studies had examined localism in any great depth in the tourism context when I was starting my research, especially in developing countries. I would argue it is still the case. Despite various spikes in popularity among women throughout the past several decades, surfing remains a male-dominated sport (Booth, 2001; Olive et al., 2012). Therefore, given my topic, and where I was conducting research (Central America), I was confident that most of my study participants would be male. However, once I got in the field, I realised I could not ignore my own gender or its role in my study. So here I am, writing a chapter on femininity in the field.

I was a Peace Corps volunteer (official title: Ecotourism Facilitator) for two years in Guatemala. Reviewers and readers of my work know because I have discussed it in all of my publications on Central America. It is part of my narrative where I position myself in the study. However, it is also important to acknowledge because that is where my desire to do research began. It is where I started to learn about Central American culture. Before I was assigned to my Peace Corps site, I received three months of intensive, cross-cultural training so that I could function and work in a culture that was different from my own. Throughout this training, Guatemalans and Americans (many of whom were married to Guatemalans) explained the culture to us: greetings, formalities, idiosyncrasies and workplace culture. As a Peace Corps volunteer, I occupied an odd position. I was not a tourist, but I was not a local. I was temporary though, not like an expatriate. I knew how to get around, I paid local prices for transportation and bargained at the markets. I was invested in my community, had relationships with local families, and deeper ties than any tourist that came through. Once you are a Peace Corps volunteer, it is hard to consider yourself a tourist in Central America. When I go back, it is more like returning to a second home than a foreign region.

One cultural aspect we were educated about was the way gender roles played out in Guatemalan culture, which were different from what many of us were used to in the United States. Women were warned about *piropos* ('catcalling'), the prominence of infidelity among Guatemalan men and the unlikely development of platonic friendships with them. The organisation was attempting to make us aware of the phenomenon known as 'machismo', which is prevalent throughout Central America (Mirande, 1997; Sternberg, 2000; Stevens, 1973). While Mirande (1997) argues that little empirical work has been done on machismo and some men may define it more positively than others (being a man means working hard, taking care of one's family, etc.), it is generally understood as a negative phenomenon (egotistical men who are unfaithful womanisers). After three months of training, the knowledge of this cultural phenomenon was fairly ingrained, despite observing exceptions to machismo, such as many of the Guatemalan male Peace Corps staff who trained us. I was assigned to an indigenous town and fortunately did not have to cope with some of the problems associated with machismo that were reportedly more common in other parts of the country. Gender roles were still rigid, but the machismo was more subtle and it was not as intrusive upon us as volunteers. However, I still dealt with sexism on a regular basis, and many Guatemalan men fulfilled the stereotypes about which we were warned.

This background is important, because I carried it with me into my academic fieldwork. I knew how to function in a culture different from my own where machismo was present. I was prepared for being hit on, cat-called and hearing sexist views because that had been my previous experience. I had a resigned acceptance to these problems instead of letting them annoy me, get under my skin or interfere with my work. I should point out that my previous experience also helped me to not feel threatened by this behaviour. I had never been physically assaulted or anything like that. Since I knew machismo tended to be part of the culture, it enabled me to brush it off much easier than another woman who might have arrived to do fieldwork in Central America for the first time. I also recognised that, while it was common, not every man engaged in these negative manifestations of machismo. Therefore, I did not give much thought to gender or its role in my study when I set out to study surfers in Central America, especially because I would probably not be interviewing many women. However, once I started my research, I realised my gender was affecting my data collection and interview content and knew it was something I would need to address when reflecting on my position as a researcher. In this chapter, I analyse the ways in which my gender played a role in my research with surfers (Usher, 2017; Usher & Gómez, 2016; Usher & Kerstetter, 2015a, 2015b) in tourism destinations in Nicaragua and Costa Rica (Figure 4.1).

Nicaragua

Doing research in Central America, I had to be conscious of my position as a 'first world' researcher working in the 'third world' in order to not reproduce the inequalities I sought to investigate (Cupples, 2002). However, my Peace Corps training and prior experience made it difficult

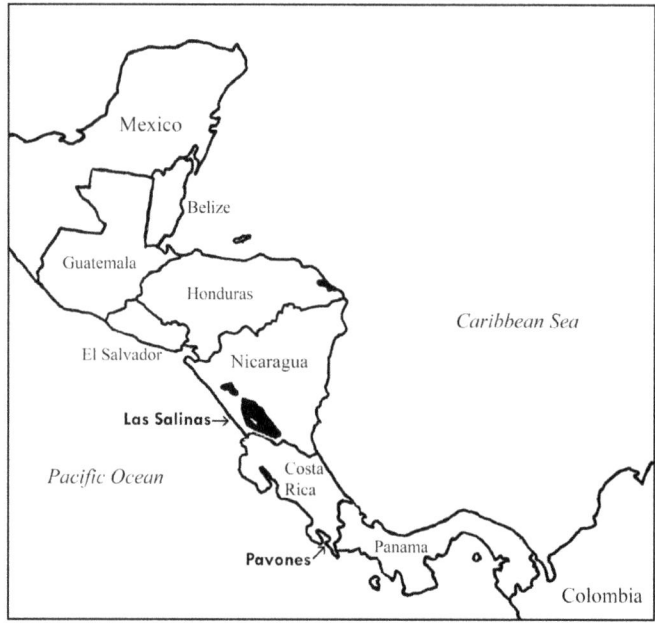

Figure 4.1 Map of Central America

to avoid 'othering' Nicaraguan men as machismo stereotypes with ulterior motives. This is apparent in my first day of surfing field notes from my research in Las Salinas, Nicaragua in 2012. After paddling out and my leash breaking, I made my way into the beach and ended up talking to a local surfer. I told him about the study and he said he could help me find participants. He also asked if I had a boyfriend and went to parties: 'I wondered if that was asking me out? I basically just assume that at this point down here. Isn't that awful?' (Excerpt from field notes, 18 May 2012). He did help me find participants within the next few days and while he never 'came on' to me in person, I did receive flirtatious text messages from him several weeks later. Similar to Cupples' (2002) experience in Nicaragua, this man was eager to assist me because he was perhaps 'sexually motivated'. Another local surfer flirted with me regularly whenever he saw me. Some of my participants asked if I went to parties. I did not go to the parties to which they referred: fiestas at the local bars or parties on the beach near the hostels and restaurants. I told men who asked that I did go to fiestas my host family had in their yard to celebrate family birthdays, but few guests attended who were not family members.

These interactions reveal the complexities of doing ethnographic research in tourism destinations. As an embedded researcher, much like a Peace Corps volunteer, I was neither a local nor a tourist. Not only was I working within another culture, but I was also dealing with stereotypes of American women based on encounters they had with tourists (Cupples,

2002). Many white women (from the US and Europe) seek out romantic encounters/relationships with Latin men during their vacations (Frohlick, 2007; Meish, 1995). White women's features are also considered attractive to some men in Latin American (Cupples, 2002; Meish, 1995). Knowing I would attract attention anyway, I covered up when I went surfing. I wore trunks and a rashguard most of the time (which also helped with skin protection in the hot tropical sun). Even this did not help; one married local surfer who lived near my host family teased me one day by asking when he would see me in a bikini. I told him no one wanted to see that and he said he did. I laughed it off and went on my way.

I did not entirely conform to local gender roles because I went surfing (at the time of the study, no Nicaraguan women from the community surfed), but members of the community were used to seeing surfing *gringas* ('gringa' is the word for white European or American women). Several surfing *gringas* had married local men in the community. These women were well-liked and had made positive contributions towards the community (such as giving art classes or helping in the local clinic). However, I avoided parties so that my intentions would not be misinterpreted and I would not fulfil the stereotype of the 'partying *gringa*'. I wanted to maintain a professional distance from my participants and demonstrate that I was not there to have a few flings while on vacation. I did not want to lose the respect I had gained from my host family and community members. Las Salinas was geographically separated from most of the tourism infrastructure in the area and the community was largely socially conservative and very religious (Catholic or Evangelical). As I had in Peace Corps, I tried to work within the cultural constraints and conform to gender norms in order to do my work. However, as Cupples (2002: 383) points out, we are still 'sexually positioned' by our host communities even if we are not pursuing sexual relationships. Therefore, despite my best intentions, my identity as a single American woman positioned me as someone to be romantically pursued by several of my participants.

Once I started looking for surfers to interview, I started to become certain some were eager to do interviews because they were interested in me romantically. Much like the example above, asking about my relationship status and party attendance became standard throughout the course of our introductions or later conversations. Had I been a male researcher, I do not know if some local surfers would have been as interested in doing an interview. They might have seen me as a rival (for waves and women) instead of someone with whom they wanted to spend more time; therefore, my gender appeared to have an advantage in helping me obtain participants.

Once I started the interviews, my female identity had an additional advantage, especially with respect to my research topic. My questions for local surfers centred on their opinions of other surfers (local and foreign), their sense of ownership and regulation over the surf break, and their surfing experiences. As locals told stories and expanded on their interactions with expatriates and tourists, they did not hold back in their complaints and frustrations with these two groups. Wondering why they had no qualms with complaining to me (an American) about American surfers, I realised that it was American men they were talking about, not women. Local surfers did not seem to view me as an American surfer. Male tourists and expatriates were the primary ones with whom they had had negative interactions. I am not sure they would have revealed all of this to a male researcher – my gender seemed to privilege me to this information. I feel as if I got more detailed and honest responses than had I been a male researcher asking the same questions. My findings revealed that while local surfers expressed ownership over the surf break, they wanted to share it with tourists and foreigners as long as these people respected locals. When tourists violated surf etiquette (widely acknowledged surfing rules concerning who has the right-of-way), it was frustrating to local surfers and they would often remind tourists of the rules.

However, locals' desire to share the space and receive respect was often superseded by their desire to display their masculinity in the surf. When I asked what happened when a surfer dropped in on (caught the wave in front of someone already riding) a local surfer, one participant told me it depended on whether it was a girl or a guy. If it was a girl, the surfer would encourage her to go and cheer her on the wave. If it was a guy, he would yell and make a fuss, possibly starting a verbal confrontation with the offending surfer. Therefore, some local surfers seemed to be constructing their own negative interactions, which may have been based on the prevalence of machismo in the culture. Some locals' desires to attract women dictated a different interaction with them in the surf; whereas men who violated rules and ruined the wave they were riding had to be shown a vocal expression of disapproval. By challenging the men who dropped in on them, they were displaying dominance in the surf break both as locals and as men (Preston-Whyte, 2002).

I experienced and observed this deference to women in the surf several times at Popoyo (the name of the surf break near Las Salinas). At the time of my fieldwork, I did not see many women surfing there on a regular basis. Sometimes a women's surf camp from a town further south would bring people to Popoyo and I saw the female owner of this camp catch a wave when many surfers were paddling for it at the same time. I suspected it was because many of the male surfers may have yielded to her. When there were a lot of locals out, they would encourage me to paddle for waves and I would catch more than usual. I think this was primarily because they knew me but also because, as previously discussed, several of them might have been interested in dating me. I got used to the familiar call of *'dale, dale, dale!'* ('go, go, go!') as I paddled for a wave. I did not feel the same attitude from tourists. Most of them seem to be competing with me and everyone else in the water for waves. The tourists probably assumed I was another tourist. Being one of the only women out in the surf much of the time also made me reluctant to approach male tourists when I was surfing and ask them for short interviews. Many of them were fairly attractive and I was worried they would think I was coming on to them. This fear may also have been rooted in my passivity in the line-up.[1]

I should take a moment to discuss my surfing background. I can surf, but my skill level was not as advanced as most of the surfers at Popoyo. I have competed in four World Championships of Surf Kayaking but I first got on a surfboard in 2008. This put me in a strange position. I was incredibly comfortable in the ocean and knew how to read and ride waves, but my skill on a board was not as good as it would have been in my kayak. So while many other surfers may have perceived me as a beginner, I have been surfing (some sort of craft) since I was 12 years old. Men also sometimes assume women are less skilled surfers anyway, simply because of their gender (Bush, 2016). Therefore, being an intermediate female board surfer in a male-dominated environment at a world-class surf break did not breed confidence. I did not catch many waves at Popoyo at all until the end of my fieldwork period. I felt intimidated and worried I would simply wipe out on a wave someone else with more skill could have ridden. I was also paranoid about dropping in on someone because I did not want to be labelled a 'kook'. Fendt and Wilson (2012) found that female surf tourists in their study experienced the same kind of self-doubt when they travelled. Also, I was preoccupied with observing other surfers, which was difficult to do if I was focused on catching waves and paddling back to the line-up. Perhaps I worried male tourists would think I was out there to get men instead of catch waves. I ended up finding tourists on the beach to interview, because for some reason I was more comfortable with that approach.

As mentioned previously, an interesting aspect of surfing at Popoyo was that no Nicaraguan women surfed there at the time of my study. The closest person to a 'local female surfer' was a highly talented, Latin American expatriate woman who had been living there for several years and was well-liked by many of the locals. I spoke to a friend (a local surfer) about this and he told me the expatriate woman had tried to teach several of the local women but they had not continued with the sport. He said they were not interested, but mentioned that his sister wanted to learn. However, I attributed their non-participation to the traditional gender roles and many household demands on women that I had observed in Las Salinas. Both women and men held jobs; however, men did not have the additional burdens of maintaining the house, cooking and caring for children that women did. Many men were able to dedicate their time off to surfing.

My gender offered an advantage in Las Salinas because it enabled me to obtain participants easily and gain more nuanced information about host and guest conflicts. Even though I experienced some negative aspects of machismo, I also better understand Mirande's (1997) characterisation of machismo as a more complex phenomenon that can have positive aspects as well. Male members of my host family, surfers I befriended and others

Figure 4.2 Nicaraguan men start to run after a school of fish they have just seen cut through the water

were respectful, kind and delightful to be around. Men with rough, leathery hands taught me to dance the cumbia. Their impeccable sense of rhythm and ability to dance was as intertwined with their masculinity as their jobs which involved hard manual labour (see Figure 4.2). My positive experiences also reinforced the care I needed to take in writing up my findings. In my reporting, I noted that 'some' (not all) male participants hit on me and not all men I encountered conformed to machismo stereotypes.

Costa Rica

With one study on localism done, I embarked on another study several years later in 2014 and followed it up with further observational work in 2015 (Usher, 2017; Usher & Gómez, 2016). I had heard there had been an incident in Pavones, Costa Rica, between a local Tico (the name Costa Ricans call themselves) and a stand-up paddle boarder, and since it was a point break[2] (reputed to be one of the longest left-breaking waves in the world), it seemed a logical place to study localism. I knew Costa Rican tourism was more developed, and it had been established as a well-known surf destination as early as the 1990s (Krause, 2013). Therefore, I was interested to find out how different it was from Nicaragua, which only began to grow as a surf tourism destination in the late 1990s and early 2000s. However, Pavones is unique in Costa Rica: the town's remote location and tormented history have not encouraged tourism development to the scale which has been seen in other parts of the country. I was curious to see how gender would play out in this destination.

When I called the local contact, a community leader whose information I had been given, he began speaking perfect English with me. He confused me with another 'Lindsay' and I corrected him and he remembered hearing about me. I was astonished because I was not accustomed to hearing fluent English being spoken by the people I worked with in Guatemala or Nicaragua. Only one or two Nicaraguan surfers from Las Salinas spoke any English. It made me realise that working in Pavones was going to be a much different experience from my time in Nicaragua. I called the 'host mom' my contact had provided, and we worked out a few logistics. A week later, after a very long two days of travelling, she met me as I got off the Pavones bus outside the *supermercado* ('supermarket'). She was wearing a tank top and shorts. That was not an outfit my Nicaraguan host mom would ever have worn and I was fairly certain they were around the same age.

As I got used to my new surroundings, I realised how different Pavones was from Las Salinas. Geographically, the town is right on the surf break. It took me five minutes to walk from my house to the beach where I typically paddled out. The salt flats I was used to trekking through, to get from Las Salinas to Popoyo, made it at least a one kilometre walk to the surf break from the community. In Pavones, *gringos* lived interspersed among the Ticos and the tourism businesses were along the tiny main strip of the town. I was invited to a baby shower the first Sunday I was there. The shower was celebrating the first baby of a Costa Rican woman and a French man. The party attendees included Ticos and *gringos*. Pavones was a transnational community and had been for some time.

Being in a transnational community meant that I was not particularly unique. As I started to find Tico surfers to interview, some were willing but several said no. They did not seem particularly interested because I was a *gringa*. There were plenty of us around. My host mom pointed out one guy at the bar while we were watching the World Cup (that year Costa Rica advanced far into the tournament, generating plenty of excitement during my time there) and said he acted like he was too good for everyone. She said he only spoke to *gringas*. However, he did not speak to me. He was one of several people who did not want to do an interview. Several Ticos did not want to answer my questions about foreign residents, which also suggested that my gender did not offer any advantage and my nationality put me at a disadvantage in obtaining Tico participants and getting a lot of information from them.

I want to return to my above statement briefly because it might have seemed unusual for me to be in a bar with my host mom. Many community members and tourists hung out at this bar and restaurant, especially during the World Cup. My adolescent host sisters would come there as well. Pavones had fairly relaxed social standards. Drinking (and some drugs for that matter) was not a big deal to most people. In describing the place to people, 'hedonistic' is a word I use frequently. According to one woman (an American born in Costa Rica), tourists had introduced the partying lifestyle to the town years ago and many local residents adopted the lifestyle as well, to their detriment in some cases. However, because of this, and the length of time during which foreigners had been living there (many of them for 20 years or more), I did not feel as though I had to be as concerned about social mores as I had been in Nicaragua. Everyone went to the bar so I was not concerned with people seeing me there. They did not seem to think less of me for it.

It was also easier to make friends with local Tico men and not have them misinterpret it as dating. I was wary of this at first, but after meeting one friend at a bar one evening and not feeling as if he expected anything, I realised it was possible. During both periods of study in Pavones, in 2014 and 2015, I befriended locals who seemed to have no intention of pursuing a romantic relationship with me. In 2015, I made a new friend with a local who been away in the capital for many years and had returned recently. One night, during my second period of fieldwork, I found myself sitting between two Tico fishermen at the bar. We conversed for a while and one joked with some younger Ticos that I was his girlfriend. We all laughed. I knew it was good-natured and bid them farewell a little while later, not concerned about leaving the wrong impression. Another aspect of being in the socially-relaxed environment of Pavones was that I did not have to worry about what I wore when I was surfing, or even out on the beach. I observed many women surfers in skimpy, barely-there bikinis, therefore I was not worried about drawing attention to myself. However, I still wore a rashguard and trunks most of the time, especially on days when the surf was bigger, which helped keep everything in place and again, protected my skin from the sun.

There were also local Tica (female) surfers in Pavones, which as I mentioned, was not a phenomenon I had come across in Las Salinas. I interviewed five of them and it was interesting to hear their perspectives on localism. I wondered if a male researcher would have pursued their perspectives as I did since some of them did not surf as much as the men. As one Tica mentioned to me, there were not many local female surfers, but they were there; one of them even wore a bikini when she surfed. These women offered important observations about gender in the surf. For example, one Tica was shy and did not provide very long answers in her interview but said arguing in the surf was something she particularly noticed with the men, women were calmer. Another Tica said that men were always competing with one another in the surf and women were not like that.

One of my goals with the Pavones study was to try and speak with more expatriates this time around and learn more about their feelings of territoriality over the surf break (not just their observations about local surfers acting territorially, which had been my focus in Nicaragua). My previous study in Nicaragua, and Krause's (2013) work in Costa Rica, indicated that foreign residents often enacted heavier localism than native locals (Usher & Kerstetter, 2015a, 2015b). My findings in Pavones confirmed these previous studies: locals, tourists and expatriates agreed that expatriates were generally more aggressive in the surf than Ticos. Expatriates were more than happy to talk to me, they gave some of the longest interviews. Probably because most of them were American, I did not think about my gender as much when I was interacting with them, but upon reflection, realised that it came out in different ways. For example, one expatriate (who fed me lunch at his house and took me to dinner) remarked that he enjoyed spending time with women because they talked about more interesting topics than how many barrels one had gotten that day. Other expatriate men would curse in their interviews and then apologise. I am not sure if they would have apologised to a male researcher or if they simply wanted to sound less crass for an interview which was being recorded.

I caught far more waves at Pavones than I ever did at Popoyo (the sheer size of the break helped to increase wave availability; Figure 4.3). The first week or so, I was intimidated by the break and stayed further down the line, closer to the inside where wave got smaller. I finally got to the point where I would position myself in the middle section. Remembering my

Figure 4.3 Author riding a wave at Pavones

experiences at Popoyo, I realised I struggled with being confident in new places. I know I am not the only woman to feel this way, based on previous research (Fendt & Wilson, 2012), but also my own observations. I noted this on my first day out in the surf at Pavones:

> It amazes me how assertive men can be in the surf. The girl who could surf was pretty good about getting waves but I could tell she would back down sometimes. It just occurred to me today: it seems as if guys can just show up at a surf break and surf. They are more aggressive and not as worried as the women seem to be about dropping in on someone. (Excerpt from field notes, 29 May, 2014)

During my second period of fieldwork I encountered another woman who I saw get a great ride on a big wave. She spoke to me when she paddled back out: 'Scary wave!' and then shook her arms as if she was carrying tension in them. I saw her the next day and she said she had been trying to get in (to the beach) for an hour and she was over it. The woman said her husband told her to just go for any wave because the person closest to the peak would not make it all the way down the line (implying the wave would break and they would wipe out). She said she always assumed they would make it. I told her I made the same assumption. These two women were probably more skilled surfers than me, and yet they also experienced doubt and lacked confidence in the surf break as I did at Popoyo and at Pavones. Male-dominated surf spaces seem to lead some women to question their belonging at a surf break and contribute to feelings of self-doubt (Fendt & Wilson, 2012; Olive et al., 2012; Waitt, 2008). Brennan (2016) even argued that oppressive masculine dominance manifests itself in the way women surf. Their movements on the wave are restricted, or not as dynamic as they could be, because the oppression causes women (consciously or unconsciously) to doubt their belonging and abilities.

Tico surfers did not offer me any special treatment as a woman in the surf, which contrasted with my experience in Nicaragua. However, in my interviews, several expatriates explained that one of their rules was that they would never drop in on a woman or a child. Corey (pseudonym) explained:

> There would be somebody out there and they would just be dropping in on girls, literally, and I can't, it's like, um, a lot of the times girls don't have the upper hand because they don't want to [have] huge muscles so they are more petite, and this is nothing to do with macho-ness, this has to do with ... how do I explain it, they just don't paddle as hard and all that so they're not, they're in the water and you have to give them the right of way because they have a hard time out there, the majority of them.

It was statements like these that made me question if he realised I was a female surfer, similar to experiences Olive and Thorpe (2011) had in their fieldwork when explicit or sexist comments were made in their presence. He followed this up by saying there was one expatriate woman who was more 'built' (muscular) than him, could paddle better than him, and caught waves easily. I will refer to her as 'Carla'. It was true; I watched Carla surfing during the big swells and she was a 'charger' as another expatriate described her. I also interviewed her: Carla was from South America but had lived off and on in Pavones for over 10 years. She was a highly skilled surfer who was well-respected in the local community. In the male-dominated world of surfing, women who have a high skill level in surfing are often compared to men: a woman who can 'surf like a man' has supposedly reached the pinnacle of surfing achievement (Bush, 2016; Comer, 2010; Waitt, 2008). While this is a highly problematic and sexist statement because it situates men's surfing as better than women's surfing and places them at the top of a hierarchy, men seemed to respect Carla because of her aggressive approach to surfing which mirrored their own surfing style. Therefore, despite a relaxed social environment which eased my interactions with men in the community, the surf break at Pavones was still a male-dominated space where women contended with sexism.

Pavones is a unique town in Costa Rica and it provided an interesting basis of comparison for my work in Nicaragua. It also was interesting because my gender did not seem to affect my research in the same ways. Years of international influence in the town affected the ways in which gender roles played out. I did not feel as socially restricted but my gender and nationality were not advantageous because of the transnational nature of the community. However, the surf break was male-dominated like it was in Nicaragua and called attention to the hierarchical way in which gender played out in the waves.

Concluding Remarks

In Wheaton's (2002) reflexive discussion of her study with windsurfers, she refers to the privileging of insider perspectives in sport ethnographies: 'I will argue that the distinction between 'insider' and 'outsider' is a misleading binary opposition rooted in an essentialist and fixed understanding of identities ...' (2002: 253). The same could be said of doing cross-cultural ethnography in sport tourism destinations. I occupied insider and outsider roles at different times with local residents, expatriates and tourists throughout both of my studies. As a woman, I was an outsider to male-dominated surf culture. As a surfer, I was an insider to my participants. However, as an intermediate board surfer, I was an outsider to the predominantly advanced surfer population I was interviewing. As a former Peace Corps volunteer, I understood the culture, spoke the language and sympathised with local residents; however, I was also an outsider to them as a privileged person from a wealthy country. As an American, I understood the culture of many tourists and expatriates and also spoke the same language. My knowledge of language and culture proved to be an advantage with Nicaraguans and Ticos. My gender was an advantage with Nicaraguans, though was not particularly helpful in my research with Ticos. Gendered comments and experiences emerged more with expatriates in Costa Rica.

Women who plan to do fieldwork in sport tourism destinations should be prepared to occupy insider and outsider roles, especially in a cross-cultural context. However, for women from developed countries working in developing ones, it is especially important that they have a constant awareness of their privilege and power and work to not reinforce inequalities. These women may find themselves subject to culturally-accepted sexist rhetoric or objectification but should not allow these experiences to overwhelm their fieldwork. I am not referring to instances in which women have been threatened or harmed in their research sites, because that is a different matter. My point is that succumbing to stereotyping, based on gendered interactions in cross-cultural settings, will not produce trustworthy findings or be beneficial to the host community that the researcher wishes to support. However, while stereotyping of participants should be avoided, female researchers can use gender stereotypes to their advantage in the field. Women are often perceived as caring people willing to listen. In my experience, participants wanted to tell their stories and were eager to find someone who wanted to hear them. Being a woman facilitated that process in the gendered environments in which I found myself. Women should acknowledge their strengths as researchers and go confidently, but humbly, into the field.

Notes

(1) The 'line-up' is the group of surfers positioned around the peak of the wave. Ideally, surfers take turns riding waves depending on their position in the line-up, but this is rarely as orderly as it should be.
(2) A point break is a wave that breaks around a point of land found in areas with mountains and hills. It is often formed by deposits from a river mouth which flows into the ocean at that location (Warshaw, 2003). There is a very distinct take-off point for surfers to congregate around, therefore a point break line-up is often easily regulated by local surfers.

References

Alessi, M.D. (2009) The customs and culture of surfing, and an opportunity for a new territorialism? *Reef Journal* 1 (1), 85–92.
Booth, D. (2001) From bikinis to boardshorts: Wahines and the paradoxes of surfing culture. *Journal of Sport History* 28 (1), 3–22.
Brennan, D. (2016) Surfing like a girl: A critique of feminine embodied movement in surfing. *Hypatia* 31 (4), 907–922.
Bush, L. (2016) Creating our own lineup: Identities and shared cultural norms of surfing women in a U.S. East Coast community. *Journal of Contemporary Ethnography* 45 (3), 290–318.

Comer, K. (2010) *Surfer Girls in the New World Order.* Durham: Duke University Press.
Cupples, J. (2002) The field as a landscape of desire: Sex and sexuality in geographical fieldwork. *Area* 34 (4), 382–390.
Fendt, L.S. and Wilson, E. (2012) 'It's a challenge, it's hard to get a wave': The impact of constraints on women surf tourists. *Tourism Review International* 15 (4), 337–348.
Frohlick, S. (2007) Fluid exchanges: The negotiation of intimacy between tourist women and local men in a transnational town in Caribbean Costa Rica. *City and Society* 19 (1), 139–168.
Krause, S. (2013) Pilgrammage to the playas: Surf tourism in Costa Rica. *Anthropology in Action* 19 (3), 37–48.
Meish, L.A. (1995) Gringas and Otavalenos: Changing tourist relations. *Annals of Tourism Research* 22 (2), 441–462.
Mirande, A. (1997) *Hombres y machos: Masculinity and Latino culture.* Boulder: Westview Press.
Nazer, D. (2004) The tragicomedy of the surfers' commons. *Deakin Law Review* 9 (2), 655–713.
Olive, R., McCuaig, L. and Phillips, M.G. (2015) Women's recreational surfing: A patronising experience. *Sport, Education and Society* 20 (2), 258–276.
Olive, R. and Thorpe, H. (2011) Negotiating the 'f-word' in the field: Doing feminist ethnographic in action sport cultures. *Sociology of Sport Journal* 28, 421–440.
Olivier, S. (2012) 'Your wave, Bro!': Virtue ethics and surfing. *Sport in Society* 13 (7/8), 1223–1233.
Preston-Whyte, R. (2002) Constructions of surfing space at Durban, South Africa. *Tourism Geographies* 4 (3), 307–328.
Sternberg, P. (2000) Challenging machismo: Promoting sexual and reproductive health with Nicaraguan men. *Gender and Development* 8 (1), 89–99.
Stevens, E.P. (1973) Machismo and marianismo. *Society* 10 (6), 57–63.
Usher, L.E. (2017) "Foreign locals": Transnationalism, expatriates and surfer identity in Costa Rica. *Journal of Sport and Social Issues*, https://doi.org/10.1177/0193723517705542
Usher, L.E. and Gómez, E. (2016) Surf localism in Costa Rica: Exploring territoriality among Costa Rican and foreign resident surfers. *Journal of Sport and Tourism.* doi: 10.1080/14775085.2016.1164068
Usher, L.E. and Kerstetter, D. (2015a) Re-defining localism: An ethnography of human territoriality in the surf. *International Journal of Tourism Anthropology* 4 (3), 286–302.
Usher, L.E. and Kerstetter, D. (2015b) 'Surfistas locales': Transnationalism and the construction of surfer identity in Nicaragua. *Journal of Sport and Social Issues* 39 (6), 455–479.
Waitt, G. (2008) 'Killing waves': Surfing, space and gender. *Social and Cultural Geography* 9 (1), 75–94.
Warshaw, M. (2003) *The Encyclopedia of Surfing.* Orlando: Harcourt, Inc.
Wheaton, B. (2002) Babes on the beach, women in the surf: Researching gender, power and difference in the windsurfing culture. In J. Sugden and A. Tomlinson (eds) *Power Games: A Critical Sociology of Sport* (pp. 240–266). New York, NY: Routledge.

5 Early Motherhood and Research: From Bump to Baby in the Field

Brooke A. Porter

Dr Brooke Porter is an early career researcher in the human dimensions of fisheries and coastal environments. Her work explores tourism as a development and conservation strategy in lesser-developed regions, with emphasis on surf and adventure tourism. She is focused on developing simple and effective development and conservation strategies for coastal communities. Her choice to combine motherhood and doctoral studies meant that, to date, the majority of her fieldwork experiences have been accompanied. Previously overlooking these influences, she has now learned the importance of exploring and contextualising the effects of accompanied fieldwork. She has worked in various capacities with NGOs, international aid agencies and educational institutions on Maui, New Zealand, the Philippines and in Africa. She currently serves as a Scientific Adviser to The Coral Triangle Conservancy, a NGO that focuses on reef protection and restoration in the Philippines and is an Adjunct Professor at the Umbra Institute in Perugia, Italy.

Introduction

There are phases of the female experience that have considerable effect on fieldwork. Motherhood, although optional, is an example. Warren (1988) suggested that motherhood may elicit a 'drift' response in the female academic, describing drift as reactions to situations, rather than an effect of planning or personal goals, that may play a significant role on the female academic career. While drift may be seen as weakening the woman's role to that of a passive participant, there are potential benefits to be gained from a drift response. First, it is noted that drift is most applicable to women who are participating in a partnership. Whereas a partnership is most commonly characterised as a relationship with a spouse or significant other, drift may also be relevant to professional relationships. Challenging the passiveness associated with Warren's (1988) description of drift, I benefited from what I will call, referring to biological categories of symbiotic relationships, a 'mutual drift'. Similar to mutualism, I suggest mutual drift is characterised by a response or adaptation to a situation that benefits both persons in the partnership. Mutual drift became a factor two semesters into my doctoral studies in New Zealand. My husband was offered an exciting position in his field in the Philippines. At this point in my doctoral studies, I had yet to define my research site. The Philippines fulfilled the requirements I was seeking, and in addition, I would be able to depend on the financial support of my husband.

I was both eager and nervous to begin fieldwork. I did not know the country to which I was moving, or its many languages. My only familiarity with Filipino customs was through travel guides, a Filipino colleague and some online research. Further, I was a novice researcher in social science fieldwork. I relied upon my supervisory team's encouraging words, which were, in sum, 'just start'. Start I did. A few months into the field, I had accomplished a successful reconnaissance visit, conducted pilot interviews, secured a study site and tested positive for pregnancy. The associated experiences with the pregnancy and the birth of our son, had obvious temporal effects on my fieldwork. It was not until the write-up stage, and at the advice of my supervisory team (notably both males), Mark Orams and Michael Lück, that I was asked to explore other biases that were a result of my childbearing abilities and thus, unique to a female research experience.

In hindsight, it is apparent that I did not give sufficient consideration to the effect of my gender on my doctoral research. I was focused solely on the completion of the task as a successful researcher, not as a successful female researcher (Frohlick, 2002). I wanted to avoid the common labels, such as weak or inept, that are often associated with the female gender. Therefore, I felt it advantageous to attempt an androgynous persona (Warren, 1988).

I attribute the oversight to three main variables, with the first being simply a lack of research experience. Second, was the subject matter. My doctoral studies focused on exploring the viability of marine tourism as an alternative livelihood for fisherfolk in less-developed regions. There is little in the fisheries or tourism literature on the effects of gender on field work. My attempts to locate relevant research experiences in the tourism literature were futile. Third, I now recognise the lack of attention I gave to gender biases as an *intentional* oversight (Frohlick, 2002; Gurney, 1985; Landes, 1986). I say this only after time away from the experience, exposure to anthropological and feminist literatures, and a deep reflection on the entire research process. I realise that it was with intent that I chose a field space full of adventure (see Bell, 1993; Frohlick, 2002). The remoteness of the fishing communities meant that multiple forms of travel were required just to reach the sites. Further, there was a roughness to the communities beyond the poverty. Cock-fighting and gambling were part of daily routines; it was not difficult to find fishermen inebriated before noon; and then there was the omnipresent risk associated with life at sea. I had hoped that these adventurous or 'masculine' attributes (Frohlick, 2002; Sparke, 1996) of my chosen field space would somehow demonstrate my dedication to the research process, as I had wanted to avoid being seen as a lesser academic (Schrijvers, 1993; Warren, 1988) as a result of gender. I was of the opinion that gastrointestinal illness resulting from sampling foreign cuisines conjures tales of ethnographic bravado, whereas leaving an interview to vomit because of morning sickness is remarkably less impressive in the field. Having had significant time away from these field experiences, I now realise the impact that my femininity, specifically motherhood, had on my research and on me as a researcher. This chapter provides a reflexive analysis of the gender biases that occurred during my doctoral field studies; it explores gender issues associated with womanhood, from pregnancy to parenting choices, over the course of a long-term research project.

The Field

I entered the field as a childless, married woman, and left the field as a married mother of two children and a Filipino street-cat. Macintyre (1993: 47) suggests that, for most academics, doctoral research accounts for the 'longest single stint of fieldwork' they will ever undertake. My time in the Philippines totalled four years. During all but the final nine months, I was engaged in my doctoral studies. My data collection was limited to four research sites in the Luzon region of the Philippines (see Figure 5.1), though many episodes from my every-day life in Manila (considered the world's most densely populated city) influenced my research; therefore, I consider it a semi-ethnographic study. Accordingly, these experiences also influenced the interpretation of my hard data. Thus, for the purposes

Figure 5.1 Map of the Philippine archipelago. The research sites were all very small islands which are not visible within a map of the entire archipelago. Therefore, general research locations (at the provincial level) are indicated with arrows. Palawan is an archipelago within the larger Philippine archipelago. Manila, the capital is indicated with a circle

of this analysis, I consider the country itself as the field. This section investigates gender-biased situations from the field in a temporal progression, beginning with a reconnaissance visit.

Bolinao

October 2011

A few weeks after arriving in the Philippines, I embarked on a reconnaissance visit to the University of the Philippines Marine Science Institute (UPMSI) in Bolinao, Pangasinan. Bolinao is accessible from the capital city of Manila via well-maintained roadways; multiple daily trips are available via public bus transportation. I travelled during daylight via public bus – a seven-hour journey. This was my first trip on a public bus in the Philippines, and despite being the only foreigner on the bus, I gave personal safety little thought. I spent five nights in the UPMSI dorms in a private room and was accompanied by the deputy director of UPMSI and students to the field area on Santiago Island, which is a 10-minute commute via a small *banca*, the traditional Filipino fishing vessel. Barangay Victory, the field site, was then a 15-minute ride via motorised tricycle. The fisherfolk of Barangay Victory on Santiago Island were familiar with the research process and have ongoing projects with UPMSI staff. It is also worth mentioning that many of the UPMSI students are 20-something, single, childless females, who by Filipino norms, would commonly be married with children. As a result, access as a married, childless female was easy. The visit was largely uneventful and the visit progressed with relative ease.

During this trip, my field journal included references to the socio-economic divide between myself and the participants. I had envisioned a mostly male sample, as the standard assumption is that it is the men who fish. This is partly true, with the men being the ones who go out to sea; however, the women have a considerable role in the fisheries, gleaning the shores daily for smaller fish and invertebrates. Arriving in the field, I decided to interview anyone who was available, regardless of gender, a choice which increased the depth of my data. In particular, I recorded notes about the wife of the village leader. She had been married for over 20 years and had borne 10 children. What struck me was that she did not have a wedding band. Comparing her domestic accomplishments to mine (at the time a meagre two years of marriage with zero children), I found myself embarrassed by my own wedding band. Similarly, Schrijvers (1993), and her husband who accompanied her in the field in Sri Lanka, described embarrassment at the socio-economic divide between them and the villagers. However, the socio-economic gap is not necessarily of the same importance to the locals. For example, Vera-Sanso (1993) found that her participants were disappointed in her lack of jewellery, for her presence and interviews conveyed higher status on the hosts than familial visitors. Schrijvers (1993) wrote that both she and her husband noticed the socio-economic divide. I discount that awareness of socio-economic differences is a direct effect of gender. Instead, I suggest that this divide would be observed in individual ways that may or may not be particularly feminine or masculine. Mead (1986) suggests empathy as a gendered affect associated with being female. Likewise, Nader (1986) describes women as having an increased ability to relate to others over their male peers. While I am unable to speak for men in general, I can say without doubt, that my husband, during a later visit, did not notice the ring-less finger of the village leader's wife and, therefore, could not share similar sentiments and feelings. Stating empathy and compassion as female traits is a gross simplification. It is possible that instances of socio-economic awareness can be coded as being more masculine or more feminine; however, spatial and temporal factors must also be considered.

November 2011

I returned to Bolinao about four weeks later to join UPMSI staff in observing and assisting with visitors from an Indonesian government fisheries organisation. During this trip, I was able to conduct pilot interviews with the help of Dr Annette Menez, my local mentor, guide and Deputy

Director of UPMSI. Due to the field logistics of this trip, it was necessary to wade through the water to access one of the meeting spaces; therefore, swimwear was compulsory. However, on this trip I found myself dressing for more coverage (i.e. full rash guard and long board shorts). I did this in an attempt to divert excessive male attention (e.g. stares, comments about appearance) away from myself and, in part, out of respect for the conservative culture of the visitors (many of the female visitors from the Indonesian group wore burkinis). This attempt to conform to the field culture by adapting dress has previously been recorded by female fieldworkers (Caplan, 1993; Golde, 1986; Oboler, 1986; Vera-Sanso, 1993). However, many of these attempts are misinterpreted or absolute failures (e.g. Vera-Sanso mistakenly dressing as a prepubescent girl in Madras, India). As such, changes in my attire did little to reduce attention from male participants as there was no changing my white skin colour (Warren, 1988).

February 2012 – 10 weeks pregnant
The third and final trip to Bolinao marked the trip with the most male attention, despite the presence of my husband for part of the visit. It was also on this trip that my previous attempts at field-androgyny, which in retrospect were already completely futile, went by the wayside and gender-related issues in my research became unavoidable (Conaway, 1986; Oboler, 1986). This visit corresponded with my first-trimester of pregnancy (and punishing nausea from morning sickness). During this visit, I had to eat a constant stream of crackers to avoid being sick during the interviews which were commonly held in quaint rural houses which were often frequented by small livestock (e.g. chickens) with larger livestock (e.g. cattle, pigs) nearby. I shared snacks with all of the participants, yet I remember a distinct feeling of guilt, that I, by comparison a wealthy, healthy white woman, was incessantly eating in front of impoverished participants. Another area of consciousness was the consumption of participants' time. My field notes from this trip stated:

> I feel the interview questions are tedious ... there was no rush or impatience on their [the participants'] behalf, but perhaps on mine as I tried not to waste their time.

Ganesh (1993), who reflected on issues of reciprocity in her Srivaikuntam research, was plagued by a similar sentiment, feeling 'guilty about taking up so much time' (1993: 136) in the early stages of her research. I view the care for participants as a form of empathy. While not exclusively a female trait, Mead (1986) surmises that the female and male field experience is quite divergent, including temporal factors as variables. She suggests:

> It is probable that women have a higher toleration for such continuous personal involvement, if only because they have identified as children

with their mothers who, as wives and mothers, were necessarily displaying it. (1986: 328)

Pregnancy is an outward gendered affect and, thus, an observable bias in the research process. Though I was still at a stage where my 'bump' could have been mistaken as excess weight, I chose to share the news of my pregnancy with all the participants. This choice, though in part due to fears of needing to quickly exit interviews due to morning sickness, was mainly to foster truth in the research process. This news of my pregnancy was welcomed by participants, who had previously questioned my childless marriage (see Vera-Sanso, 1993). The shift in understanding is supported by the experiences of Oboler (1986) who found that her pregnancy improved her rapport with female participants, creating a shared experience. Likewise, Caplan (1993) found that motherhood opened the proverbial doors to new fields of data. On this trip, I collected unsolicited data about infant nutrition (see Porter & Orams, 2014). I attribute the sharing of this specific information to be a result of my forthcoming parenthood (Levey, 2009).

Despite my gravidity, the male attention continued. One male participant said, 'I am happy because you are beautiful to see. It's a new look and a new face'. My husband joined me after a few days in the field, yet prior to this, others inquired about my marital status. Another male participant stated to me, 'I am happy when someone like you comes', and continued to my husband, who had joined me for the last few days in the field, 'Excuse me if I'm a joker, but your wife is beautiful'. Revisiting these comments, I disagree with Mead who stated, 'actual beauty is less important than the attitudes a woman has toward her own looks' (1986: 321). Constantly queasy, sweaty and incessantly exhausted, I felt far from beautiful during this time. Instead, I attribute the continued male attention to me being a 'novelty' (Ganesh, 1993: 135). Comments about my appearance made me slightly uncomfortable. An appropriate response to sexism in the field remains unclear (Back, 1993; Warren, 1988). Back (1993) suggests that overlooking sexist comments may be a form of collusion with the subjects, yet, addressing such comments may be patronising to the participants. Collectively, Back (1993) called for the development and subsequent analysis of the cultural construction of masculinity, a construct that, over two decades later, remains a fringe component of the literature.

Zambales

April 2012 – 18 weeks pregnant

A little over a month later, my husband joined me on a trip to observe a key informant's surf tourism project in Zambales, a three-hour drive from Manila. Despite my husband's repeated attempts to convince me that staying in a hostel was a bad idea as we were not young (being in our 30s), and with me pregnant, I again found myself attempting to be something of a 'field warrior'. Admittedly, he was right. Bongo drums late into the night combined with dealing with morning sickness in a communal bathroom was too much. I had been defeated by the so-called masculinity of the field. Noted by Tripp (2002: 794), in reference to international fieldwork, 'academic expectations and norms were not established with academic mothers in mind, nor have they been sufficiently modified as more women have entered academia'. Beyond issues of general comfort (Cornet, 2013), a number of other factors were considered in this choice, particularly, access to appropriate medical care, and personal safety (Ortbals & Rincker, 2009). Pregnancy and the field were seeming arch enemies (see Cornet, 2013). Soon after this trip, and with the full support of my supervisors, I chose to take a formal leave of absence from my studies and focus on the birth of our son.

Palawan
January 2013 – Orlando age 4-months, Coron

Childbearing, a gendered affect, introduced a definitive temporal bias to the research process. This section of the chapter resumes following the birth of our son, Orlando. It is here that I explore how parenting philosophies (see Tripp, 2002), particularly breastfeeding (e.g. Frohlick, 2002) and childcare (e.g. Amadiume, 1993; Cornet, 2013), require that a young child be brought into the field or that the research be postponed. Exclusive breastfeeding was a personal choice that came relatively easily for us. Childcare was a more debatable issue for my husband and me. Domestic help was affordable in comparison to the USA (also noted by Cornet, 2013; Tripp, 2002). My husband was willing to explore the idea of domestic help beyond our part-time cleaner to avoid overburdening me while I resumed my research. However, I was extremely fearful of forfeiting even partial control of childrearing after witnessing others' *yayas* (nannies) trying to bestow their cultural norms (e.g. fatten babies with sugary foods) on foreign children (see also Cornet, 2013), and hearing stories of kidnappings arranged by *yayas*. After many discussions, my husband and I agreed that I would take responsibility for day-to-day childcare while he was at the office. In her explanative account of the issues associated with international research and parenting, Tripp (2002) stated that spousal support and cooperation is imperative in international research where children are a factor. My husband was (and continues to be) incredibly supportive of my research endeavours. He scheduled time off work so that he could accompany us into the field. Reaching the field base required a one to two-hour taxi ride (depending on traffic), a one-hour flight, 45 minutes by van to the port and a one-hour boat ride via a *banca*, the traditional Filipino fishing vessel. It was an all-day affair. The field site was another two-hour boat ride from the base. As Bell (1993), whose two children accompanied her in Australia notes, 'whatever I did in the field entailed planning for the children, carrying a swag (bedding) for three, provisions for three, always thinking through likely conflicts of needs, and taking actions to minimise or obviate problems' (1993: 36). Whereas fieldwork during pregnancy required medical-clearance visits prior to leaving for the field (Ortbals & Rincker, 2009), I found the logistics associated with entering the field with an infant required extensive preparation. With the exception of a few staples (e.g. water, eggs and oil), we had to pack in a week's worth of food. I packed and prepared to the best of my ability (Bell, 1993; Cornet, 2013) considering logistics that I would have otherwise disregarded such as safety floatation devises, noise concerns from the *banca* diesel engine, and infant-safe sun protection (see Figure 5.2). At four months, my son was exclusively breastfed; therefore, I was not concerned with his nutritional needs during the journey. I did, however, take special care in packing first aid

Figure 5.2 Travelling with my husband and son between research sites on a *banca*. Sun protection was a concern as our son was below the recommended age for sunscreen. A salvaged tarpaulin sign provided only minimal shade depending on the direction of travel and time of day, so we also covered him in long sleeves and pants. To minimise engine sound, I used mouldable, wax ear plugs and held a towel around our son's ears while we were underway (Photo credit: Scott Countryman)

supplies including the basics, as well as a syringe and a vial of epinephrine in the event of a box jelly sting or other anaphylaxis events. More common safety measures, such as a car seat, were not an option due to the field dynamics. Had my son incurred any medical issues beyond a mild fever or cut, I would have abandoned my fieldwork (Bell, 1993), as even the most rudimentary medical facility was hours away.

With little exception, Orlando was in an Ergobaby™ carrier (see Figure 5.3) on the boat, in the field and during interviews. Baby carriers are an ideal form of transport for infants and toddlers in the field (see Cornet, 2013; Frohlick, 2002). Despite the convenience of the carrier, this meant that Orlando was an omnipresent element in the fieldwork (Bell, 1993). I had feared that doing interviews with Orlando in tow would detract from the research, especially as I seemed to be constantly making rocking and bouncing motions (the movements mothers or caregivers tend to do out of habit, even in the absence of a child). Despite my sways and bounces during interviews, in reflecting on the experience, his presence positively influenced access to an otherwise wary audience (Caplan, 1993; Cornet, 2013; Schrijvers, 1993). As an extension of myself, he literally lessened the space between the subjects and me. He normalised my presence in the communities and humanised the overall field experience for

Figure 5.3 Orlando, 7 months, in the Ergobaby™ carrier. The outrigger boats, constructed of wood and bamboo did not have any mentionable safety features; therefore, it was necessary to hold or keep Orlando in the Ergobaby™ during transit (Author's photo)

the subjects (Levey, 2009). The presence of my infant son allowed me access to information that would have otherwise been difficult to acquire, a process Levey (2009: 317) refers to as 'wedging knowledge'. It was, in fact, women anthropologists who first documented female specific roles (see Nader, 1986).

Given his young age and lack of adherence to any predictable feeding schedule, I breastfed him during some interviews. As reported by Cornet (2013), many of the local women wanted to learn more about my son, who was much chubbier and larger than the local children his age. It was common for female participants to ask questions about my infant nutritional choices; all were visibly surprised to find that his size was maintained solely by breast milk.

Our first trip into the field as a family was successful. Other than a few engine stalls, the trip was flawless. I attribute the success to multiple factors including personal adaptability and attitude towards the research process (Cornet, 2013), spousal support (Tripp, 2002) and parenting philosophy (e.g. breastfeeding). Though we were in the remote field for a comparably shorter stint, unlike Schrijvers (1993) and Amadiume (1993) my child was well and did not suffer from the gastrointestinal illnesses common in lesser-developed regions. Like Frohlick (2002), I recognised the health benefits and convenience of breastfeeding in the field.

April 2013 – Orlando 7-months old, Busuanga

Following the success of the first field trip with my 'mini-assistant' I did not think twice about taking Orlando into the field again. My husband was unable to join us on this trip due to work commitments, and instead I hired a trusted local friend and colleague, Joanne Garcia, as a field assistant. My only expectation of her was to assist with the data collection though translation; however, her assistance was invaluable, and without it, I doubt I would have lasted the week. Unexpectedly, yet most welcome, she immediately assumed the caretaker role of *áte*, a Tagalog word for older sister, to Orlando. She was eager to hold him, to fan him when the Filipino summer became unbearable and provided security when I needed to divert my attention away from parenting responsibilities. After realising that suitable safety floatation devices were scarce, I packed a bit differently, as indicated in an email to my mother:

> 8 April 2013
>
> You'll be happy to know, I invested in an inflatable baby life ring that I will take on the boat with us – I figured it was more practical (and comfortable and likely safer) than a baby life vest. It's one of those rings that the baby sits in. I'll be sure to pack it and begin inflation at the first sign of trouble. Remember we're in the tropics and it takes quite a while for a boat to sink, hence why my plan is fool-proof :)

Otherwise, in comparison, this trip was also favourable. My son was a considerable influence on access to participants (Caplan, 1993; Cornet, 2013; Schrijvers, 1993); a phenomenon Levey (2009) describes as a wedge, which my son provided with his presence. Just as before, the babbling presence of Orlando meant that we were never refused an interview, and I was able to collect [unsolicited] data on infant nutritional choices. Taking Orlando into the field without my husband created not only a sense of personal achievement, but also reaffirmed an academic embodiment of me as field mother.

Discussion

Serendipitously, I was able to draw upon and compare field experiences spanning from childless to with child within a single research project. At the onset of my doctoral studies, I had been cautioned against combining motherhood and academia (see also Schrijvers, 1993). Wanting both a PhD and children, I did not entertain the notion that combining academia and reproductive responsibility could have potential effects on the research (Oboler, 1986). Honestly, I found the combination of reproductive responsibilities with doctoral studies beneficial. Though arduous at times (Cornet, 2013), motherhood significantly increased my productivity. Academic deadlines took on new meaning, with parenting duties and impending births as significant variables (see Figure 5.4).

The influence of gender had obvious effects on my research and having revisited the experiences in depth, gender issues were deserving of more attention in my thesis. Warren (1988: 13) suggested four themes as part of gender-fieldwork literature: entrée; finding a place within the culture; sexuality and the body; and sexual politics. Five themes, some of which mirror those defined by Warren (1988), resulted in the most noticeable gendered affects: (1) sexual politics; (2) drift; (3) logistics; (4) access; and (5) embodiment. I have explained the components associated with these themes earlier in the chapter; therefore, here, I will discuss the themes as more general, and hopefully transferable, constructs. Specifically, I explore the presence, or lack thereof, of these themes in my doctoral thesis and how they compare when viewed under a gendered 'lens'.

During the described experiences, sexual politics included mainly sexual objectification. In my thesis, I wrote of potential gender bias towards the researcher, 'As a female researcher investigating a predominately male occupation (with the exception of the shore-based fisheries) there were incidences of male participants displaying masculinity towards the researcher' (Porter, 2014: 307). It is worth noting that I ignored these comments or immediately dismissed them with a smile. Although in my thesis I noted that these comments were limited to a single research site, I failed to explore this as an effect of motherhood. I did not experience any sexist comments as a mother with an infant in tow. Thus, I concluded that neither personal appearance nor marital status (including the presence of

Figure 5.4 The day of my doctoral examination in Auckland, New Zealand. My then 2-year-old son and I travelled together from the Philippines to New Zealand. The examiners and the Auckland University of Technology worked together to move my defence date forward a couple of weeks so I was able to attend before pregnancy travel restrictions were placed in effect (Photo credit: Nana/Linda Porter)

my husband) significantly affected sexual objectification in the field, and instead, propose motherhood and the presence of a child as an influencing factor in curbing sexual objectification.

The progression of my doctoral research and the entire field experience itself was a result of 'mutual drift'. Warren (1988) suggests drift as a gendered response and this likely holds true even in the case of mutualism. At first, the partner was my husband; by the end, the partners included my children. In the early years of motherhood, it is often the woman who is the primary caregiver. The choice to breastfeed limited the amount of time I could be away from my children, thus introducing a forced adaptation to the situation. In my thesis, I labelled the adaptation as pragmatism. Conceivably, the two are one and the same. An early advocate of pragmatism, William James (1907: 22) stated that pragmatism, 'has no objection whatever to the realising of abstractions, so long as you get about among particulars with their aid and they actually carry you somewhere'. I propose that, as academics, we go beyond a pragmatic label and embrace the role of gender in drift responses, giving them specific ontological attention in the literature.

Logistics as a gendered effect were most prominent throughout. However, logistics notably changed as 'I' became 'we'. Some variations, such as field supplies and equipment, and increased travel expenses due to the presence of another human, were clear. Others components of personal safety were less obvious. For my field studies, the university required I have a safety protocol, which focused on keeping my supervisors aware of my movements. Other than this standardised procedure, I did not refer to personal safety in my thesis. Prior to pregnancy, my concerns were with avoiding physical attack. With pregnancy and motherhood, medical access took priority. Reflecting on this experience, I think my focus on keeping my child safe and healthy diverted my attention away from personal safety in general. The Philippines is considered the third most dangerous country in which to defend environmental rights (Global Witness, 2014); crime rates are high (Overseas Security Advisory Council, 2015). During our time in the Philippines, I was, and still am, most affected by the murder of an advocate against illegal fishing, Gerlie Menchie Alpajora. As reported by *Bicol Today*, the murder was connected to her work; she 'was brutally slain while sleeping beside her two minor children' ('Environmental Group Seeks Justice', 2015). This news came at a pivotal point, affirming a decision we had made only two weeks earlier. Deciding to prioritise quality of life, we decided to leave the Philippines. I, we, needed a break from the field.

Though not the only variable, I attribute the presence of my son as a significant factor in gaining access and securing participants. He invoked an affectionate curiosity in the locals, thus, increasing access. Additionally, his presence was a form of reciprocity. By welcoming the interview process, the participants were able to be in close contact with my light-skinned, considerably 'healthy' baby. Motherhood provided a commonality between the researcher and the participants (Caplan, 1993; Cornet, 2013; Ganesh, 1993; Macintyre, 1993; Schrijvers, 1993; Vera-Sanso, 1993). Though fieldwork would have been physically simplified had I been alone (Cornet, 2013), I cannot fathom the mental stress I would have endured through leaving my firstborn, coupled with the logistics of having to express milk to maintain my supply. I was more comfortable in the field with my child than without (Frohlick, 2002).

Bell (1993) found difficulty in constructing a field-self due to the presence of her children; however, I believe this is an effect of the field remaining as a masculine construct (Cornet, 2013; Frohlick, 2002). Attention to this and to the theoretical significance of family in the field is still largely absent from the literature (Cornet, 2013; Flinn, 1998; Frohlick, 2002). By sharing and analysing gender as an outward bias in the research experience, I have come to realise the need for gender as a standard ontology. Not only is it necessary to disclose influential variables as part of the scientific process, but in doing so we foster connectivity between the researcher and the participants. Motherhood is one of many sources of connectedness available to us as researchers. In writing this chapter, and revisiting the experiences through conversations with my husband, we agreed that taking an infant into the field was not necessarily the safest parenting choice. However, we agreed that, for us, and in so many ways, it was the best choice. My now five-year old, enjoys revisiting his first field experience through stories and photographs. Some of the people who we met in the field, still ask for photographic updates of our family. Rather than call special attention to a gendered ontology, I suggest that we, as researchers, validate our research practices by normalising gender as yet another variable with indisputable effects on the research process.

References

Amadiume, I. (1993) The mouth that spoke a falsehood will later speak the truth: Going home to the field in Eastern Nigeria. In D. Bell, P. Caplan and W.J. Karim (eds) *Gendered Fields: Women, Men and Ethnography* (pp. 182–198). London: Routledge.

Back, L. (1993) Gendered participation: Masculinity and fieldwork in a south London adolescent community. In D. Bell, P. Caplan and W.J. Karim (eds) *Gendered Fields: Women, Men and Ethnography* (pp. 215–233). London: Routledge.

Bell, D. (1993) Yes Virginia, there is a feminist ethnography. In D. Bell, P. Caplan and W.J. Karim (eds) *Gendered Fields: Women, Men and Ethnography* (pp. 28–43). London: Routledge.

Caplan, P. (1993) Learning gender: Fieldwork in a Tanzanian coastal village, 1965–85. In D. Bell, P. Caplan and W.J. Karim (eds) *Gendered Fields: Women, Men and Ethnography* (pp. 168–181). London: Routledge.

Conaway, M.E. (1986) The pretence of the neutral researcher. In T.L. Whitehead and M.E. Conaway (eds) *Self, Sex, and Gender in Cross-Cultural Fieldwork* (pp. 52–63). Chicago: University of Illinois Press.

Cornet, C. (2013) The fun and games of taking children to the field in Guizhou, China. In S. Turner (ed.) *Red Stamps and Gold Stars: Fieldwork Dilemmas in Upland Socialist Asia* (pp. 80–99). Vancouver, CA: UBC Press.

'Environmental group seeks justice in death of Bicoloan anti-illegal fishing activist' (17 August 2015) See http://bicoltoday.com/2015/08/17/environmental-group-seeks-justice-in-death-of-bicolana-anti-illegal-fishing-activist/ (accessed 15 June 2016).

Flinn, J. (1998) Introduction: The family dimension in anthropological fieldwork. In J. Flinn, L. Marshall and J. Armstrong (eds) *Fieldwork and Families: Constructing New Models for Ethnographic Fieldwork* (pp. 1–21). Honolulu: University of Hawaii Press.

Frohlick, S.E. (2002) 'You brought your baby to base camp?' Families and field sites. *The Great Lakes Geographer* 9 (1) 49–58.

Ganesh, K. (1993) Breaching the wall of difference: Fieldwork and a personal journey to Srivaikuntam, Tamilnadu. In D. Bell, P. Caplan and W.J. Karim (eds) *Gendered Fields: Women, Men and Ethnography* (pp. 128–142). London: Routledge.

Global Witness (2014) *Deadly Environment: A Rising Death Toll on Our Environmental Frontiers is Escaping International Attention* [Report]. London: Global Witness.

Golde, P. (1986) Odyssey of encounter. In P. Golde (ed.) *Women in the Field: Anthropological Experiences* (2nd edn, pp. 67–96). Los Angeles, CA: University of California Press.

Gurney, J.N. (1985) Not one of the guys: The female researcher in a male-dominated setting. *Qualitative Sociology* 8 (1) 42–62.

James, W. (1907) Lecture II: What pragmatism means [PDF]. In W. James (ed.) *Pragmatism: A New Name for Some Old Ways of Thinking*. See http://iws.collin.edu/amiller/William%20James%20-%20Pragmatism.pdf

Landes, R. (1986) A woman anthropologist in Brazil. In P. Golde (ed.) *Women in the Field: Anthropological Experiences* (2nd edn, pp. 117–139). Los Angeles, CA: University of California Press.

Levey, H. 2009 'Which one is yours?': Children and ethnography. *Qualitative Sociology* 32 (3) 311–331.

Macintyre, M. (1993) Fictive kinship or mistaken identity? Fieldwork on Tubetube Island, Papua New Guinea. In D. Bell, P. Caplan and W.J. Karim (eds) *Gendered Fields: Women, Men and Ethnography* (pp. 44–62). London: Routledge.

Mead, M. (1986) Field work in Pacific Islands, 1925–1967. In P. Golde (ed.) *Women in the Field: Anthropological Experiences* (2nd edn, pp. 292–331). Los Angeles, CA: University of California Press.

Nader, L. (1986) From anguish to exultation. In P. Golde (ed.) *Women in the Field: Anthropological Experiences* (2nd edn, pp. 67–96). Los Angeles, CA: University of California Press.

Oboler, R.S. (1986) For better or worse: Anthropologists and husbands in the field. In T.L. Whitehead and M.E. Conaway (eds) *Self, Sex and Gender in Cross-Cultural Fieldwork* (pp. 28–51). Urbana, IL: University of Illinois Press.

Ortbals, C.D. and Rincker, M.E. (2009) Embodied researchers: Gendered bodies, research activity, and pregnancy in the field. *PS: Political Science and Politics* 42 (2) 315–319.

Overseas Security Advisory Council (OSAC) (2015) *Philippines Crime and Safety Report*. See https://www.osac.gov/pages/ContentReportDetails.aspx?cid=17461

Porter, B.A. (2014) Marine tourism as a supplemental livelihood: An exploration of remote fisheries-based communities in the Philippines. Doctoral dissertation, Auckland University of Technology.

Porter, B.A. and Orams, M.B. (2014) Exploring tourism as a potential development strategy or an artisanal fishing community in the Philippines: The case of Barangay Victory in Bolinao. *Tourism in Marine Environments* 10 (1) 49–70.

Schrijvers, J. (1993) Motherhood experienced and conceptualised: Changing images in Sri Lanka and the Netherlands. In D. Bell, P. Caplan and W.J. Karim (eds) *Gendered Fields: Women, Men and Ethnography* (pp. 143–158). London: Routledge.

Sparke, M. (1996) Displacing the field in Field work: Masculinity, Metaphor and space. In N. Duncan (ed.) *Body Space* (pp. 212–233). New York, NY: Routledge.

Tripp, A.M. (2002) Combining intercontinental parenting and research: Dilemmas and strategies for women. *Signs* 27 (3) 793–811.

Vera-Sanso, P. (1993) Perception, East and West: A Madras encounter? In D. Bell, P. Caplan and W.J. Karim (eds) *Gendered Fields: Women, Men and Ethnography* (pp. 159–167). London: Routledge.

Warren, C.A.B. (1988) *Gender Issues in Field Research* (Qualitative Research Methods Series 9). Newbury Park, CA: Sage Publications.

6 'Mummy, When Are We Getting to the Fields?' Doing Fieldwork with Three Children

Antonia Canosa

Dr Antonia Canosa is a social anthropologist and recent PhD graduate from the Centre for Children and Young People at Southern Cross University, Australia. After being a stay-at-home mum for several years looking after her three children, she decided to go back to academia to complete a PhD in Education. Her own childhood growing up in the popular tourist destination of Positano on the Amalfi Coast (Italy) and the experience of raising three children in the Australian tourist destination of Byron Bay, provided an emic view and unique angle of vision to conduct her doctoral research. Antonia's thesis explores how children negotiate a sense of identity and belonging when growing up in a tourist destination. The study employs ethnographic, participatory and visual methodologies to privilege young people's voice and agency. Her research interests also include the anthropology of tourism, children's rights and participation, ethical issues in researching with children and youth cultures.

Introduction

In this chapter, I describe the *embodied entanglements* of doing doctoral research accompanied by my own children. Common perceptions of the solo and childless men or women researchers who leave their families behind to carry out fieldwork away from home have perpetuated the myth of research as a 'disembodied practice' (Frohlick, 2002). Even in the recounting of fieldwork narratives, the role of accompanying family members has often been erased. Previous research, particularly from a feminist perspective, has strived to overcome these common biases surrounding what *legitimate* fieldwork constitutes and has highlighted the important role of our subject positions (class, race, gender, sexuality, disability, etc.) (Dombroski, 2011; Drozdzewski & Robinson, 2015; Farrelly *et al.*, 2014; Flinn, 1998; Frohlick, 2002; Gilbert, 1994; Staeheli & Lawson, 1994).

In an effort to overcome such biases, I discuss how my role as a *mother* of three young children influenced my choice of field site as well as my fieldwork practices during doctoral research. Subconsciously, my gendered subjectivity has influenced my research from the very start and has led me to make important choices and adaptations throughout the fieldwork. Rarely, in tourism studies, as in other social sciences, have accompanying family members been featured in research accounts (Dombroski, 2011; Drozdzewski & Robinson, 2015; Flinn, 1998; Frohlick, 2002). In this chapter, I present an autobiographical account of my fieldwork experiences, focusing on how these experiences are uniquely female, and discussing some of the opportunities and difficulties that arose from embracing rather than concealing my role as a 'mother in the field'.

Fieldwork as an Embodied Practice

In the past, doing fieldwork – particularly ethnographic fieldwork with its emphasis on participant observation – was an objective and scientific endeavour which resulted in the analysis and interpretation of reality and ultimately the creation of theory (Flinn, 1998). Nevertheless, postmodern and poststructuralist influences felt around the 1980s instigated a *crisis of representation* whereby the authority of the researcher in ethnographic research and translation was increasingly being questioned and challenged (Clifford, 1986; Marcus & Fischer, 1986). Anthropologists, for example, realised that there is 'no Archimedean point' (Clifford, 1986: 22) from which to represent the world, as our subject positions increasingly shape our interpretation and representation of reality (Moore, 1999).

With the propagation of postmodern and feminist scholarship, fieldwork is increasingly being acknowledged as a highly experiential and embodied practice (Flinn, 1998; Frohlick, 2002; Gilbert, 1994). Flinn (1998) argues that fieldwork is not just a set of procedures but 'an intense, deeply emotional experience' (1998: 7). The fieldworker is thus not a neutral observer but a 'positioned subject' (2008: 7) who enters the field with a host of subject positions or embodied selves (Dombroski, 2011; Frohlick, 2002). Although there has been a reluctance in the past to acknowledge the impact of our subject positions on fieldwork practices (Flinn, 1998), the importance of personal experience (and a reflexive engagement in the field) is crucial both to the production of knowledge and to defining and mapping our *theoretical journeys* (hooks, 1994).

This reluctance to merge the personal and professional/academic spheres is evident in the lack of fieldwork accounts about accompanying family members. Frohlick (2002) argues that it is somewhat considered taboo 'to blur and even violate the boundaries of our field sites with visible traces of our personal lives' (2002: 52). Although the decision to travel with or without our family members undoubtedly shapes our fieldwork experiences and the production of knowledge, there has been an entrenched assumption that researchers, whether men or women, travel alone to the field (Frohlick, 2002). Nevertheless, the myth of the lone/solo, childless fieldworker/ethnographer is increasingly being challenged by the growing scholarship in this space (Dombroski, 2011; Drozdzewski & Robinson, 2015; Farrelly *et al.*, 2014; Flinn, 1998; Frohlick, 2002; Gilbert, 1994; Staeheli & Lawson, 1994). Among these, accounts of mothering in the field and the embodied experiences of combining *fieldwork* and *carework* are noticeable (Dombroski, 2011; Drozdzewski & Robinson, 2015; Farrelly *et al.*, 2014; Frohlick, 2002).

Reflexive and autobiographical accounts of fieldwork with accompanying family members are still, however, few and far between in tourism studies (Frohlick, 2002). Even more scarce is literature that addresses gender biases specific to women researchers (as this edited book suggests). According to some, 'despite three decades of study and a recent increase in papers, tourism gender research remains marginal to tourism enquiry' (Figueroa-Domecq *et al.*, 2015: 87). This leaves considerable scope to explore the role of gender and gender embodiment in the production of knowledge (Chambers & Rakić, 2015; Pritchard *et al.*, 2007; Small, 2016). In this chapter, I discuss the embodied experience of doing fieldwork 'at home' accompanied by my three children. Taking a reflexive and autobiographical stance (Chang, 2008), I discuss how my roles as an *ethnographer* and as a *mother* merged while doing fieldwork in an Australian tourist destination.

Being a Mother in the Field

Although there is an underlying assumption that gender inequity is a thing of the past (Glazer-Raymo, 2001), women in academia are often faced with considerable challenges including combining motherhood and fieldwork. My experience of carrying out doctoral research was indeed gendered and uniquely female, as I grappled with the same issues that other female academics encounter (Drozdzewski & Robinson, 2015). From the very start, I made decisions about what to research, how and where to carry out my fieldwork based on my role as a mother of three young children. In hindsight, these decisions where subconsciously taken, yet, reflecting back on them, I can now see how the topic I chose to research and the choice of field site were guided by my gendered subjectivity (Dombroski, 2011).

In late 2012, after a long break as a 'stay-at-home' mum, I decided it was time to return to academia and do what I love best – research. At the time my children were seven, five and three and my need to 'be there' for my family (Farrelly *et al.*, 2014: 33) influenced both the topic I chose to research and where I carried out fieldwork. As a mother of children who are growing up in a tourist destination – and having grown up in a popular holiday destination myself (Canosa, 2014) – I was drawn to this area of research. I soon discovered there was a lack of research focused on children and young people growing up in host communities, and their perceptions and attitudes towards tourism (Canosa *et al.*, 2016). Hence my interest in exploring how children and young people negotiate a sense of identity and belonging amid the continuous flow of visitors to their community (Canosa *et al.*, 2017).

Living in the popular tourist destination of Byron Bay (see Figure 6.1), I decided that doing research 'at home' would be an ideal way of combining fieldwork and care-work (Drozdzewski & Robinson, 2015). In

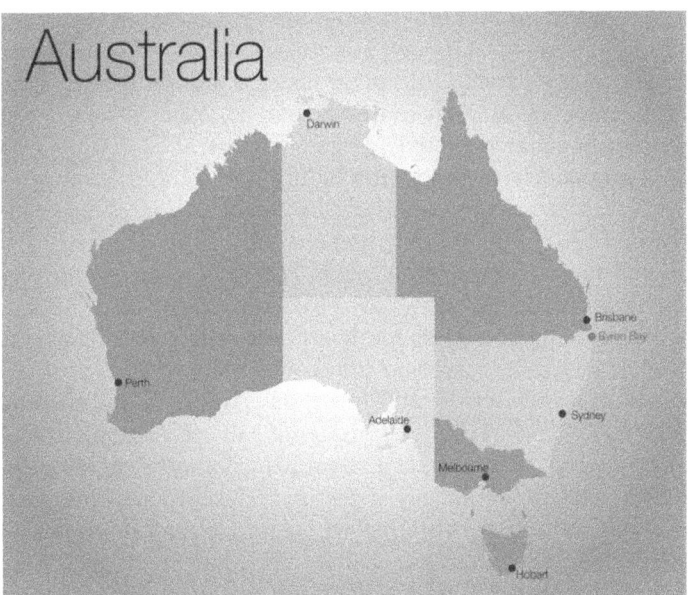

Figure 6.1 Map of Australia showing the location of Byron Bay

addition, I felt the same feelings of 'guilt' that other researchers have written about when making decisions about how to carry out meaningful fieldwork and still fulfil my role as a mother (Farrelly *et al.*, 2014; Frohlick, 2002). Having completed 12 months of ethnographic fieldwork, I can now relate some of the effects of femininity in the field and the subsequent opportunities and challenges of negotiating motherhood and fieldwork.

Advantages of researching with accompanying family members

As discussed, researchers are usually reticent about disclosing how personal/family decisions impact and shape field experiences. In my experience, fieldwork was a deeply emotional process which involved juggling day-to-day family activities (e.g. sport, homework, household duties, etc.) with typical fieldwork activities such as organising interviews and focus groups; attending community events; facilitating participatory projects with young people in the community; and generally establishing the relationships and networks essential to meaningful ethnographic research. While at first I struggled to combine fieldwork and care-work and often felt overwhelmed by the intensity of both activities, I now realise how having my children with me positively shaped the research process and enhanced my opportunities for meaningful engagement in the field, which would not have been possible otherwise (see also Dombroski, 2011; Farrelly *et al.*, 2014; Flinn, 1998).

My research strategy involved recruiting participants outside school in order to challenge the balance of power which is heavily skewed towards adult supervision in such contexts (Hart, 1992; Kellett, 2004). This meant I often had to organise interviews and focus groups in the afternoon with my own children with me. Initially, I tried to organise these interviews when my partner was at home so that I could go alone; however, it quickly became apparent that my participants felt more at ease when I had my children with me. My role as a *mother* and not just a *researcher* actually made me more 'accessible' to them by 'dismantling power relations' (Farrelly *et al.*, 2014: 26). Rather than concealing my identity as a mother my gendered subjectivity actually created the grounds for a more embodied and relational engagement in the field.

My status as an adult and a foreigner (my Italian accent being a defining factor) often had an 'othering' effect which was at odds with the kind of relationship I wanted to establish with my participants. I soon realised that my role as a mother created considerable interest among the children I was interviewing. When I talked about being a mother of three children who attend a local school, my participants were much more at ease. Likewise, when I had my children with me (and had to attend to their needs) participants would often relax and be more talkative. My identity as a mother thus rendered relationships with my participants more equal and facilitated the kind of relational and dialogical approach so important when doing ethnographic fieldwork. As Farrelly *et al.* (2014) argue, 'children in the field can help establish the identity of the fieldworker ... [they] enable the fieldworker to occupy a role which community members can relate to' (2014: 26).

In addition, having the children with me facilitated access to participants and resulted in the collection of valuable data. Having to care for my own children while doing fieldwork meant I had access to young people in the community who would have otherwise remained inaccessible (e.g. at sporting events, youth groups). I often took advantage of the time spent – for example, watching my children play sport – to talk to other young people about my research and organise to meet for formal interviews/focus groups. I quickly understood that embracing my role and identity as a mother – and the 'embodied entanglements' (Frohlick, 2002: 50) that resulted – made my fieldwork experience more meaningful and improved my chances of producing interesting and innovative research.

In a sense, my children kept me grounded and created the basis for a (peculiar) balance to my fieldwork days. Having to collect my children after school also gave me a clear deadline; come 3 o'clock I knew all desk-based work had to end. This I think, although frustrating at the time, gave me focus and increased my productivity in those morning hours. In addition, manual jobs such as meal preparation and household chores resulted in crucial thinking time which I would have otherwise spent in the field or at my desk had my children not been with me during fieldwork. This would have left me feeling drained and unable to make important connections between raw data and theory. For my children it was also fun to be involved in 'mummy's work'. As the following statement suggests, they often positively commented on being involved even though at first they had no idea what my work entailed (Figure 6.2):

> It was really good, it was really fun ... at first I thought it meant going into the sugarcane fields to chop down some sugarcane ... but then I realised it meant going to do interviews and all that ... it meant doing your PhD. (Davide, age 10)

For me personally, ethnography as a methodology involved an 'embodied, relational engagement with a *site*' (Dombroski, 2011: 26), the boundaries of which extended to my personal life and involved blending and merging my identity as a *researcher* with my identity as a *mother*. Viewing fieldwork as an *embodied space* highlights the effect of our femininity on the research process and the inherent gender biases that unfold in the field. This in turn challenges the common misperceptions of the 'disembodied researcher' who erases traces of accompanying family members from his/her research accounts (Dombroski, 2011; Frohlick, 2002). Combining fieldwork and care-work does, however, create considerable challenges.

Figure 6.2 Photograph taken by David Hickson, artist and film producer during the participatory filmmaking activity. I am pictured in the top left-hand corner with my arm around my son Davide

Complexities of negotiating fieldwork and care-work

Choosing to do fieldwork 'at home' has the obvious advantage of not having to travel elsewhere for data collection; my children did not miss school, they were not uprooted from their network of friends and my partner did not need to take time off work. Nevertheless, I struggled throughout my PhD (but particularly during fieldwork) to legitimise my work with family and friends. Often my family could not grasp the importance of *being in the field* – talking to people, attending community events and generally doing what an ethnographer does, being embedded in the community. I often felt guilty about dragging my children along with me for work when we might have spent the day in other ways. I think this stems from my own upbringing and entrenched cultural assumption that the mother must be the primary carer and 'always present' for her children.

At times, the fieldwork also produced considerable disruption to family routines as I tried to juggle after-school activities with fieldwork activities. I often had to pack voice recorders and ethics paperwork as well as think about snacks and games to entertain my own children (Figure 6.3). Combining care-work and wage-work produces considerable 'physical, emotional and time-management challenges' for mothers in the field (Drozdzewski & Robinson, 2015: 375).

In addition, prior to having children, my ethnographic field experiences consisted of long periods of uninterrupted time to immerse myself

Figure 6.3 My daughter, Sara, helping during fieldwork

in the community, meet people, ask questions and participate in community events (see Canosa, 2014). After having children, fieldwork has meant combining *care-work* with *fieldwork*, limiting my full participation in the ethnographic site. My interview recordings are evidence of the many interruptions I experienced during interviews when attending to the needs of my children (e.g. toilet trips, providing snacks or just the usual 'mummy look at me!'). Although this was annoying at the time, it became obvious that my participants where amused by these interruptions and were often more open and forthcoming in their discussions as a consequence.

As Farrelly *et al*. (2014) argue, mothering is a highly 'sensory' and 'tactile' experience, and my ability to 'see, touch, feel, hear and breathe' (2014: 44) my children provided that emotional balance that would have been impossible if I had been worrying about the children left at home. Although my 'embodied vulnerability' as a mother caused certain limitations, coming to terms with and accepting this vulnerability created the grounds for a relational engagement in the field (Dombroski, 2011). The gendered role of researchers in tourism studies is rarely acknowledged, as is the effect of femininity in the field and the biases specific to women researchers. The physical and emotional challenges that women in the field encounter are also often neglected in tourism research. Hopefully, with the propagation of a critical/feminist and reflexive tourism scholarship we can promote dialogue across disciplinary boundaries to address common issues and biases encountered by 'women in the field' (Ateljevic et al., 2005, 2007; Fullagar & Wilson, 2012; Pritchard et al., 2011).

Final Reflections

This chapter presents an autobiography of my experiences negotiating fieldwork and motherhood during doctoral research. I have discussed how having accompanying family members in the field has been both challenging and rewarding. Positive aspects include facilitating the rapport-building process with participants; accessing valuable data; and generally providing a 'healthy sense of both self and family' (Flinn, 1998: 17). Although challenging at times, having my children with me actually promoted a dialogical encounter with research participants. Looking back, I am certain that had I pursued a PhD before having children my research topic and approach would have been different. Motherhood has, in a sense, shaped the choice of topic, how the research was carried out and the underlying philosophical stance I have taken (see also Castle & Woloshyn, 2003).

Even before entering the field I was aware of the limitations I would encounter as a woman and mother; however, it was not until I embraced my status as a 'mother in the field' that I was able to reap the benefits of *accompanied fieldwork*. At first I was, in fact, reluctant to disclose elements of my personal life to research participants and I went to great lengths to try and organise interviews without my children being present. Nevertheless, the involvement of my children in fieldwork activities, and the many interruptions they created, actually facilitated the breaking down of power relations and made me – 'the adult researcher' – more accessible to my young participants.

I do want to acknowledge, however, that researching children's lived experiences provided a suitable *field environment/space* for my children to be present. In other areas of research or with adult participants it may have been unsuitable and unpractical to have 'kids in tow'. Ethical implications must also be considered, particularly in relation to anonymity and confidentiality during interviews. Generally, I tried to engage my children in other activities (e.g. riding their scooters or playing nearby) and thus they were not in close proximity during the interviews. Nevertheless, my *professional* and *personal* worlds would often get entangled during fieldwork. During the participatory film component of my research (Canosa et al., 2017), for example, my son (aged 10 at the time) and daughter (aged 7) expressed a desire to be involved in both the creation of the animation films and the research discussions (see Figure 6.2).

From an ethical point of view, I considered my own children no different from the children I was interviewing. The child-centred reflexive approach embedded in my research strategy, and closely informed by the international Ethical Research Involving Children (ERIC) framework (Graham *et al.*, 2013), guided my fieldwork practices (Canosa & Graham, 2016). To respectfully and ethically involve children (including my own) in the research, I employed the three 'Rs': Reflexivity, Rights and Relationships. This framework is useful in guiding research towards a *relational* approach, to recognise children's *rights* – as enshrined in the United Nations Convention on the Rights of the Child (UNCRC) – and to strive for a *reflexive* engagement in the field in order to negotiate the ethically challenging moments during fieldwork (Powell *et al.*, 2016). Conducting ethnographic and participatory research with children is often a 'messy' process which necessitates a degree of ethical mindfulness that can only come from a reflexive engagement in the field. This was achieved through a careful process of journaling (see also Holland *et al.*, 2010) and through continuous reflection on how my children's presence in the field shaped the production of knowledge.

Since the call for more reflexively-oriented approaches to tourism research (Ateljevic *et al.*, 2005; Feighery, 2006; Franklin & Crang, 2001; Phillimore & Goodson, 2004; Pritchard *et al.*, 2011; Wilson & Hollinshead, 2015; Wilson *et al.*, 2012), little has been written about how gender impacts our fieldwork experiences. Reflective accounts of our gendered experiences are few and far between (Matthews, 2012; Mura, 2015). Even more scarce are accounts of how women experience fieldwork in tourism research and the biases we encounter (Frohlick, 2002). This edited collection is an exciting opportunity for cross-disciplinary dialogue in this space. It may also shed light on why research on families and children in tourism has to date mainly come from women rather than men. According to Schänzel and Carr (2016: 2), this may point to a 'continued gender-biased discrimination' in academia where families and children are seen predominantly as a 'woman's' research topic.

Our individual voices and stories provide a starting point for a collaborative dialogic analysis of femininity in the field (Castle & Woloshyn, 2003; Frank, 2002). I feel that turning the *reflexive gaze* upon ourselves to explore how our gendered subjectivities create biases (both positive and negative) during our fieldwork practices can be a powerful tool in understanding how gender impacts the production of knowledge. Only through cross-disciplinary reflexive inquiry on a global scale can we collectively address the gaps in tourism knowledge and contribute to 'ignite' feminist and 'gender-aware' approaches in tourism research (Figueroa-Domecq *et al.*, 2015: 99).

References

Ateljevic, I., Harris, C., Wilson, E. and Collins, L.F. (2005) Getting 'entangled': Reflexivity and the 'critical turn' in tourism studies. *Tourism Recreation Research* 30 (2), 9–21.

Ateljevic, I., Pritchard, A. and Morgan, N. (eds) (2007) *The Critical Turn in Tourism Studies: Innovative Research Methodologies*. Oxford: Elsevier.
Canosa, A. (2014) The role of travel and mobility in processes of identity formation among the Positanesi. *Tourist Studies: An International Journal* 14, 182–202.
Canosa, A. and Graham, A. (2016) Ethical tourism research involving children. *Annals of Tourism Research* 61, 219–221.
Canosa, A., Moyle, B. and Wray, M. (2016) Can anybody hear me? A critical analysis of young residents' voices in tourism studies. *Tourism Analysis: An Interdisciplinary Journal* 21, 325–337.
Canosa, A., Wilson, E. and Graham, A. (2017) Empowering young people through participatory film: A postmethodological approach. *Current Issues in Tourism* 20 (8), 894–907.
Castle, J.B. and Woloshyn, V. (2003) Motherhood and academia: Learning from our lived experience. *Journal of the Motherhood Initiative for Research and Community Involvement* 5 (2), 35–46.
Chambers, D. and Rakić, T. (2015) Conclusion: Reflections beyond existing research frontiers. In D. Chambers and T. Rakić (eds) *Tourism Research Frontiers: Beyond the Boundaries of Knowledge* (Vol. 20, pp. 167–176). Bingley: Emerald.
Chang, H. (2008) *Autoethnography as Method*. Walnut Creek, CA: Left Coast Press Inc.
Clifford, J. (1986) Introduction: Partial truths. In J. Clifford and G.E. Marcus (eds) *Writing Culture: The Poetics and Politics of Ethnography* (pp. 1–26). London, England: The University of California Press.
Dombroski, K. (2011) Embodying research: Maternal bodies, fieldwork and knowledge production in North-West China. *Graduate Journal of Asia-Pacific Studies* 7 (2), 19–29.
Drozdzewski, D. and Robinson, D.F. (2015) Care-work on fieldwork: Taking your own children into the field. *Children's Geographies* 13, 372–378.
Farrelly, T., Stewart-Withers, R. and Dombroski, K. (2014) 'Being there': Mothering and absence/presence in the field. *Sites: A Journal of Social Anthropology and Cultural Studies* 11 (2), 25–56.
Feighery, W. (2006) Reflexivity and tourism research: Telling an(other) story. *Current Issues in Tourism* 9, 269–282.
Figueroa-Domecq, C., Pritchard, A., Segovia-Pérez, M., Morgan, N. and Villacé-Molinero, T. (2015) Tourism gender research: A critical accounting. *Annals of Tourism Research* 52, 87–103.
Flinn, J. (1998) Introduction: The family dimension in anthropological fieldwork. In J. Flinn, L. Marshall and J. Armstrong (eds) *Fieldwork and Families: Constructing New Models for Ethnographic Fieldwork* (pp. 1–21). Honolulu, Hawaii: University of Hawaii Press.
Frank, A.W. (2002) Why study people's stories? The dialogical ethics of narrative analysis. *International Journal of Qualitative Methods* 1, 109–117.
Franklin, A. and Crang, M. (2001) The trouble with tourism and travel theory? *Tourist Studies* 1, 5–22.
Frohlick, S. (2002) You brought your baby to base camp? Families and field sites. *The Great Lakes Geographer* 9, 49–58.
Fullagar, S. and Wilson, E. (2012) Critical pedagogies: A reflexive approach to knowledge creation in tourism and hospitality studies. *Journal of Hospitality and Tourism Management* 19, 1–6.
Gilbert, M.R. (1994) The politics of location: Doing feminist research at 'home'. *Professional Geographer* 46, 90–96.
Glazer-Raymo, J. (2001) *Shattering the Myths: Women in academe*. Baltimore, MD: JHU Press.
Graham, A., Powell, M.A., Taylor, N., Anderson, D.L. and Fitzgerald, R. (2013) *Ethical Research Involving Children*. See http://childethics.com/

Hart, R.A. (1992) *Children's Participation: From Tokenism to Citizenship*. Florence: UNICEF Innocenti Research Centre.
Holland, S., Renold, E., Ross, N.J. and Hillman, A. (2010) Power, agency and participatory agendas: A critical exploration of young people's engagement in participative qualitative research. *Childhood* 17, 360–375.
hooks, b. (1994) *Teaching to Transgress: Education as the Practice of Freedom*. New York, NY: Routledge.
Kellett, M. (2004) 'Just teach us the skills please, we'll do the rest': Empowering ten-year-olds as active researchers. *Children and Society* 18, 329–343.
Marcus, G.E. and Fischer, M.M. (1986) *Anthropology as Cultural Critique: An Experimental Moment in the Human Sciences*. London, England: The University of Chicago Press.
Matthews, A.L. (2012) 'Write' of passage: Reflecting on the fieldwork process and its contribution to critically orientated tourism research. *Journal of Hospitality and Tourism Management* 19, 1–8.
Moore, H. (1999) *Anthropological Theory at the Turn of the Century*. Cambridge: Polity Press.
Mura, P. (2015) 'To participate or not to participate?': A reflective account. *Current Issues in Tourism* 18, 83–98.
Phillimore, J. and Goodson, L. (eds) (2004) *Qualitative Research in Tourism: Ontologies, Epistemologies and Methodologies*. London: Routledge.
Powell, M.A., Graham, A. and Truscott, J. (2016) Ethical research involving children: Facilitating reflexive engagement. *Qualitative Research Journal* 16 (2), 197–208.
Pritchard, A., Morgan, N. and Ateljevic, I. (2011) Hopeful tourism: A new transformative perspective. *Annals of Tourism Research* 38, 941–963.
Pritchard, A., Morgan, N., Ateljevic, I. and Harris, C. (eds) (2007) *Tourism and Gender: Embodiment, Sensuality and Experience*. Wallingford: CABI.
Schänzel, H.A. and Carr, N. (2016) Introduction: Special issue on children, families and leisure – part three. *Annals of Leisure Research* 19, 381–385. doi: 10.1080/11745 398.2016.1201241
Small, J. (2016) Holiday bodies: Young women and their appearance. *Annals of Tourism Research* 58, 18–32.
Staeheli, L.A. and Lawson, V.A. (1994) A discussion of 'women in the field': The politics of feminist fieldwork. *Professional Geographer* 46, 96–102.
Wilson, E. and Hollinshead, K. (2015) Qualitative tourism research: Opportunities in the emergent soft sciences. *Annals of Tourism Research* 54, 30–47.
Wilson, E., Small, J. and Harris, C. (2012) Editorial introduction: Beyond the margins? The relevance of critical tourism and hospitality studies. *Journal of Hospitality and Tourism Management* 19, 48–51.

7 The Dissemination of the Feminine: An In-depth Analysis of Independent Travel

Gisele Carvalho

Gisele Carvalho holds a Master of Science in Education and Environmental Management and is in the final stages of her PhD in tourism at University of Aveiro. Orginally from Brazil, the experience of living alone in Portugal has transformed her in the personal and professional dimensions. Gaining this independence has been vital in exploring the theme of her thesis about independent travel of females. She believes that being single and childless has provided her with opportunities for a greater introversion, and has revealed a new vision for her mission as educator and researcher. The depth that she has gained from her studies about gender, leisure, spirituality and independent travel have increased her commitment to promote these subjects, in particular, in the Amazon region where she lives and works. She considers women's empowerment through personal development as necessary to confront gender inequality that arises from human relations.

Women in the Field (Other Studies)

The research presented in this chapter involved 15 Brazilian women who had travelled on their own at least once for the purpose of leisure. Some were interviewed face-to-face and others via Skype. The latter was used both due to its current use as a communication tool as well as to minimise travelling expenses. As such, a more feminist approach was thought to be appropriate to gather information about the interviewees' experiences and give the women a voice (Harding, 1987), which is considered more of a help than a hindrance by Smith (1992). In research and fieldwork in the area of gender studies, ethnographic knowledge is very relevant and is generally based on studies in the areas of anthropology and the social sciences (Bell *et al.*, 1993; Golde, 1970; Whitehead & Conaway, 1986).

Judith Butler is considered one of the most expressive and complex thinkers on the various questions which are raised when it comes to performance and gender. Her research is underpinned and influenced by such authors as Foucault, Derrida, Lacan, Spinoza and Irigaray. According to Butler (2004), gender is a concept which goes beyond social norms and the notion of woman, which enables us to reflect upon sex and gender in relation to societal norms, thus giving it a political dimension.

There is a notable predominance of female researchers in the area of gender studies. Either individually or collectively, women act on various fronts – in the family, in the labour market, in politics and in a range of formal and informal institutions – and these numbers may increase proportionally as they acquire more knowledge on the subject (Hanmer & Klugman, 2015). In addition, these researchers have shown that the education of women is strongly associated with empowerment, which can be seen in many walks of life: the importance of cognitive transformation, such as increased confidence, greater autonomy, feelings of self-worth and respect and motivation are emphasised on both fronts (Hanmer & Klugman, 2015: 239).

My research follows the principles laid down by Wilson (2004), although it focuses more on the different dimensions of independent travel. In Wilson's (2004) study about Australian women who travel alone, the focus was on the constraints and vulnerabilities that a woman faces when travelling alone. She states that the feminist paradigm requires a more detailed and complex description of the data, and allows women to use their own words to talk about their experiences and the constraints they experience as independent travellers.

To some extent, there is vulnerability in both the role of interviewer and interviewee. This is a feature of social relationships and corresponds to the role each person or group plays in the process, with reciprocal feedback between us and the outside world (Butler, 2004). According to the author, there is a psychic resistance to vulnerability, where the subject claims their right to their place in society, equality, mobility and safety; all of which were observed in the discourse of these women (Butler, 2015).

When writing about the issue of vulnerability, Butler explains that there are many ways in which performativity can become an example of resistance; for example, in movements where differences do not construct a unified identity (Butler, 2015). Therefore, without the constraints of social norms, people may be open to new possible alliances as a result of something they have in common, and in this way the body, through action, expresses itself both implicitly and explicitly, in performative resistance. This can be observed in independent travel, where women resist certain pressures societies impose upon them by treating them as if they did not have the right to move around freely.

We are in an era of fluidity, transition and change, which requires greater involvement and commitment with gender-difference focused policies; in other words, a political attitude which pays closer attention to the subjectivity of individuals, taking into account their own characteristics and specificities. In this way, during my fieldwork, my objective was to create an environment which was conducive to the interviewees revealing information about themselves in an authentic way. In this context, it is important to state that identity is not a fixed process, but rather a dynamic one, where experiences are potential opportunities for people to (re)produce their individual personalities. This can be particularly relevant during independent leisure trips, especially because the women interviewed have greater freedom of choice when travelling compared to other aspects of their everyday lives (Graburn, 1983; Neulinger, 1981).

Consequently, if on one hand there is vulnerability, on the other there is resistance. It is also important to highlight that there is a paradox within the concepts of violence, vulnerability and resistance, because by resorting to the law to challenge violence, many times we legitimise it (Butler, 2004). In truth, no-one wants to be perceived as vulnerable, which is clearly reflected in the discourse of the women interviewed in this study. When I interviewed women who had been on a greater number of journeys, I became aware of their need to portray themselves as strong and courageous women, which in turn made me feel somewhat intimidated and challenged because I did not have a similar profile to them. Perhaps it is inevitable that a comparison between my experiences and theirs be drawn, and that feeling of inadequacy was not present when I interviewed women who had not travelled as much.

The women interviewed react to the subtle social prejudices and stereotypes of being female, single and/or alone, childless, Brazilian and Latin, and describe some of their experiences in a more aggressive manner. However, the more they focus on the differences, the more powerful those differences become due to the fact that resistance requires women to overcome their own vulnerability (Butler, 2015).

In relating performance to leisure, Cohen (2013) explains that the contemporary theory of leisure has taken on notions of performance and performativity used to exemplify how spaces and discourses are created, reproduced, resisted and transformed. From this viewpoint, a performative perspective recognises that individuals are able to perform in various ways and have a range of mutable selves. In other words, personal identities are not fixed but rather in the process of being created. As a result, individuals are able to produce and reproduce their sense of personal identity (Cohen, 2013).

The Experience Moves Me

> 'Travel to find your own boundaries. Travel. Grow. Spend time blending in. To keep what is yours'.
> (A.F., 26 years old, interviewee)

After conducting some of the interviews, I have come to believe that the practice of independent travel provides a range of information which can be used to reflect upon such areas as gender issues, the vulnerability of human relationships and subjectivity. My interest in studying Brazilian women who travel alone arose after my first independent trip outside Brazil, due to the fact that it raised a number of issues about the challenges and benefits of travelling solo as a woman.

Therefore, my own doubts and questions as a researcher are all interconnected with the dimensions of self and performance. People want to tell their stories and experiences and to talk about what they have learnt in life as a result of the places they have travelled to. They long to share how happy (or not) they were and what they felt. However, what motivates them to do this? And are people interested in finding out how a woman feels as she ventures out into the world on her own?

While trying to understand what independent travel meant to the women who were interviewed, I became a part of the complexity of these women's reflections, particularly because I had experienced a process of profound reflection during the interviews. As stated by one woman, with regard to what she had learnt when she travelled alone: *'Travel to find your own boundaries. Travel. Grow. Spend time blending in. To keep what is yours'* (A.F., 26 years old). This engagement between me and interviewees occurred in a very fluid way throughout the whole process, especially in the face-to-face interviews. It was as if the interviewees and I were friends having a conversation in a bar, with a level of intimacy created from common experiences and ideas. During the Skype interviews, that empathy took longer to emerge, perhaps due to the impersonal nature of virtual communication.

Being Brazilian and single and travelling alone abroad can take on many different meanings. The Brazilian culture is by nature a chauvinistic one, which for a very long time dictated women's behaviour. With globalisation, access to a digital world without borders and higher qualifications, Brazilian women have had the opportunity to enter traditionally male-dominated areas and broaden their horizons, an example of which is independent travel. Nowadays, Brazilian women are more financially independent and are in a position to travel more.

The accounts provided by the women interviewed show the intensity and complexity of everything that underpins their experience of independent travel. During each interview, I was able to reflect upon things to the extent that they sometimes made me question my own personal choices. Therefore, in order to understand how productive the connection and feeling of empathy between myself and the interviewees was, it is important to briefly contextualise the period of time, location and the circumstances under which the meetings with these women took place.

It was with a certain level of sensitivity towards gender issues that I approached this study. My own personal path helped me to acquire knowledge which resulted in an interest in pursuing research in this area, in particular the effects travelling has on people's lives, as well as increasing my understanding of the benefits gained through independent travel, in terms of learning experiences, challenges and benefits. My experiences, as well as those of the interviewees were taken into consideration, from the selection of the participants and the development of the interview script, to the personal (and virtual) meetings with the subjects and the analysis of the data gathered. The dynamic nature of the process resulted in a dramatic shift in the way I feel, the way I perceive myself as a woman and a researcher, how I relate to others and my understanding of gender differences and similarities.

The Path

This section explores the researcher's role in 15 in-depth interviews carried out with adult Brazilian women who have travelled alone at least once to international destinations, for leisure and tourism. In essence, these women chose their destinations and had the experience of being alone in a country other than their own.

Stage one: Preparing the interview

> *'Travel to find your own boundaries. Travel. Grow'.*

After having identified women who had the correct profile for this study, I made contact with them via email and/or telephone in order to tell them about the objectives of the study and what would be expected of them. Once I had received feedback from them, I arranged a face-to-face or Skype meeting to interview them, according to their availability.

In the majority of the face-to-face meetings, I suggested the place but I was also open to any possible suggestions from them. The objective was to create a place which was comfortable and had a quiet and welcoming environment, or at least with as little extraneous noise as possible in order to record the conversation. Perhaps if the interviewees had been male, I would have been more careful, I might have sought less intimate and more public meeting places such as a library or a café. I might also have called on the help of an assistant to be with me during the interviews to avoid potentially uncomfortable moments. As I felt secure in my relationship with the interviewees, all the places used were favourable and contributed to the interviews being both dynamic and fluid. Two interviews were carried out in study rooms in the University of Aveiro Library, another two in my house, three in the interviewees' homes and one in a restaurant.

The methodology used was a non-probability snowball sample, which focuses more on the relationships between the sample, the object and the empirical *corpus*, rather than on the technical rules of sampling (Poupart *et al.*, 2008). This type of sampling is the most frequently used and is based on the precise characteristics the researcher wants to analyse. The method consists of creating a network of social relationships among the people being interviewed, who then provide names of other potential subjects (Poupart *et al.*, 2008).

The starting point was my network of personal acquaintances, with some suggestions made by the interviewees themselves. I also felt a certain amount of resistance when arranging the interviews, seeing as the process required the respondents to give of their time and they needed to have some interest in and sensitivity to the subject. At the beginning, finding women with the desired profile was difficult because I was living in Portugal and needed to carry out in-depth interviews, which would take time. Curiously, however, after I had already carried out the interviews and while discussing the issue with other people, I met many other Brazilian women who fit the profile. This happened a lot when I mentioned my research, and I also found new potential interviewees who fit the profile. I was able to see that the theme of this study is a growing trend and it is increasingly common to find women with similar characteristics.

The women who I planned to interview via Skype showed interest in the subject, but I also became aware of some resistance on their part, perhaps because they did not know me personally. The interviews lasted on average one hour, and at the beginning it was important to make the women feel as comfortable as possible to earn their trust in order for them to open up to me. If the interviewees had been men, perhaps the interviews would have been shorter with more objective replies to the questions I asked.

The aim of the study is to understand what the experiences and challenges of independent travel mean to these Brazilian women through the analysis of their feelings and perceptions of what they had been through.

However, in order to minimise bias in the interviewees' discourse, the information provided at the beginning was limited to explaining the objective of the study: a personal reflection of the experience of independent travel. This approach favoured the spontaneous and direct exchange of information, as well as time for the interviewees to reflect upon the answer to a particular question.

It is no surprise, therefore, that the data provided by the interviewee can be considered a co-construction, where both the interviewee and the interviewer participate (Poupart et al., 2008). I agree with Oliveira's (2006) opinion that interviews have the advantage of creating a personal relationship between the researcher and the subject, thus increasing the possibility of widening the discussion beyond the questions in the script. This was the case between the interviewees and me, perhaps because we were women and because of the similarities between us, which made the interaction more fluid. The interviews took place within an 11-month period, from January to November 2014. Throughout this time, I noticed interesting differences in my own performance, both during the interviews and with regard to the increase in my awareness of the issue, which overlaps with my own personal life, resulting in a mixture of perceptions between the participants and myself. At the end of the first three interviews I took notes in my field diary of my personal feelings about how the interviews had gone and my impressions of the interviewees' body language (gestures and behaviour). The habit of taking notes waned as the interviews progressed; however, I am aware that if I had continued to take notes, they could have been very useful while I was analysing the data collected.

Stage two: The interview

'Spend some time blending in'

In-depth or semi-guided interviews can reveal both the intensity and complexity of social relationships because they are capable of raising issues about what occurs in different areas of everyday life (Poupart et al., 2008; Quivy & Campenhoudt, 1992). The same happened throughout the interview process. Although some of the questions were guided, the women interviewed were allowed to speak freely, honestly and spontaneously, using their own words, about what they felt was most important with regard to the question asked. I believe that this process favoured greater reflection on the part of these women.

Even though each woman's case was unique, I tried in all of the interviews to create a light-hearted environment in which they felt at ease. Initially my fieldwork was supposed to take place in Brazil with face-to-face interviews. However, in order to reduce the expense of this type of fieldwork and to optimise my time, as well as overcome the difficulty of finding women who fit the profile, I decided to find Brazilian women who were living temporarily in Portugal, seeing as I was doing my PhD there. In addition, as I had a scholarship from a Brazilian research-oriented agency (CAPES), it was important to carry out my PhD in its entirety in Portugal. The idea of carrying out fieldwork in Portugal was to reduce costs; however, I realise that interviewing women face-to-face in their homes could make the experience richer and create more empathy because the interviews were carried out in a comfortable and familiar place, which could contribute to a more fluid and dynamic experience. From a researcher's perspective, going out to meet the interviewees was more challenging.

With regard to any expenses the subjects had to pay, the women were interviewed face-to-face in Portugal and via Skype, therefore no costs were involved. From an ethical point of view, anonymity and confidentiality of the women's personal information and their social environment were also ensured. In general, I became aware of the feeling of comfort and well-being on the part of the subjects while they shared their travel experiences, because they were spontaneous and showed interest and openness during the interviews. Furthermore, the interviews provided an opportunity for the women to discuss social issues, as well as to come up with multiple interpretations of their own discourses (Poupart *et al.*, 2008). There was genuine interest in hearing what they had to say and in unravelling some of the contexts and interpretations which go beyond discourse (Quivy & Campenhoudt, 1992).

Stage three: After the interview

'To keep what is yours'.

During the analysis of the data collected, my objective was to understand and analyse the content of the interviews from a transdisciplinary perspective, linking various fields of knowledge and constructing connections from and between different areas of study (Morin, 1989). This transdisciplinary approach to the research created the opportunity for a more subjective analysis of the data. At the same time, I attempted to be as faithful as possible to the theoretical underpinnings, and my own personal experiences and vision of the world, which acted as a common thread for the observation, analysis and interpretation of the data collected during the interviews.

While the data were being analysed, due to the fact that I was very close to and conscious of the content of the interviews, my supervisors suggested that I ask two external female reviewers to look at the interviews in order to find any common denominators in the profiles of the women interviewed. This required a certain amount of flexibility on my part as a researcher, especially in the construction, deconstruction and reconstruction of my object of study (Poupart *et al.*, 2008).

The path taken to consolidate the dialogue between me and the women interviewed was an experience which I reflected upon throughout the whole research process. I tried to make myself aware of all the subjective factors which could affect and influence the framework and analysis of the findings.

Interpretative researchers point out that the development of knowledge and trust are social constructs in which the researcher is perceived as an essential part of the process – with all their subjectivity, opinions and ideologies – in the interpretation of the dialogue which takes place with the interviewee (Rey, 2005). Taking this concept as a starting point, during the interviews I tried to create empathy with the participants, with whom I found numerous affinities, particularly when we spoke about the constraints and learning opportunities experienced during independent travel.

Gender was an important aspect when interviewing other women. As a woman, I was able to better understand the diverse range of settings in which women find themselves in their personal and social lives. For decades, feminist voices have produced significant guidance for the politics of modern society. Furthermore, due to its emancipatory and critical nature, feminist research empowers women, thus strengthening the demands they make based on their own personal realities, and opening an intellectual and emotional space where women can find their place in society (Hesse-Biber, 2012). For me, research on independent travel was an opportunity for the women interviewed, as well as myself, to have a voice and express ourselves freely. It was a space where they could discuss their grievances and suggestions for change, with a view to creating equal access to leisure activities for everyone.

The statements provided by the interviewees revealed that a woman who travels alone challenges a series of institutionalised paradigms and deep-rooted prejudices, which results in her being judged by society. In this way, for me personally, my research brought to the fore a discussion which includes other ostracised groups and minorities, with a view to fighting such issues as sexism, racism and homophobia, as well as developing a more complex knowledge of the issue (Hesse-Biber, 2012). This study falls within the scope of this type of research due to its contextual, inclusive, experiential and socially-relevant nature, which goes beyond my role as a researcher who is involved in an intimate and in-depth relationship with my object of study (Reinharz, 1992).

So, What is Mine?

For me personally, it was very gratifying to write about this process because by reflecting upon my path in this study, I relived milestones I had experienced during the four years I lived in Portugal, and reflected upon my own learning curve from the beginning of my thesis up to this point. Inspired by previous studies, I believe that the fact that I am a woman and a qualitative researcher contributed to a new way of reflecting upon research carried out in the field of gender issues.

As with life, irrespective of the gender of the researcher, research is a mindful and flexible path which may lead to inner reflection, to deconstructing paradigms and resolutions, adaptation and alienation to find oneself and the Other. In a subjective way, exchanging information and feelings with the world outside may gradually minimise the prejudices which still exist with regard to women (Brown, 2006). Just as a mirror reflects our own image, the Other shows us where we are and who we are in our lives. In this context, I increasingly contemplate the mysticism of the female gender because I understand personal factors to be fundamental in research, such as the connection between the researcher and the subject of their research and the personal and ideological reasons which drive them to carry out their work in the field. Gender theory makes all the sense in the world when I listen to the accounts of the women who participated in this process, because they raise important issues of everyday human relationships, which should be more widely discussed and developed, in addition to the increased empowerment the experience brought to my own personal life.

The common thread in this study was feminist research and it provided me, as a female researcher, with a strong need to find myself and an opportunity for in-depth self-analysis. During the interviews, I reflected upon my identity as a woman, my beliefs about what it is to be a woman, what it is to be a man and about personal and professional relationships. Each step made me more aware of my own path and my understanding of the issue became clearer with regard to personal gains and the fruits of my labour in this field.

After having carried out the research, I feel more empowered and conscious of my role as a researcher and better prepared to increase my knowledge about other areas related to gender issues. I am more aware of my subjectivity and have a better understanding and a more open mind to a world of possibilities for future professional projects.

For the women who were interviewed, independent travel is a form of resistance when taking into account the context in which they find themselves and has the capacity to promote transformation, which may in turn create a more egalitarian society (Henderson, 2002). It is clear that the behaviour of these women during their trips is influenced by the social structures which are in place. However, they accept the challenges and the responsibilities which stem from their freedom to choose, even if that means exposing their physical and emotional integrity, clearly described in the constraints experienced during their independent travels.

As a researcher, increasing awareness of issues such as gender and performance in the context of qualitative research raised many personal issues too, including being Brazilian, a woman, single, someone who is academically-qualified and having travelled alone. This brought me significantly closer to the interviewees and contributed to a more fluid and authentic dialogue. At various times, the lines between myself and the object of my research became blurred because, as I was listening to the accounts of the interviewees, I also analysed by own life, my personal choices and my experiences. Without a doubt, these reflections resulted in many learning opportunities which helped shape some of my personal life choices from then on.

There are numerous variables and behaviours resulting from those relationships which had a significant influence on me, such as gender, nationality, socio-economic class and civil status. The ability a person has to freely choose and perform their gender occurs after the establishment of existing social norms, making them more susceptible and vulnerable to those same norms. As previously mentioned, the fact that I am a female researcher and that I have travelled abroad alone, as well as other affinities with the subjects of this study, may have enhanced the empathy created between us.

Both my role as a researcher and the role of the women interviewed were not completely free because performativity is not limited to free will, particularly because we are vulnerable to and affected by discourses which are imposed upon us and subject to categorisation and what is expected of us in terms of behaviour (Butler, 2015). That means that there are expectations with regard to behaviour, both by me as a researcher and by the women as subjects of the study, and the roles which we implicitly agreed to carry out.

This study was developed within the context of exposing vulnerability, performative acts and the deconstruction of paradigms. The expansion of the feminine within the context of independent travel demonstrates this resistance, as described by the subjects of this study, who strongly demand their place in society and the recognition of their right to the mobility of their bodies within political and social spheres. In addition, upon reflection after the interviews, I sought inspiration in the lives of the women I interviewed to overcome my internal and personal conflicts which arose throughout the research process.

One of my motivations for this study is to widen the scope and perceptions of Brazilian women, who are increasingly independent and empowered, and follow a cultural trend of equal rights and opportunities, which is clearly reflected in independent travel. The in-depth interviews also helped to give those women a voice and allowed them to participate actively in a developing consumerist market. Moreover, my research aims to intensify the resistance to gender prejudice by exposing the sexist behaviour and attitudes which arise when a woman travels alone. As a woman, I understand that we cannot show our vulnerability or our sensitivity out of fear that we will be perceived as inadequate, fragile or untrustworthy.

The performances, both mine and those of the interviewees, are subject to male-dominated social circumstances, both in public and in private spheres. As such, our everyday relationships and behaviours are shaped by society's expectations of the female gender. The practice of women travelling alone is one which raises a range of ethical and gender issues and which corroborates and gives continuity to a subtle transformation of established standards, with particular emphasis on people's individual freedom. At the end of the process, I was able to understand independent travel from other perspectives and incorporate new ways to perform the feminine within me.

All in all, I found that there was a certain level of reciprocal legitimacy and identification between myself and the subjects of this study. We are all connected, which means that because we are all dependent on our social relationships, there is relational vulnerability. Therefore, all gender issues and discourses affect and limit us within the norms of societal behaviour, which in turn limit our inner self, as well as the more existential sense of being and becoming.

References

Bell, D., Caplan, P. and Karim, W.J. (eds) (1993) *Gendered Fields, Women, Men and Ethnography*. New York, NY: Routledge.
Brown, B. (2006) Shame resilience theory: A grounded theory study on women and shame. *Families in Society: The Journal of Contemporary Social Services* 87, 43–52. doi: 10.1606/1044-3894.3483.
Butler, J. (2004) *Undoing Gender*. New York, NY: Routledge.
Butler, J. (2015) *Relatar a si mesmo: crítica da violência ética*. Belo Horizonte: Autêntica Editora.
Cohen, S. (2013) Leisure, identities and personal growth. In S. Elkington and S. Gammon (eds) *Contemporary Perspectives in Leisure: Meanings, Motives and Lifelong Learning*. London, England: Routledge.
Golde, P. (ed.) (1970) *Women in the Field Anthropological Experiences*. Chicago, IL: Aldine Publishing Company.
Graburn, N. (1983) The anthropology of tourism. *Annals of Tourism Research* 10 (1), 9–33.
Hanmer, L. and Klugman, J. (2015) Exploring women's agency and empowerment in developing countries: Where do we stand? *Feminist Economics* 5701 (November), 1–27. doi: 10.1080/13545701.2015.1091087.
Harding, S. (1987) *Feminism and Methodology*. Bloomington, IN: Indiana University Press.
Henderson, K. (2002) Ocio y Género: ¿Un Concepto Global? In L. Setién and A. Marugán (eds) *Mujeres y Ocio: Nuevas Redes de Espacios y Tempos* (pp. 21–38). Bilbao: Universidad de Deusto.
Hesse-Biber, S. (2012) *Handbook of Feminist Research: Theory and Praxis* (2nd edn). Thousand Oaks, CA: Sage.
Morin, E. (1989) *Ciência com consciência*. Rio de Janeiro, Brazil: Bertrand Brasil.
Neulinger, J. (1981) *To Leisure: An Introduction*. Boston, MA: Allyn and Bacon.
Oliveira, R. (2006) *O trabalho do Antropólogo* (Paralelo 15, Ed.) (2ª). Brasília, Brazil: São Paulo Editora UNESP.
Poupart, J., Deslauriers, J., Groulx, L., Laperrière, A., Mayer, R. and Pires, A. (2008) *A pesquisa qualitativa: Enfoques epistemológicos e metodológicos*. Petrópolis, Brazil: Vozes.

Quivy, R. and Campenhoudt, L. (1992) *Manual de investigação em ciências sociais*. Lisboa, Portugal: Gradiva.
Reinharz, S. (1992) *Feminist Methods in Social Research*. New York, NY: Oxford University Press.
Rey, F. (2005) *Diferentes Momentos do Processo de Pesquisa qualitativa e suas exigências metodológicas. Pesquisa qualitativa e subjetividade: os processos de construção da informação*. São Paulo, Brazil: Pioneira Thomson Learning.
Smith, D. (1992) Sociology from women's experience: A reaffirmation. *Sociological Theory* 10 (1), 88–98.
Whitehead, T.L. and Conaway, M.E. (eds) (1986) *Self, Sex and Gender in Cross-cultural Fieldwork*. Champaign, IL: University of Illinois Press.
Wilson, E. (2004) A 'journey of her own'?: The impact of constraints on women's solo travel. Unpublished PhD thesis. Southern Cross University, East Lismore, Australia.

8 Gender Bias and Marine Mammal Tourism Research

Emmanuelle Martinez and Catherine Peters

Dr Manue Martinez is an early career researcher. Her main interest lies with the mitigation and management of the effects caused by human activities on marine mammals and the marine environment. Originally from France, Manue completed both her undergraduate and postgraduate studies overseas, in the United Kingdom and New Zealand, respectively. Although her postgraduate research has focused on the endemic and endangered Hector's dolphins and the effect of tourism activities, she has collaborated with colleagues working on a range of other cetacean species across the Pacific over the past two decades. Her passion and independence from any family duty have also given her the opportunity to travel and work (including fieldwork) in various capacities within the Pacific Region, from NGOs, government agencies, and educational institutions. She is currently based in Northland, New Zealand, lecturing in the Conservation and Environmental Management programme at Northland polytechnic.

Cat is a PhD candidate in the final stages of completing her thesis. Her work is focused on understanding factors affecting marine mammal conservation to better enhance management frameworks in New Zealand. She currently studies the Bay of Islands coastal bottlenose dolphins (a nationally endangered species) and the tourism industry which is built around viewing and swimming with them. Her goals include enhancing protection of both the bottlenose dolphins and an industry that has been described as a major tourism draw card for New Zealand by working closely with the industry and stakeholders. The field location where her current research is based has meant overcoming many logistical constraints synonymous with remote locations. One such hurdle has been to regularly train new team members; this included training her own partner, who has, at times, joined her in the field. Cat remains passionate about sharing her experiences with new students and aiding in their development of skill sets vital for successful fieldwork.

Note: As friends and colleagues, Manue (EM) and Catherine (CP) also conducted similar doctoral research projects in the field of marine mammal tourism. The authors naturally supported each other as well as shared, discussed, and reflected upon their experiences over the years. This chapter is a combined voice of the challenges they faced during their fieldwork relating to gender bias.

Introduction
Women in life sciences

Even in the 21st century, the cultural stereotypes and misconceptions that shape people's attitudes towards women still strongly permeate our societies. In the field of science, is the playing field equal, or is there a tendency for women in science to be undervalued? Gender and equity, with the marginalisation of women, was only officially recognised as a crucial issue in science education in the 1990s (Baker, 2002), and is yet to be resolved. Unfortunately, the mass media culture (Davies *et al.*, 2002) and education system (including at faculty level; Moss-Racusin *et al.*, 2012) continue to contribute to the negative and widespread cultural stereotypes about women: that they hold inferior social status (Walker, 1998), are less competent in sciences, lack leadership aptitude and are more likely to be emotional (Cadinu *et al.*, 2005; Crocker *et al.*, 1998).

Life sciences, as opposed to physical sciences, are considered more 'women-friendly', as well as less 'scientist scientist' (as termed by school girls – normally referred to as 'hard scientists'), and are, therefore, more often studied by women (Baker & Leary, 1995: 18). Female scientists may subtly, or not so subtly, be encouraged into this field (Etzkowitz *et al.*, 1994). Exploring why gender issues and the masculine image of science are affecting the recruitment and retention of women into the science, engineering, and technology fields (Etzkowitz *et al.*, 1994; Moss-Racusin *et al.*, 2012) is beyond the scope of this chapter. However, it is important to note that these gender issues extend beyond the classroom into the workplace (e.g. Acejo & Abila, 2016; Davies, 2002; Prokos & Padavic, 2002; Thomas, 2004) and into fieldwork (e.g. Green *et al.*, 1993; Lumsden, 2009; Moser, 2008).

Marine mammal tourism research

Since the 1950s, cetacean-watching as a commercial endeavour has experienced spectacular growth (O'Connor *et al.*, 2009). There are, however, increasing concerns regarding the sustainability of this industry in many locations around the world, including New Zealand (e.g. Parsons, 2012). Indeed, evidence indicates that swimming-with and watching dolphin activities affect free-ranging cetacean populations both in the short- and long-term, which can have conservation implications (e.g. Bejder *et al.*, 2006). Our doctoral research aimed at assessing the potential effects of such activities on two nationally endangered species (Baker *et al.*, 2016): the coastal bottlenose dolphins (*Tursiops truncatus*) in the Bay of Islands (CP) and the endemic Hector's dolphins (*Cephalorhynchus hectori*) in Akaroa Harbour (EM; Figures 8.1 and 8.2).

Our fieldwork locations were directly linked to the tourism industry, being the most popular sites at which to watch and swim-with dolphins in

112 Femininities in the Field

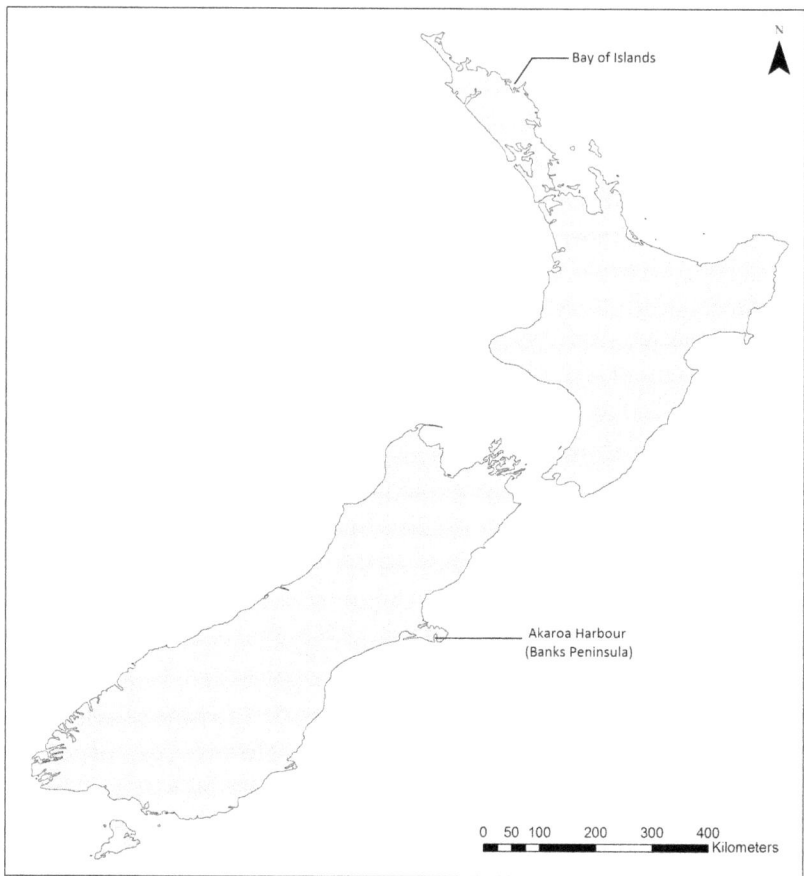

Figure 8.1 Map showing the field site locations in New Zealand: The Bay of Islands and Akaroa Harbour, Banks Peninsula

the North and South Islands, respectively. Our platform selections were primarily based on the most appropriate method for our studies (e.g. Bejder & Samuels, 2003), taking into account our research questions, field site topography and budget. These included land-based station(s) or a vessel, either from a platform of opportunity (POP; e.g. commercial tour boat) or a research vessel (RV). Although Akaroa Harbour offered excellent vantage points for land-based surveys (EM), the Bay of Islands topography was more challenging and the use of a RV was deemed the best method (CP). Interactions with tour operators and the public were typically minimal from land-based platforms, with the main issue being site accessibility, while the likelihood of such interactions was highest on POPs. As a result, most of our personal and shared experiences with friends and colleagues in this field occurred primarily from vessel platforms.

Figure 8.2 Two species of nationally endangered dolphins found in New Zealand: (a) the coastal bottlenose dolphin *Tursiops truncatus* (Photo credit: F. Vivier/C. Peters); and (b) the endemic Hector's dolphin *Cephalorhynchus hectori* (Photo credit: M. Mariani/E. Martinez)

Is there gender inequity in marine mammal tourism research?

When assessing the potential effects of watching and swimming-with dolphins, we, as scientists, see it as an opportunity to help better manage such activities, making them more sustainable, while minimising any effects on target species. Those in the industry, however, may perceive this improved management as having the potential to cause loss of revenue. This loss may be realised through a change in permit conditions (i.e. a reduction in daily trips) or permits being revoked. Facing hostility in the field was, therefore, not surprising regardless of our gender. Factors such as ethnicity, class, age and gender can, however, be important in shaping how we interact with others while in the field (Edwards, 1990). Gender inequity, whether conscious or subconscious, can take many shapes and forms. This can include denigration, harassment and 'sexual' treatment (Gurney, 1985). It can also affect rapport building and personal safety. This made us ponder whether subtle and subconscious prejudices introduce bias towards women's research on tourism, and, in particular, on field data collection. Can a woman be appreciated as a scientist as well as a woman, rather than one or the other, or even worse as neither? We believe that it is possible, yet, it is dependent upon a multitude of variables. It depends on location, colleagues, and personal attitude as well as age, ethnicity, and cultural background. Personally, we have learnt to identify and deal with gender inequity, navigate the political minefields, and be oblivious to what is expected of us as women. We achieved this by acting professionally, keeping our integrity, and earning respect to get the data required to complete our research. Through practice, we have found that preparing for gender bias leads to better field experiences and research outcomes.

In this chapter, we provide a self-reflection drawing upon a diverse range of combined field experiences as female researchers. In doing so, we reflect upon whether conscious and subconscious prejudices linked to our gender may have introduced biases into our field data collection and overall research. While these did not undermine our data *per se*, it is important for female researchers to be aware of and acknowledge that we will need to manage the gender-based challenges routinely faced while conducting fieldwork. We also discuss the various mechanisms we used to successfully overcome gender inequity. Finally, we conclude by exploring how tourism research, and female tourism researchers, might move forward.

Gender Inequity in the Field

The large majority of the public as well as the crew of various tour operators were supportive of our research projects and genuinely kind towards us. However, we cannot deny that we were occasionally subject to gender inequity, as illustrated by the examples below. While women around the world face some of these issues, others were more specific to our field.

Gendering, denigration and sexual harassment

The maritime industry is considered traditionally as an 'exemplar of masculinity' (Connell, 2005: 187). Working aboard passenger vessels, such as tour boats, might not conflict with notions of femininity as much as on board cargo ships (Thomas, 2004) or offshore overnight vessels, meaning that women might be more readily accepted as skippers, steward and crew. Nevertheless, as female researchers, fitting into a male-dominated culture proved to be challenging due to the stereotyped view that women are vulnerable, with the tendency to be denigrated, treated as sex objects and subjected to sexual advances (Golde, 1970; Gurney, 1985; Lumsden, 2009). According to Easterday *et al.* (1982), a young female researcher is likely to encounter 'hustling' in such a setting. 'Hustling' is defined as ranging from 'flirtatious behaviour and sexually suggestive remarks to overt sexual propositioning' and 'involves statements or actions which place the female researcher in an inferior or devalued position' (Gurney, 1985: 46). While not rampant, we (including our female interns) dealt with 'hustling' that was similar to what women have reported as seafarers (Thomas, 2004) and in the Police Academy (Prokos & Padavic, 2002). Demeaning labelling (e.g. *'dolphin girls'*) and name-calling included both affectionate (e.g. *'sweetheart'*, *'hey babe'*) and derogatory terms (e.g. *'dolphin bitches'*). Because none of us wore a wedding ring, we were also questioned about our private lives. Common questions included: *'Do you have time for a personal life?'*; *'Let me know if you'd like to go for a coffee sometime'*; *'Why is an attractive woman like you not married?'* Some men preferred to resort to flattery: *'You look great, do you work out?'* Others preferred to use unwelcomed humour such as *'make sure you put lots of sunscreen on girls'*, while having a clear view of the female crew from a higher vantage point.

Occasionally, we also experienced inappropriate body language and discreet, but unwanted, physical contact, the most classic ones being buttock pinching, hair grabbing and the 'paternal squeeze' (Green *et al.*, 1993: 630). The same authors and Thomas (2004) reported that similar overt sexual harassment while in the field often occurred in a public setting in an attempt to embarrass or humiliate. Such situations can lead to anxiety given the uncertainty of the duration and the potential escalation of the harassment, especially when the victims have no control. To illustrate, our female team, while washing the RV or vehicle, was told to take photos with our wet tee-shirts to raise funds for our research, while men would stop working to watch or comment, *'it is nice to have young female researchers'*. For us, this represented gender bias as, from our experience, male researchers are less likely to be subject to such derogatory comments. Our responses to this type of heckling included calling out such behaviour or simply ignoring it. Doing so, repetitively, eventually cemented our position in the hierarchy of a male-dominated boat yard. Future boat washes became subsequently easier once it was made clear that we would not be discouraged or rise to the taunting remarks – a process that took about a year.

'Hegemonic masculinity' and 'sexist treatment'

The notion that men are superior to women still exists in contemporary western society, with the dominant process reinforcing men's power on cultural and collective levels labelled 'hegemonic masculinity' (Connell,

2005: 77). Hegemonic masculinity can take many forms (Burris, 1996), including subordination of women, heterosexism, authority, competitive individualism and aggressiveness (Connell, 1995, 2005). During our fieldwork experiences, gender caused our roles and abilities as skippers, scientists and team leaders to be questioned.

Skipper abilities

During fieldwork, our driving (Lumsden, 2009) and skippering skills were subject to gender-related 'sexist treatment' (Gurney, 1985: 44). The belief that women cannot drive a car, let alone a boat and a trailer, still exists. A whole female crew on a RV was often seen as an oddity. For example, one bystander remarked, '*I saw the boat being launched this morning and was impressed. I then noticed that it was a female skipper and crew so I had to wait to tell you how impressed I was*'. This type of comment, even though seemingly complimentary, underlines a subtle, yet strong gender bias. The undertone being that as opposed to a female, a male skipper would be expected to know what to do. It was common for men to stop at a boat ramp and watch our RV dock, probably due to curiosity. Some would genuinely and kindly offer help to drive the trailer for us, while others would outright tell us what to do. Having to perform a challenging boat manoeuvre in front of a crowd can be nerve wracking, especially when familiarising yourself with a new location. Such treatment, in the form of unwelcomed instruction, can be very unsettling, daunting, and lead to a depletion of self-confidence. Should we women make a minor mistake, typical derogatory comments about our abilities would ensue: '*they let anyone drive a boat these days*'. Despite our experience and abilities, we often did not get the respect we deserved as a result of gender prejudice.

Scientific abilities

Our capability for leading and conducting proper research, as well as the validity of our methods, were, at times, overtly questioned by both tour operators' staff and members of the public. This could be expected given the sensitivity of our research and its potential impacts on the local economy, but it also seemed a result of the view of women as intrinsically less competent and qualified (Prokos & Padavic, 2002). This gendered interpretation was further supported by some of our male interns who adopted the misconception that statistical analyses and programming are too complex for women. Despite being well-educated and accustomed to the presence of female classmates, especially in life sciences, these male interns continually questioned our ability.

Furthermore, our credibility as scientists was sometimes diminished by the use of colloquial names. While some name-calling can appear subtle, genuine and humorous, we were often referred to as the '*sorority girls*', a term used regularly in a derogatory manner, portraying girls as snobs and airheads. *'Dolphin girls'* was another label commonly used – is there such a thing as a *'dolphin boy'*? There is a traditional expectation that women on board tour vessels serve as naturalists rather than true scientists, as it is a role that requires less scientific training and fieldwork skill. We were often perceived as *'dolphin huggers'*, especially when the research crew happened to be all women, though this could not have been further from the truth. We were also often asked whether we had had any *'magical and spiritual moments with the dolphins'*, a question unlikely to be asked of a male researcher. In fact, in neither of our research teams was this question ever asked of a male researcher, despite it regularly being asked of female team members. Once people have labelled or categorised someone as 'lesser', it becomes challenging to change their opinions. These gender-related, preconceived biases from the field can later affect how the research findings are received.

Leader abilities

Another aspect stemming from hegemonic masculinity is the view, both consciously and unconsciously, that women are unable to hold positions of power and that their authority can be disregarded (Prokos & Padavic, 2002). To illustrate, members of the public and/or crew, when meeting for the first time, would often address a male intern assuming that he was in charge of our research project. Some skippers did not hesitate to confront us when they did not like something, expecting us to back down because we were viewed as the 'weaker' sex: *'are you sure you know what you are doing?'* Though rare, we also experienced issues asserting our authority over and commanding respect from our male interns (particularly with those older than us).

Being considered as less competent may in some situations prove advantageous. Women tend to be portrayed as weaker and less threatening (Easterday *et al.*, 1982). In the field, ethnographers can choose to 'play upon the role of naïve researcher or "acceptable incompetent" to their advantage' (Lumsden, 2009: 509). Similarly, as *'pretty, young'* female researchers, we appeared to be more popular with the general public, perhaps being perceived as more approachable and likeable. This gendered effect allowed us to convey conservation messages more effectively than an older, hairier, and/or bearded man, for example, would.

Overcoming the Issues and Succeeding

According to Gill and Maclean (2002: para. 4.5), 'a woman entering a male-dominated setting is often the target of innuendo, rumour and boasting. A female ethnographer, though, is expected to deal with this situation such that the research does not suffer'. This expectation, while unjust, applied to us. Confronting sexist behaviours might have affected relationships with the tour operators, the community at large, and/or potentially jeopardised our research. Here, we share the main mechanisms we applied to successfully complete our fieldwork, given our personalities, personal backgrounds, locations and research topic. Building a professional identity and maintaining professionalism at all times proved to be our best weapons, both in and out of the field.

Professional identity

At the core of fieldwork experience is the identity management process or display of character (Tewksbury & Gagné, 1997; Van Maanen, 1982). While this process is associated with social science fieldwork, we believe it is also applicable to our field, particularly when relying on POPs and/or the collaboration of tour operators in order to gather data. The importance of a strong and positive rapport is intensified when the research involves a sensitive topic (here tourism activities) or a stigmatised population (Renzetti & Lee, 1993). Presentation of self, in and out of the field (within the local community and with tour operators, government agencies, and colleagues), is, therefore, an important part of managing a research project as a female researcher. Indeed, women are often made to feel that they have to be careful how they present themselves, or that they must put in more professional effort in order to be taken seriously, and/or to gain the same respect as their male peers (Etzkowitz *et al.*, 1994). These ideas raise many questions. Is toughening up to survive in a harsh male-dominated environment the solution? Are we not tough enough yet too tough? Do we appear too aggressive, too '*bitchy*', by being ambitious? Although, if we are too soft, will we be trampled on, chewed up, and spat out? Balancing the demands of fieldwork (including our professional identity) and private lives can be challenging. This becomes particularly pertinent when based remotely in the field for logistical reasons for months at a time (EM) or year round (CP), where isolation (physical and social) is likely. Similar sentiments have been noted in the literature on female shipboard researchers (Belousoy *et al.*, 2007; Sampson & Thomas, 2003). According to Van Maanen (1982: 112), 'a good part of fieldwork is simply being attentive to the impressions one's presence and activities cast off'. A researcher is, therefore, positioned by her/his gender, age, ethnicity, sexual identity, and so on, as well as by her/his biography, all of which may inhibit or enable certain research processes in the field (England, 1994). Consequently, assumptions about researchers' identities are commonly made, frequently deduced from our interests, associates, or appearance (Tewksbury & Gagné, 1997).

Appearance and femininity

An important question to ask is whether women need to dress and act a certain way to be taken seriously as a scientist. Is the field a place in

Figure 8.3 Conservative and practical work clothing attire giving a professional image while collecting data in the field (Photo credit: T. Guérin)

which to be feminine? According to Steele *et al.* (2002), people often see themselves in terms of the social identity that is the most stigmatised in their current environment. Not surprisingly, women in male-dominated professions often face a conflict between their femininity and the dictates of their selected career (Acejo & Abila, 2016; Coffey *et al.*, 1992; Lumsden, 2009). Women commonly de-feminise themselves in a work setting in an attempt to reduce unwanted sexual attention and advances (e.g. Acejo & Abila, 2016; Green *et al.*, 1993; Lumsden, 2009; Thomas, 2004). Appearance plays a major factor in our professional identity construction, both in and out of the field. As rightly highlighted in Acejo and Abila's (2016: 131) study, the aim of female researchers on board vessels was 'to conduct research and as such, make sure that the seafarers recognised an appearance that expressed more of that purpose instead of my gender'. We wore gender-neutral clothing (neither very masculine nor too feminine or conservative, and not form-flattering; Figure 8.3), with minimal or no make-up, hair tied back, and no perfume. This ensured that we were not only comfortable in the field, but also served the secondary purpose of supporting a professional image for us, while we interacted with skippers and crew.

Professional attitude

As women, we automatically have a target on our back, questioning our capabilities. The younger and blonder we are, the bigger the target! Likewise, Kyle and Mahler (1996) demonstrated that biases regarding personal appearance, such as hair colour – especially blonde – and cosmetic use, affected judgments about a female applicant's ability. Thus, despite our efforts to maintain professional demeanours and stay sensitive to power relations, gender bias issues remained unavoidable.

Sexism is symptomatic of myths in our society concerning women (e.g. driving abilities); dealing with it can be stressful (Lumsden, 2009). Choosing to ignore behaviours that conflict with our own values can have a moral cost (Keith, 1992). How do we cope with such situations given that no ready prescriptions for female researchers exist (Gurney, 1985)? Where do we draw the line? Do we remain silent and ignore it? If so, our silence might be 'condoning the re-enactment of the gender stratified order, allowing these particular participants to relate to us in a stereotypical fashion' (Arendell, 1997: 358). However, rather than a betrayal of our beliefs (Sampson & Thomas, 2003), choosing not to challenge sexism and 'hustling' may be the only practical and safe way to conduct research in a male-dominated environment (Gurney, 1985). There is, indeed, a certain obligation to be 'nice' (Green, 1993: 632) to the tour operators for fear of potentially jeopardising our field research (e.g. access to POPs). In our case, we attempted to first minimise potential 'hustling' by avoiding situations that may be perceived as potentially inappropriate (e.g. avoiding any one-to-one interactions in a private setting). Furthermore, we retreated into professionalism when dealing with very unprofessional behaviours by staying calm, collected, and polite. The same applied to our female interns: when one of them was screamed at and told she was 'useless', she simply told the person 'thank you for your time' and walked away. Consequently, sexual innuendos diminished over time. In some cases, unfortunately, 'hustling' was too much to handle for some of our younger interns, who lacked the confidence to deal with such situations. As a result, the roster had to be changed so that only male interns collected data when certain skippers were on board. Our data collection could have been jeopardised had we been unable to recruit male interns, given that the large majority of applicants were female (personal observation). Dealing with this type of situation taught us important skills, such as flexibility and adaptability, that were needed to successfully conduct our fieldwork.

When experiencing inequality at work, women usually report working much harder to perform comparatively better than their male counterparts in order to be accepted, be seen as capable (Thomas, 2004), and be successful (Etzkowitz et al., 1994). Prejudice and difficulties can be approached from a more positive side: they can provide women with a tangible obstacle to overcome. Once accomplished, women are aware that they possess the strength and capabilities to achieve what they set out to do. This, in turn, can further boost their confidence. We worked hard in the field to avoid making any mistakes, as we were determined to both succeed and establish ourselves as professional female scientists with integrity.

Rules

Even when not acting in any stereotypical feminine way, we found ourselves treated as 'fragile' entities. This further emphasised the view that women are not as qualified to conduct proper research (similar to Prokos & Padavic, 2002). Consequently, there was a need to constantly provide proof that we rightly deserved to be in the field conducting research. Situational cues linked to the likelihood of encountering identity threat in a setting (e.g. sexism, gender bias) can prompt heightened cognitive and physiological vigilance and a decreased feeling of belonging. Modification of the environment may, therefore, foster perceptions of identity safety (Murphy *et al.*, 2007). In addition to physical appearance, we implemented rules (for both ourselves and our research team) to address these 'threats' by remaining professional at all times. The standard rules were:

- maintaining professionalism in and outside the field;
- avoiding making inappropriate comments or public criticism, including on social media);
- refraining from any relationships with the commercial and government personnel to avoid any potential conflict of interest; and
- avoiding revealing clothing on board vessels.

These rules made us feel safer and reduced the probability of being 'hustled', facing awkward situations, and having our capabilities and integrity questioned. However, the rules resulted occasionally in a team leader being called a 'matron' as she was deemed unfair by some crewmembers.

Building good rapport

Building a professional identity and cultivating good rapport with tour operators and the public was paramount for the success of the type of research we conducted. Building a necessary positive rapport can, however, be challenging for female researchers in a male-dominated environment. As previously mentioned, the objectification of women in the maritime industry highlights the entrenched sexism, making it challenging for women to integrate (Acejo & Abila, 2016). Sampson and Thomas (2003) also noted the complexities of establishing rapport with seafarers. Sexism and long-term containment on board can potentially motivate seafarers to opportunistically attempt to derive some form of sexual power over female researchers. Luckily, our fieldwork did not require spending months at sea. As such, by forging and fostering a professional identity, as well as by working hard, we managed over time to build relationships, establish trust, and earn respect. This, in turn, generated more support for our research projects. Given that the maritime industry is an 'exemplar of masculinity' (Connell, 1995: 187), building a good rapport with local operators would have taken less time for male researchers.

Moving Forward

Our experiences, which might resonate with other female researchers, represent some of the dilemmas women face while conducting fieldwork in a male-dominant environment (e.g. Acejo & Abila, 2016; Green *et al.*, 1993; Moser, 2008; Thomas, 2004). While all types of fieldwork encounter some issues, the large majority of challenges we experienced originated from gender inequity. It is doubtful that a male researcher would have had to deal with the same challenges we had to face. The issues we experienced and have reported here usually related to only a minority of people, as the majority we interacted with were very supportive and genuinely interested in our research projects. Although most incidents could be considered as relatively minor, they still point to the 'continuous challenges posed by the underlying reality of the presence and dynamic of gender in the field' (Arendell, 1997: 362). This influenced our, and that of our female interns', fieldwork experiences. The most notable issues were denigrating comments and the reluctance to accept us as capable scientists. These are both common themes reported in traditionally male-dominated professions, including the police force (Prokos & Padavic, 2002) and seafaring (Acejo & Abila, 2016; Thomas, 2004).

To our knowledge, academia is not teaching female researchers in our discipline how to deal with the challenges linked to gender during fieldwork. Perhaps it is not something that can always be taught in a classroom environment, but rather has to be gained by experience (Tewksbury & Gagné, 1997). According to Moser (2008), the solution is to only engage in fieldwork that uses our own strengths rather than changing our personality to fit a given fieldwork situation. We are not all equally suited to or capable of conducting particular types of fieldwork (Mills & Withers, 1993). We suggest, however, that training or guidance that provides us with a deeper knowledge of our emotional abilities and strengths can guide female researchers towards making appropriate choices in fieldwork. In the end, it will all come down to attitude, motivation, determination, ambition and ultimately individuality.

We, as female researchers, need to understand and acknowledge our feelings, whether they be positive or negative. Ignoring our emotions is denying that they may have an effect on us and, consequently, on our research (Coffey, 1999). Only by first accepting and acknowledging that gender bias is present in the field, can we then better position ourselves to discuss those issues and begin to break down stereotypes. When witnessing direct harassment of women and other gender bias issues, men rarely challenged it. This implied acceptance by these men, whether conscious or unconscious, of the discrimination against, or harassment, and intimidation of women. The same can be said about women. It is as much about our attitude as women as it is men's attitude towards us. As women, we may justify or diminish the problem: '*I am sure he did not mean it that way*'. Should female researchers challenge gender issues? Should these issues, for example, be addressed in the limitations section of research outputs? Arendell (1997: 364) argued that in doing so, we can be 'dismissed as "one of those overly-sensitive women" or "feminists", out to prove an agenda and further "emasculate men"', and, therefore, not be taken seriously with respect to our research. Yet, by remaining silent, we are part of the problem and not the solution. Young women might be more inclined and inspired to become scientists in a traditionally masculine domain if environments are created in which they can work and study without the threat of being reduced to a negative stereotype (Crocker *et al.*, 1998). The issue of gender bias is societal and can be unconscious for both genders (Jenkins, 2016). 'Legislator, affirmative action, and policies will not change culture, people change culture. […] We are all responsible for a solution' (Jenkins, 2016: n.p.). Men and women who are aware of gender issues, including members of academia, should, therefore, speak up, lead by example and inspire change. Like any other issues in research, reporting these challenges in the literature would certainly highlight the bias. The important question is whether the scientific community would embrace and acknowledge a non-quantifiable, and in some cases, embarrassing bias as a true bias. Would reporting inappropriate sexism eventually lead to change?

Overall, it is important to remember that, as researchers, we are highly educated women; we should behave and act with confidence, professionalism, and rise above gender bias. We treated anyone involved in our research projects as we would like to be treated (i.e. with respect and courtesy). This is how, with time, we gained respect from most. We women excel at reading situations and acting appropriately, so let us use those skills to be aware of and adapt to the situation accordingly and successfully complete our research. In the end, how we deal with a situation will depend upon our own unique life experience and personal determination. It is our hope that by sharing our field experiences and acknowledging the issues we faced as female researchers, we have shed some light on how these might be overcome and how we can move forward, together, and in the right direction.

References

Acejo, I.L. and Abila, S.S. (2016) Rubbing out gender: Women and merchant ships. *Journal of Organizational Ethnography* 5 (2), 123–138.
Arendell, T. (1997) Reflections on the researcher-researched relationship: A woman interviewing men. *Qualitative Sociology* 20 (3), 341–368.
Baker, D. (2002) Where is gender and equity in science education? *Journal of Research in Science Teaching* 39 (8), 659–663.

Baker, C.S., Chilvers, B.L., Childerhouse, S., Constantine, R., Currey, R., Mattlin, R., van Helden, A., Hitchmough, R. and Rolfe, J. (2016) Conservation status of New Zealand marine mammals, 2013. *New Zealand Threat Classification Series* 14. See www.doc.govt.nz.

Baker, D. and Leary, R. (1995) Letting girls speak out about science. *Journal of Research in Science Teaching* 32 (1), 3–27.

Bejder, L., Samuels, A., Whitehead, H., Gales, N., Mann, J., Connor, R., Heithaus, M., Watson-Capps, J., Flaherty, C. and Krützen, M. (2006) Decline in the relative abundance of bottlenose dolphins exposed to long-term disturbance. *Conservation Biology* 20 (6), 1791–1798.

Bejder, L. and Samuels, A. (2003) Evaluating the effects of nature-based tourism on cetaceans. In N. Gales, M. Hindell and R. Kirkwood (eds) *Marine Mammals: Fisheries, Tourism and Management Issues*. Collingwood, Australia: CSIRO Publishing.

Belousov, K., Horlick-Jones, T., Bloor, M., Gilinskiy, Y., Golbert, V., Kostikovsky, Y., Levi, M. and Pentsov, D. (2007) Any port in a storm: Fieldwork difficulties in dangerous and crisis-ridden settings. *Qualitative Research* 7 (2), 155–175.

Burris, B.H. (1996) Technocracy, patriarchy and management. In D.L. Collison and J. Hearn (eds) *Men as Managers, Managers as Men*. London: Sage.

Cadinu, M., Maass, A., Rosabianca, A. and Kiesner, J. (2005) Why do women underperform under stereotype threat?: Evidence for the role of negative thinking. *Psychological Science* 16, 572–578.

Coffey, A. (ed.) (1999) *The Ethnographic Self: Fieldwork and the Representation of Reality*. London: SAGE.

Coffey, S., Brown, J. and Savage, S. (1992) Policewomen's career aspirations: Some reflections on the role and capabilities of women in policing in Britain. *Police Studies* 15 (1), 13–19.

Connell, R. (ed.) (1995) *Masculinities*. Berkeley, CA: University of California Press.

Connell, R. (ed.) (2005) *Masculinities* (2nd edn). Berkeley, CA: University of California Press.

Crocker, J., Major, B. and Steele, C.M. (1998) Social stigma. In D. Gilbert, S.T. Fiske and G. Lindzey (eds) *Handbook of Social Psychology* (4th edn, pp. 504–553). Boston, MA: McGraw-Hill.

Davies, G., Spencer, S.J., Quinn, D.M. and Gerhardstein, R. (2002) Consuming images: How television commercials that elicit stereotype threat can restrain women academically and professionally. *Personality and Social Psychology Bulletin* 28 (2), 1615–1628.

Easterday, L., Papademas, D., Schorr, L. and Valentine, C. (1982) The making of a female researcher: Role problems in fieldwork. In R.G. Burgess (ed.) *Field Research: A Sourcebook and Field Manual* (pp. 62–67). London: Routledge.

Edwards, R. (1990) Connecting method and epistemology: A white woman interviewing black women. *Women's Studies International Forum* 13, 477–490.

England, K.V.L. (1994) Getting personal: Reflexivity, positionality, and feminist research. *Professional Geographer* 46 (1), 80–89.

Etzkowitz, H., Kemelgor, C., Neuschatz, M., Uzzi, B. and Alonzo, J. (1994) The paradox of critical mass for women in science. *Science, New Series* 266 (5182), 51–54.

Gill, F. and Maclean, C. (2002) Knowing your place: Gender and reflexivity in two ethnographies. *Sociological Research Online* 7 (2). See http://www.socresonline.org.uk/7/2/gill.html (accessed June 2016).

Golde, P. (ed.) (1970) *Women in the Field: Anthropological Experiences*. Chicago, IL: Aldine.

Green, G., Barbour, R.S., Barnard, M. and Kitzinger, J. (1993) 'Who wears the trousers?' Sexual harassment in research settings. *Women's Studies International Forum* 16 (6), 627–637.

Gurney, J.N. (1985) Not one of the guys: The female researcher in the male dominated setting. *Qualitative Sociology* 8 (1), 42–62.

Jenkins, L.M. (2016, May 27) Unconscious gender bias: Everyone's issue. *The Huffington Post*. See http://www.huffingtonpost.com/lisa-marie-jenkins/unconscious-gender-bias-e_b_7447524.html

Keith, M. (1992) Angry writing: (Re)presenting the unethical world of the ethnographer. *Environment and Planning D: Society and Space* 10 (5), 551–568.

Kyle, D.J. and Mahler, H.I.M. (1996) The effects of hair color and cosmetic use on perceptions of a female's ability. *Psychology of Women Quarterly* 20 (3), 447–455.

Lumsden, K. (2009) Don't ask a woman to do another woman's job: Gendered interactions and the emotional ethnographer. *Sociology* 43 (3), 497–513.

Mills, C.A. and Withers, W.J. (1993) Teaching qualitative geography as interpretative discourse. *Journal of Geography in Higher Education* 16, 159–165.

Moser, S. (2008) Personality: A new positionality? *Area* 40 (3), 383–392.

Moss-Racusin, C.A., Dovidiob, J.F., Brescollc, V.L., Grahama, M.J. and Handelsmana, J. (2012) Science faculty's subtle gender biases favour male students. *PNAS Early Edition* 109 (41), 16474–16479.

Murphy, M.C., Steele, C.M. and Gross, J.J. (2007) Signaling threat: How situational cues affect women in math, science, and engineering settings. *Psychological Science* 18 (10), 879–885.

O'Connor, S., Campbell, R., Cortez, H. and Knowles, T. (2009) Whale watching worldwide: Tourism numbers, expenditures and expanding economic benefits. A special report from the International Fund for Animal Welfare, Yarmouth, MA: Prepared by Economists @ Large.

Parsons, E.C.M. (2012) The negative impacts of whale-watching. *Journal of Marine Biology 2012*, Article ID 807294.

Prokos, A. and Padavic, I. (2002) 'There oughtta be a law against bitches': Masculinity lessons in police academy training. *Gender, Work and Organization* 9 (4), 439–459.

Renzetti, C. M. and Lee, R. M. (eds) (1993) *Researching Sensitive Topics*. Newbury Park, CA: Sage.

Sampson, H. and Thomas, M. (2003) The social isolation of seafarers: Causes, effects, and remedies. *International Maritime Health* 54 (1/4), 58–67.

Steele, C.M., Spencer, S. and Aronson, J. (2002) Contending with group image: The psychology of stereotype and social identity threat. In M.P. Zanna (ed.) *Advances in Experimental Social Psychology* (Vol. 34, pp. 379–440). San Diego, CA: Academic Press.

Tewksbury, R. and Gagné, P. (1997) Assumed and presumed identities: Problems of self-presentation in field research. *Sociological Spectrum: Mid-South Sociological Association* 17 (2), 127–155.

Thomas, M. (2004) Get yourself a proper job girlie!: Recruitment, retention and women seafarers. *Maritime Policy and Management: The Flagship Journal of International Shipping and Port Research* 31 (4), 309–318.

Van Maanen, J. (1982) Fieldwork on the beat. In J. Van Maanen, J.M. Dabbs Jr. and R.R. Faulkner (eds) *Varieties of Qualitative Research*. Beverly Hills, CA: Sage.

Walker, L. (1998) Chivalrous masculinity among juvenile offenders in Western Sydney: A new perspective on young working class men and crime. *Current Issues in Criminal Justice* 9 (3), 279–293.

9 The Effect of Motherhood on Tourism Fieldwork with Young Children: An Autoethnographic Approach

Catheryn Khoo-Lattimore

Dr Catheryn Khoo-Lattimore is a Senior Lecturer at Griffith University, Australia. Catheryn's current research interest is on tourist and guest behaviour, with a passionate focus on women, families and young children. She is also particularly interested in understanding these segments from an Asian perspective, and how their travel experience and behaviours differ cross-culturally. She is Second Vice-Chair of The Council for Australasian Tourism and Hospitality Education (CAUTHE). She is also the founder and chair of Women Academics in Tourism (WAiT), and dreams of the day when our tourism academy will become a level playing field for all. Catheryn likes to think that she lives in a resort-like home in a bayside suburb with her husband and their three young children, where she plans all their travel adventures.

Introduction

Although the influence of children in family travel decision-making has been recognised (Carr, 2011; Khoo-Lattimore *et al.*, 2015; Lawlor & Prothero, 2011; Nickerson & Jurowski, 2001; Thornton *et al.*, 1997; Wang *et al.*, 2004), scholars have also acknowledged the dearth of research which takes into account the voices of children in tourism (Canosa *et al.*, 2016; Poria & Timothy, 2014). Reasons for this have been attributed to the presumed difficult processes of gaining ethical approval for research concerning minors (Carr, 2011); the supposition that researchers should possess particular skills for working with children (Poria & Timothy, 2014); and the lack of unconventional research methods that engage children as participants (Nanda *et al.*, 2007). Most recently, three studies have attempted to address this methodological gap. Schänzel and Smith (2011) employed the use of auto-driven photo elicitation in their study with children between the ages of six and 16; Khoo-Lattimore (2015) suggested the use of appropriate props and prompts that recognise pre-schoolers' rights during data collection; while Canosa *et al.* (2016) endorsed the use of participatory film in uncovering tourism realities from young people. Although most methodological discussions on including children's voices in research tend to focus on the participants rather than the researcher, there is an increasing call for tourism scholars to be reflexive about their role and its connection to method (Finlay, 2002; Hall, 2004; Mura, 2013; Mura & Pahlevan Sharif, 2015; Westwood *et al.*, 2006).

This chapter therefore aims to explore the extent to which the researcher's identity as a mother influences research work with children. Publications on constraints women face in academia are growing, and motherhood has been cited repeatedly as one of these challenges (Acker & Armenti, 2004; Armenti, 2004; Castaneda & Isgro, 2013; Metcalfe *et al.*, 2008; Raddon, 2002). In addition to these obstacles, in this chapter, I discuss motherhood as an advantage in conducting tourism fieldwork with young children. I hope my experiences as a mother-researcher during data collection benefit other mother-researchers, and provide insights for those seeking access to participants and quality data.

Situating the Researcher in the Research

At this early point, it is important that I declare my epistemological interests as an outsider located within the tourism academy, but also as an insider studying myself as a research subject. I am an Asian academic whose research interest is in tourist and guest behaviour, with a particular focus on women, families and young children. Not coincidentally, I am also a mother of three young children aged between six months and seven years. I travelled rather extensively prior to being a mother and, afterwards, crossed many immigration checkpoints and stayed in countless holiday accommodations with my children in tow. All my children had received their passports before they turned a month old. As a family with young children, we have travelled on planes, buses, trains, cars, taxis, boats, chair lifts, cable cars, gondolas, tuk-tuks and trishaws. We have had vacations on cruises, beaches, mountains and lakes and in gardens, parks, deserts, forests, museums, zoos, theme parks and amusement centres. In naming these tourism sites, I am locating my research, myself and my own experiences with young children within the conceptual approaches of reflexivity and identity. Figures 9.1 to 9.3 further serve to situate the self in this chapter.

My personal and family travel biographical events, which intersected with parenting and motherhood have undoubtedly motivated my work involving families and children, and in particular, young children. As a mother, I have had varied family holiday experiences both positive and negative, while as a researcher, I am engaged with my participants in comparable discourse. As an Asian mother, the family holiday sites and activities I choose for my children can sometimes challenge the 'way it's done' for my white, western husband, while as a researcher, I recognise this cultural duality in my approach to 'parenting' the young participants in my study. For example, while my husband would always 'go with the flow' of destination offerings, I would deliberately seek out educational-type activities of particular tourism sites at a destination and painstakingly work our

Figure 9.1 2013 – at the Hartsfield-Jackson Atlanta International Airport from New Zealand with a toddler and 10-week-old baby in tow. This was the beginning of a six-month travel-cum-research trip which took us as a family from Georgia to South Carolina, New York, California, Florida, the Bahamas and Mexico

Figure 9.2 2014 – the young family in Mexico

travel schedules around these. I accept that my experiences as an individual can hardly be translated into large-scale generalisations but I also recognise that my knowledge will resonate with other people, particularly mothers, so I highlight this for future methodological consideration.

Motherhood and Identity

Driven predominantly by feminist scholarship, motherhood is the subject of a rapidly growing body of literature, and studies on motherhood identity alone cover wide-ranging topics from maternal well-being (Arendell, 2000) and marketing (Carrigan & Szmigin, 2004) to social inequalities (McDermott & Graham, 2005) and the management of human resources at work (Riad, 2007; Wyatt, 2002). Within tourism, motherhood has been discussed as a disruption in women's holidays (Davidson, 1996; Schänzel, 2016; Small, 2005). For example, Davidson (1996) investigated the holiday experiences of mothers with young children and found that these women continued to perform the domestic chores of cooking, cleaning and organising throughout the period of their

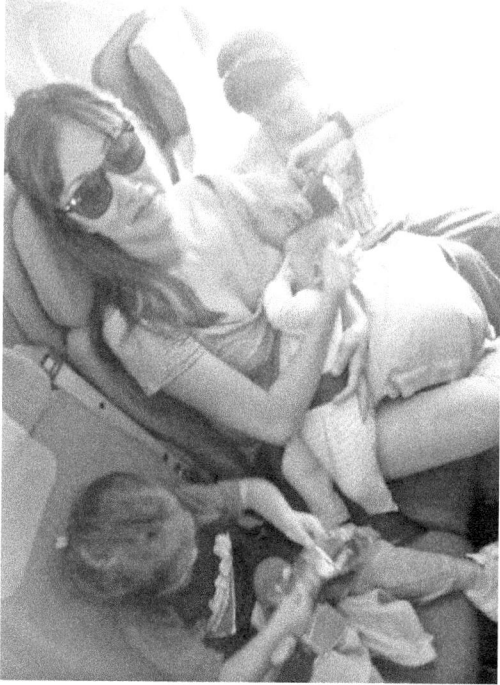

Figure 9.3 2016 – travelling to Sydney with three young children

family holidays. Despite being on holiday, which is often associated with freedom and time away from work, the women in her study were conscious of their identity as mothers first and foremost, and worked to ensure that the holiday was a happy and successful experience for their family members. Almost a decade later, Small (2005) found that little has changed for mothers with children, that the mother-identity dominates that of the tourist, and that the notion of a 'real' holiday 'was reserved for those who holidayed without their children' (p. 149). Another decade after Small's work, Schänzel (2016) revealed that mothers are still seeking relief from domestic work during family holidays. However, the women in this recent study seem somewhat more assertive in their needs for personal time, showing some forms of resistance against the traditional discourse and identity of motherhood; in a way, they began to prioritise pockets of their own leisure time over the needs of other family members.

Despite these publications on the impact of motherhood on tourism experiences, none of the researchers have written themselves into their research. Consequently, we know very little about how (and if) the researchers' own identities as mothers impacted on the data collection processes (and consequently the data) they had collected from the mothers they were researching. While these studies have provided insights into how motherhood changes the way women experience holidays over the decades, our knowledge remains limited of how the dual roles of motherhood and researcher changes research on holiday experiences.

The study that started it all

My study on children in tourism started with what was to me a stimulating (yet in hindsight, credulous) project in 2013 with the aim of understanding children's preferences for accommodation attributes during their family holidays. A focus-group method was planned with children between the ages of five and six in a private pre-school in the city of Subang Jaya, Malaysia. Three researchers other than myself were appointed as facilitators, who would be responsible for eliciting data from the young respondents. As a method of collecting data, the facilitators got the children to draw pictures of their family holidays and then used these drawings as entry points into their thoughts and opinions on travel and tourism. The project was deemed unsuccessful because the yielded data were too shallow and insignificant for analysis. Reasons for this were reported in an earlier publication (see Khoo-Lattimore, 2015). With an obligation to the funding institution, a second study was conducted in 2014, with the goal of acquiring more substantial data. Given that this follow-up study was investigative in nature, I did not engage other researchers and instead went into the field myself. I did, however, use the same semi-structured interview protocol as the facilitators used in 2013. The second study returned richer data, which raised reflexive questions on the way data were collected.

Autoethnography

Using autoethnography as the research method was an obvious choice, because it focuses on the embodied experience of the situated researcher (Fleming & Fullagar, 2007) and engages in life stories as a technique for producing theoretical understanding of highly personal events (Ellis & Bochner, 2000). Importantly, autoethnography allows the researcher to study the self as the self relates to others (Chang, 2008). This is to say that autoethnography allows the researcher to carefully self-examine the investigated issue at hand in order to understand, empathise and connect his or her personal experiences to others and consequently contribute to the growing social narratives at work and/or in society (Adams et al., 2015). In the last decade, there has been a growing conviction of the importance of autoethnography as a valid and important research tool (Allen, 2015; Grenier, 2015) and an increasing number of tourism scholars have used it (Barbieri et al., 2012; Fox et al., 2014; Kwek et al., 2014; Mackenzie & Kerr, 2013; Noy, 2008; Yang, in press).

In this chapter, I adopt a dual role: as a participant as well as the investigator. The participant role is that of a female mother-researcher, while the investigator in me becomes immersed in the field in order to elucidate for my participants (and for myself), the impact motherhood has on conducting focus groups with young children. In doing so, autoethnography functions as a method, and the focus is on understanding how motherhood can assist in enhancing the data collection experience. My autoethnographic data are in the form of my experiences with the studies conducted in 2013 and 2014, my memories, my reflection and, subsequently, my understanding of those experiences.

The Findings
Motherhood and research ethics

As noted earlier, one of the challenges in doing research with children revolves around gaining ethical approval. In most research with children, it is common for consent forms to be signed by the respondents' parents (Greenfield, 2004), and this study has gained parental consent in both stages of data collection. Motherhood influenced the ethics of the study. Based on my personal parenting philosophy, I had presumed that mothers of potential participants, too, would unquestionably want to know if their child was involved in a research project. I had assumed that seeking the parents' consent was the most logical and necessary administrative procedure towards the interview process because I had let my identity as a mother take over my role as a researcher. As a researcher, rigour would suggest that I consult the literature on doing research with children and consider the needs of the child participant. For example, it is possible that that the child may not have wanted to participate in the research project despite his or her parent's consent. As a researcher, I should have noted more critically the child's agency as an active research participant, rather than treating the child from the lens of motherhood. As a researcher, I should have, in addition to the parents' consent, sought the children's, because as a researcher, I would have known that a research participant as young as four years old is 'competent and capable regarding giving consent' (Hedges, 2002: 39).

Motherhood and access to tourism data

Okumus *et al.* (2007) noted that, 'little has been written on this area [access to respondents] in the tourism field, as most scholars do not seem to disseminate their experiences of gaining access' (2007: 8). This is also true in research with children, as researchers do not typically detail their points of entry into accessing their respondents. This is somewhat surprising as the issue of access is very much related to ethics, and its implications on minors are significant. In my fieldwork in Malaysia, motherhood played an advantageous role in the research team's access to the young respondents. This entry point was easily negotiated with the principal of a private pre-school, because one of the research team members had a son enrolled in the same school, thereby bypassing the critical rapport-building stage of gaining access. In addition, the information sheet for consent to parents also highlighted that one of the researchers is the mother of a child in the school. This inclusion was deliberate to facilitate the trust and cooperation of other mothers and parents in allowing their children's participation in the research project. This notion of trust among mothers has been established in virtual communities (Doty & Dworkin, 2014; Hall & Irvine, 2009) but also discussed in the context of data collection and access. Cornet (2013), for example, described how the presence of her 11-month-old daughter during her nine-month field trip facilitated an almost immediate affinity with the Dong people in China and fostered researcher-participant trust over the course of her fieldwork. Furthermore, being first seen as a mother by the teachers in the school who were tasked with selecting the participants for this study also meant that access to participants was primarily uneventful.

The role of motherhood in participant-researcher relationship

Given that the researcher is the central person collecting data from respondents in qualitative research (Denzin & Lincoln, 2000), reflecting on the researcher-respondent relationship becomes even more imperative. This importance is heightened in not only the adult-child relationship where the adult is often deemed to hold more power over the child, but also in an Asian context where social and cultural oriental values instinctively and unconsciously ascribe authority to the older person in group dynamics and relationships (Sung, 2001). As mothers, women are inherently protective of their children. In the 2013 data collection, this mother–child relationship was observed between a young respondent and one of the researchers, who was herself a mother to a pre-schooler at the time. On the topic of food in holiday resorts, the respondent expressed dislike for papaya. The mother-researcher responded with, 'You don't like papaya? Papaya is good! Why don't you like papaya?' In this case, the mother-researcher's concern and food ideals may have altered the course of data and data quality. It could also have, for instance, intimidated the child and other children within that focus group and, consequently, inhibited more forthcoming responses. Therefore, I argue that as noble as the intention of that motherly response was, there is a need during research design to consider more thoughtfully the researcher's identity as a mother and her role as a researcher, particularly when the studies involve children. As Hall (2011) has cautioned, the researcher's identity could have already been developed in relation to not only the self, but also existing social constructs, long before the data collection process begins.

Motherhood as an epistemological element

Epistemology is a framework for knowledge generation and, in the research process, one of the key epistemological considerations is the intellectual autobiography of the researcher (Stanley, 1993). As a mother to young children, attention to regular snack and meal intervals has become a regular cognitive demand to the extent that they have become almost unconsciously programmed. In contradistinction to the first study, my latter participation and identity as a mother-researcher accorded me the foresight to schedule the focus group interviews with the children after their morning snack time. This decision yielded a significant difference in the data quality between the two study phases, hence validating motherhood as an important epistemological element for thinking about the foundations of knowledge generation – particularly under what conditions it is generated. Given that the researched were pre-school children, power is first and foremost accorded to the researchers as adults in the research setting. This presumed power is even more entrenched in Malaysia, where the culture dictates a subdued acceptance of hierarchical status in society – Malaysia scores the maximum 100 points in the power distance dimension on Hofstede's cultural values paradigm (Hofstede, 2016; Hofstede's cultural dimensions have been used widely in multidisciplinary research on culture). In this context, the passionate and caring epistemological elements of motherhood become instrumental in the knowledge generation of children's experiences in tourism.

Another example of motherhood epistemology demonstrated in this study is concerned with the means by which the knowledge was generated. As a mother who travels extensively with her children, I would prepare 'busy bags' to help keep my children occupied during our flights and drives. These busy bags contained items such as finger puppets, stickers, playdough, pegs, paper clips, colour-coded cards and felt furniture. I would carry more than a few busy bags on any one flight, and strategically use them one by one as the flight progressed. When I went into the pre-school to conduct the focus group interviews, I had instinctively brought with me some busy bag articles such as blocks, playdough and a hand puppet in the form of a cow. I placed the blocks and playdough at the start of the focus group interviews to encourage a familiar play setting for the children and introduced the cow puppet to them as 'MooMan'. I also intermittently used MooMan (see Figure 9.4) to call the children to attention and pose questions to the children. This reduced any initial threat from my adult presence as an authority figure, and encouraged enthusiasm from the children for voicing their thoughts about aspects of their family holidays that they did and did not enjoy. Poggenpoel and Myburgh (2003) have warned that, 'The researcher as instrument can be the greatest threat to trustworthiness in qualitative research if considerable time is not spent on preparation of the field [and the] reflexivity of

Figure 9.4 MooMan and me

the researcher' (2003: 320) – thus, the results from the second study support the mother-researcher as being epistemologically advantageous for studies involving younger participants.

Implications and Conclusion

This chapter contributes to the current discourse on qualitative research in three specific ways. Firstly, the work could be read as a reflexive study of an Asian mother researching family tourism, from the children's perspectives. As a mother-researcher, I have identified with the mothers of my participants and could anticipate many of the parental concerns about the research. In contrast to Macintyre (1999), who found motherhood to be a source of mutual identification between herself and her mother-respondents, my identity as a parent in my research on family tourism has, in part, overshadowed the researcher during the research process. However, I must now also argue that while some might describe these situations as mistakes, they are also unavoidable facets of doing research. In most part, motherhood has the place of the personal within research. My presence as a mother-researcher, 'as an ordinary human being with the usual complement of human attributes, can't be avoided. Because of this, we must devise research of a kind which can utilize this presence, rather than pretend it doesn't happen' (Stanley & Wise, 2002: 151). As a result of this reflexive work, I have come to recognise the mother in me which in turn uncovered two complementary yet contradicting realisations. To be specific, it is through the lens of motherhood that I became aware of the need to obtain the children's consent. Although I am still upset that I had not done so, I am more forgiving of this 'oversight' because I am conscious of my mother-researcher identity and accept that I was also a 'mother' to my young participants and always had their interests at heart.

Secondly, this chapter has contributed to the work on motherhood in tourism. Numerous works have documented the impact of motherhood on travel and family tourism (Davidson, 1996; Schänzel, 2016; Small, 2005), but this is an initial attempt to outline how motherhood can impact the way tourism knowledge is generated. This chapter addresses a particular challenge of the current tourism publication climate: that tourism research on Asians and/or by Asian scholars is still seen as being 'religiously devoted to the most conventional rules dictated by positivist academic circles' (Mura & Pahlevan Sharif, 2015: 12). Here, I have challenged these conventional rules by demonstrating how motherhood comes into play for an Asian mother during my many phases of the research process from entering the field, to gaining access, and conducting the focus group interviews. In addition, I employed a critical approach and presented my own travel biography as a mother to young children that highlights motherhood as the trigger for conceptualising the research idea in the first place. Motherhood affects the mother-researcher, and her work should be incorporated into the conventions of academic writing, not treated as unscientific.

Finally, and directly linked to the above, this chapter also serves to expand conversations on epistemology. Within the context of motherhood and researcher identity, I provide epistemological discourse from the perspective of a mother that adds to our existing understandings of knowledge and knowledge generation. In doing so, I have not attempted to categorise these epistemological emergences into a specific origin. Rather, I have deliberately left them open for future scholarship, with an aim to diversifying current research ideologies and ontologies.

References

Acker, S. and Armenti, C. (2004) Sleepless in academia. *Gender and Education* 16 (1), 3–24.
Adams, T.E., Jones, H.S. and Ellis, C. (2015) *Autoethnography: Understanding Qualitative Research*. New York, NY: Oxford University Press.
Allen, D.C. (2015) Learning autoethnography: A review of autoethnography: Understanding qualitative research. *The Qualitative Report* 20 (2), 33–35.
Arendell, T. (2000) Conceiving and investigating motherhood: The decade's scholarship. *Journal of Marriage and Family* 62, 1192–1207.
Armenti, C. (2004) Women faculty seeking tenure and parenthood: Lessons from previous generations. *Cambridge Journal of Education* 34 (1), 65–83.
Barbieri, C., Santos, C.A. and Katsube, Y. (2012) Volunteer tourism: On-the-ground observations from Rwanda. *Tourism Management* 33, 509–516.
Canosa, A., Wilson, E. and Graham, A. (2016) Empowering young people through participatory film: A postmethodological approach. *Current Issues in Tourism*. Advance online publication. doi: 10.1080/13683500.2016.1179270

Carr, N. (2011) *Children's and Families' Holiday Experience*. Abingdon: Routledge.
Carrigan, M. and Szmigin, I. (2004) Time, uncertainty and the expectancy experience: An interpretive exploration of consumption and impending motherhood. *Journal of Marketing Management* 20, 771–798.
Castaneda, M. and Isgro, K. (2013) *Mothers in Academia*. New York, NY: Columbia University Press.
Chang, H. (2008) *Autoethnography as Method*. Walnut Creek, CA: Left Coast Press.
Cornet, C. (2013) The fun and games of taking children to the field in Guizhou, China. In S. Turner (ed.) *Red Stamps and Gold Stars: Fieldwork Dilemmas in Upland Socialist Asia* (pp. 80–99). Vancouver: UBC Press.
Davidson, P. (1996) The holiday and work experiences of women with young children. *Leisure Studies* 15 (2), 89–103. doi: 10.1080/026143696375648
Denzin, N. and Lincoln, Y. (eds) (2000) *The Sage Handbook of Qualitative Research*. Thousand Oaks, CA: Sage.
Doty, J.L. and Dworkin, J. (2014) Online social support for parents: A critical review. *Marriage and Family Review* 50, 174–198.
Ellis, C.S. and Bochner, A. (2000) Autoethnography, personal narrative, reflexivity: Researcher as subject. In N. Denzin and Y. Lincoln (eds) *The Sage Handbook of Qualitative Research* (pp. 733–768). Thousand Oaks, CA: Sage.
Finlay, L. (2002) Negotiating the swamp: The opportunity and challenge of reflexivity in research practice. *Qualitative Research* 2, 209–230. doi: 10.1177/146879410200 200205
Fleming, C. and Fullagar, S. (2007) Reflexive methodologies: An autoethnography of the gendered performance of sport/management. *Annals of Leisure Research* 10, 238–256.
Fox, K.M., Humberstone, B. and Dubnewick, M. (2014) Cycling into sensoria: Embodiment, leisure, and tourism. *Tourism Review International* 18 (1), 71–85.
Greenfield, C. (2004) 'Can run, play on bikes, jump the zoom slide, and play on the swings': Exploring the value of outdoor play. *Australian Journal of Early Childhood* 29 (2), 1–5.
Grenier, R.S. (2015) Autoethnography as a legitimate approach to HRD research: A methodological conversation at 30,000 feet. *Human Resource Development Review* 14, 332–350.
Hall, C.M. (2004) Reflexivity and tourism research: Situating myself and/with others. In J. Phillimore and L. Goodson (eds) *Qualitative Research in Tourism: Ontologies, Epistemologies and Methodologies* (pp. 137–155). London, England: Routledge.
Hall, C.M. (2011) Fieldwork in tourism/touring fields: Where does tourism end and fieldwork begin. In C.M. Hall (ed.) *Fieldwork in Tourism: Methods, Issues and Reflections* (pp. 7–18). Abingdon: Routledge.
Hall, W. and Irvine, V. (2009) E-communication among mothers of infants and toddlers in a community-based cohort: A content analysis. *Journal of Advanced Nursing* 65, 175–183.
Hedges, H. (2002) Beliefs and principles in practice: Ethical research with child participants. *New Zealand Research in Early Childhood Education* 5 (3), 31–49.
Hofstede, G. (2016) *Country Comparison*. See 6 October 2016, from https://geert-hofstede.com/countries.html
Khoo-Lattimore, C. (2015) Kids on board: Methodological challenges, concerns and clarifications when including young children's voices in tourism research. *Current Issues in Tourism* 18, 845–858. doi: 10.1080/13683500.2015.1049129
Khoo-Lattimore, C., Prayag, G. and Cheah, B.L. (2015) Kids on board: Exploring the choice process and vacation needs of Asian parents with young children in resort hotels. *Journal of Hospitality Marketing and Management* 24, 511–531. doi: http://dx.doi.org/10.1080/19368623.2014.914862

Kwek, A., Wang, Y. and Weaver, D.B. (2014) Retail tours in China for overseas Chinese: Soft power or hard sell? *Annals of Tourism Research* 44, 36–52.

Lawlor, M.-A. and Prothero, A. (2011) Pester power: A battle of wills between children and their parents. *Journal of Marketing Management* 27, 561–581. doi: 10.1080/0267257X.2010.495281

Macintyre, M. (1999) Fictive kinship or mistaken identity?: Fieldwork on Tubetube Island, Papua New Guinea. In D. Bell, P. Caplan and W.J. Karim (eds) *Gendered Fields: Women, Men and Ethnography* (pp. 44–62). London, England: Routledge.

Mackenzie, S.H. and Kerr, J.H. (2013) Can't we all just get along? Emotions and the team guiding experience in adventure tourism. *Journal of Destination Marketing and Management* 2 (2), 85–93.

McDermott, E. and Graham, H. (2005) Resilient young mothering: Social inequalities, late modernity and the 'problem' of 'teenage' motherhood. *Journal of Youth Studies* 8, 59–79.

Metcalfe, B.D., Woodhams, C., Gaio Santos, G. and Cabral-Cardoso, C. (2008) Work-family culture in academia: A gendered view of work-family conflict and coping strategies. *Gender in Management: An International Journal* 23, 442–457.

Mura, P. (2013) 'To participate or not to participate?': A reflective account. *Current Issues in Tourism* 18, 83–98. doi: 10.1080/13683500.2013.790879

Mura, P. and Pahlevan Sharif, S. (2015) The crisis of the 'crisis of representation': Mapping qualitative tourism research in Southeast Asia. *Current Issues in Tourism* 18, 828–844. doi: 10.1080/13683500.2015.1045459

Nanda, D., Hu, C. and Bai, B. (2007) Exploring family roles in purchasing decisions during vacation planning: Review and discussions for future research. *Journal of Travel and Tourism Marketing* 20, 107–125. doi: 10.1300/J073v20n03_08

Nickerson, N.P. and Jurowski, C. (2001) The influence of children on vacation travel patterns. *Journal of Vacation Marketing* 7, 19–30. doi: 10.1177/135676670100700102

Noy, C. (2008) The poetics of tourist experience: An autoethnography of a family trip to Eilat. *Journal of Tourism and Cultural Change* 5, 141–157.

Okumus, F., Altinay, L. and Roper, A. (2007) Gaining access for research: Reflections from experience. *Annals of Tourism Research* 34, 7–26.

Poggenpoel, M. and Myburgh, C. (2003) The researcher as research instrument in educational research: A possible threat to trustworthiness? *Education* 124, 418.

Poria, Y. and Timothy, D.J. (2014) Where are the children in tourism research? *Annals of Tourism Research* 47, 93–95. doi: 10.1016/j.annals.2014.03.002

Raddon, A. (2002) Mothers in the academy: Positioned and positioning within discourses of the 'successful academic' and the 'good mother'. *Studies in Higher Education* 27, 387–403.

Riad, S. (2007) Under the desk: On becoming a mother in the workplace. *Culture and Organization* 13, 205–222.

Schänzel, H.A. (2016) A time and space of one's own: Women's resistance to the motherhood discourse on family holidays. In C. Khoo-Lattimore and E. Wilson (eds) *Women and Travel: Historical and Contemporary Perspectives* (pp. 51–66). Oakville, Canada: Apple Academic Press.

Schänzel, H.A. and Smith, K.A. (2011) Photography and children: Auto-driven photo-elicitation. *Tourism Recreation Research* 36, 81–85. doi: 10.1080/02508281.2011.11081664

Small, J. (2005) Women's holidays: Disruption of the motherhood myth. *Tourism Review International* 9, 139–154. doi: 10.3727/154427205774791645

Stanley, L. (1993) On auto/biography in sociology. *Sociology* 27, 41–52.

Stanley, L. and Wise, S. (2002) *Breaking Out Again: Feminist Ontology and Epistemology*. London: Routledge.

Sung, K.-T. (2001) Elder respect: Exploration of ideals and forms in East Asia. *Journal of Aging Studies* 15, 13–26.

Thornton, P.R., Shaw, G. and Williams, A.M. (1997) Tourist group holiday decision-making and behaviour: The influence of children. *Tourism Management* 18, 287–297. doi: 10.1016/S0261-5177(97)00017-4

Wang, K.-C., Hsieh, A.-T., Yeh, Y.-C. and Tsai, C.-W. (2004) Who is the decision-maker: The parents or the child in group package tours? *Tourism Management* 25, 183–194. doi: 10.1016/S0261-5177(03)00093-1

Westwood, S., Morgan, N. and Pritchard, A. (2006) Situation, participation and reflexivity in tourism research: Furthering interpretive approaches to tourism enquiry. *Tourism Recreation Research* 31 (2), 33–41.

Wyatt, S.N. (2002) Challenges of the working breastfeeding mother: Workplace solutions. *Workplace Health and Safety* 50 (2), 61–66.

Yang, C.L. (in press) Risk perception of Asian solo female travelers: An autoethnographic approach. In C. Khoo-Lattimore and E. Wilson (eds) *Women and Travel: Historical and Contemporary Perspectives*. Oakville, Canada: Apple Academic Press.

10 Subjectivities Implode: When 'The Lone Male' Ethnographer is Actually a Nursing Mother …

Lisa Cooke

Dr Lisa Cooke is an associate professor of anthropology in the Department of Sociology and Anthropology at Thompson Rivers University in Kamloops, BC, Canada – so while she still thinks herself very new at this, she finds herself firmly in the mid-career phase of her academic life cycle. As an anthropologist interested in Indigenous-settler relations in Canada, Lisa happened upon studying tourism. 'In the field' exploring people's place-based narratives, her ethnographic gaze was drawn to the ways that touristic places are produced in particular ways, guided by select (often dominant settler colonial) narratives, and come to shape many of the terms of encounter between Indigenous and settler peoples in Canada. Interested first in ideas of North in Canadian national–cultural imaginaries, she now spends her time examining ski resorts on unceded, unsurrendered Indigenous territories in British Columbia. Both of these research areas have emerged out of personal connections to places, landscapes and the things that she likes to do outside. Her research is guided by an attempt to better understand her own relationship to place, and the historically loaded, settler colonial privilege that positions her in them in particular ways. Her son, Norry, born 'in the field' in the Yukon, continues to explore place, space and relations with his mom.

'I am an Anthropologist'

I am an anthropologist. Given the interdisciplinary, multidisciplinary and postdisciplinary tone of contemporary scholarship, this kind of statement feels a bit dated. Add to this that I situate my work within the dynamic fields of Indigenous, settler colonial and tourism studies, I feel even more self-conscious about such a declaration. And yet, here I am, an anthropologist. All of my degrees are in anthropology. I hold a faculty position teaching anthropology in an anthropology department. I am trained *in* anthropology, by anthropology. I am an anthropologist.

As an anthropologist, I learned, and I teach, about lineages. Is a group matrilineal or patrilineal? How is descent traced to a shared ancestral figure (mythic or real)? We draw diagrams with circles and triangles denoting sets of relations that make up lineage descent groups. We then use these as unit of analysis of social, political and economic organisation. Lineages create structures of relations, roles and responsibilities. We use them to trace connections to shared roots (Durrenberger & Erem, 2007).

This contemplation of *Femininities in the Field* has me thinking about anthropology, lineages, mythic disciplinary ancestral figures from whom we trace descent, and the networks for relations that make up this thing/place called 'the field'. There is perhaps no disciplinary construction within anthropology more powerful than 'the field'. 'Going to the field' is a formative rite of passage for anthropologists-in-training (Robben & Sluka, 2012). It is 'in the field' that we become 'real' anthropologists.

In what follows, I invite you to join me as I look back over my shoulder to my own time spent 'in the field' as a graduate student/anthropologist-in-training *and* woman turned mother. I headed 'to the field' in search of a PhD dissertation. I came back with both data and a baby. This posed a problem for me – not because I could not conduct fieldwork as a pregnant woman or nursing mother. I could and I did. But rather because, as an anthropologist, I had been taught that:

> ... field work represents mystery, opportunity, and excitement ... The student knows that this is a challenge he will have to face, a major rite de passage that will provide him the opportunity to prove his ability, courage, and temperamental suitability for the profession ... Success in field work proclaims manhood and generates a major transformation: a student of culture becomes an anthropologist. (Freilich, 1970: 16)

There is no doubt that my experiences 'in the field' were transformative. Just not in the way suggested by Freilich. He, manhood. Me, mother. To be sure, even as an undergraduate student I had the ability to critically deconstruct the gendered assumptions presented in this passage. And yet, somehow, in real time, 'in the field', there was something in the deeply rooted disciplinary imaginary of fieldwork as masculine and anthropologists as male that haunted me. This is my contemplation of how ...

'Rites of Passage'

Setting out 'to the field' for my doctoral dissertation research involved packing up my grad-student furniture, boxes and boxes of grad-student books, borrowing a Volkswagen camper van from my parents, and relocating from Toronto to Whitehorse, Yukon, a territory in the far northwest corner of Canada. As graduate students in a department of Social Anthropology, my classmates and I chatted often about 'the field' – 'when are you going to the field?' 'How was the field?' 'How long will you be in the field?' Many of my colleagues were conducting research in the city where we lived. 'The field' for them was not all that far from home. And yet, 'going to the field' was for all of us, regardless of the geographic location of said 'field', a fundamentally important part of our collective graduate-training-accreditation as 'real' anthropologists. We were to 'head out into the field' and then come up with something insightful to say about what we had observed and experienced. This was our 'rite of passage' in our journeys of becoming proper (read: real/serious) anthropologists.

As aspiring anthropologists, we had all been well trained in the lineages of the discipline's ethnographic traditions. As undergraduate students, we had read Bronislaw Malinowski's *Argonauts of the Western Pacific* (1922) and been told that he was a 'founding father' of the disciplinary practice of fieldwork. Malinowski had insisted that if we were to understand people and culture, we needed to participate in and observe what people did. We could not do this in museums or at a distance. We needed to go there, and experience things first hand. And so emerged 'the field' as an anthropological construction of the site of those we sought to understand, and 'fieldwork' as a foundational practice of 'doing' anthropology.

The website, *Discover Anthropology* (2016), reads:

> Since Malinowski's time, fieldwork – traditionally, away from one's own society – has been regarded as an essential and necessary part of an anthropologist's professional training. Fieldwork over an extended period – typically 1–2 years – has been thought of as particular to social anthropology, and part of what distinguishes the discipline from other social sciences.

As graduate students, we felt this requirement. We were preoccupied with its implications – ethics, funding, logistics. To be sure, as graduate students we had also critically deconstructed Malinowski's 'field' and anthropology's entanglements with colonialism, its contribution to the making of 'the Other', and the problematics inherent in the cannon of the discipline. And yet, no matter how 'post' any of us were – postmodern, postdisciplinary, postcolonial, postfeminist, posthumanist – we were products of our training in these lineages. There remained something particularly sacred about 'the field'.

There is also something particularly masculine about this 'field'. To be sure, there are women in the canon of ethnographic literature. We read Margaret Mead and Ruth Benedict as undergraduates too. In graduate school I spent hours poring over beautiful feminist ethnographic reflections that clearly situated women 'in the field'. Still, regardless of the critical vocabulary made available to me through these works, 'the field' remained in my mind a masculine space, and 'the fieldworker' a lone male figure. Just as the quote cited earlier suggests, doing anthropology meant doing fieldwork and doing fieldwork meant doing it like a man. You needed to go alone. It needed to be far away and exotically different. You needed to endure hardship and discomfort. And you needed to stay a long time. (Even if your 'field' was a housing project 15 minutes from your apartment.)

This 'lone male ethnographer' archetype is somewhat akin to a patrilineal descent line's originary male ancestor – picture a Malinowski-esk figure. He's white and male and as a Western-trained anthropologist, I feel somehow, like it or not, related to him (as mythic figure or actual person). He. Manhood. Thinking about *Feminities in the Field* alongside my colleagues in this collection has been a journey in tracing lineages (mythic and real) to the disciplinary roots that shaped my experiences as a woman 'in the field'. It has led me to consider not just how deeply I had internalised the importance of the lone-male ethnographer archetype to the *doing* of anthropology but how limiting this figure is to my actual practice of *being* an anthropologist.

By letting him go, and with him the notion that 'the field' is a performative zone of masculinity, a liberating space emerges – where my subjective positionalities as woman and new mother granted theoretical and ethnographic insight that continue to shape how I do anthropology (and motherhood, citizenship and scholarship for that matter).

'Heading to the Field'

The telling of the story to my classmates in Toronto of 'heading to the field' in Yukon made it sound far more exciting and adventurous than the actual event itself. My 'field' was far away, seemed exotic and met the narrative requirements of 'the field's' hardcore-ness. On arrival in Whitehorse, a place that I had lived twice previously, I moved into a suburban house, reconnected with a community of lovely friends, and went about my daily life. I paid bills, made dinner and did the dishes. I had come to Whitehorse to explore what it was about Yukon and ideas of 'North' that captured a touristic imagination. What made people travel, usually by road, so far to this northern point in North American? As a Canadian, I grew up hearing tales of 'The North'. I read books about its romance and lure. On completion of my undergraduate degree, I had felt the pull and moved myself to Yukon in search of something … adventure probably, maybe love, perhaps both. I met a lovely collection of others on the same quest. Many are still there.

As my journey took me to graduate school, I could not shake the question – what is it about this place that draws people to it? And how does this place, Yukon, present itself in response to this collective lure and lore? So, in 2006, comprehensive exams and coursework behind me, I headed North again. This time North was 'the field' and I went in search of something to say about it. By the end of my first summer 'in the field' (which really is code for, living my life in a place that I was doing research), I found myself pregnant. This, I had not included in my dissertation research proposal or research funding timeline. I had not listed 'have a baby' as an 'expected scholarly outcome' of my fieldwork. I had no accessible vocabulary for processing this turn of events in my academic world. This was not something that my grad-student colleagues and I had discussed in our discussions about the rigours of fieldwork. We were all to head to 'the field' to collect 'data', not have babies.

It took months to get the courage to send an email to my supervisor and committee telling them about my 'situation'. Even at the time, I recognised fully that my self-consciousness at having to 'admit' that I was pregnant was rooted in an imaginative incompatibility that I had internalised. How could I be a serious anthropologist 'in the field' (meaning: lone and male) and be a pregnant woman? My feminist-self was annoyed at my sheepish-self's deep internalisation of a patriarchal (and deeply problematic) image of the lone-male (colonial, othering) ethnographer. I had a vocabulary for problematising the tension. What I did not have, were the words to actually articulate what this meant to me in real time.

None of this was lost on me as I sat at my kitchen table in Whitehorse attempting to write an email to my supervisor and committee 'confessing' to being pregnant. Eventually, I crafted a ridiculously long email – written only in a way that someone who has never actually had (or spent much time with) a baby could – carefully explaining that yes, I was pregnant, but that no one was to fret or be concerned about my ability to keep up with my proposed timeline, as I had it all worked out. The baby would be born in the spring. May to August were the busiest months of interview and participant observation data collection. The baby would be small and portable during this and so I would just bring him/her along and that would be that. I would complete my fieldwork on schedule, produce a dissertation and graduate as planned.

This email, and the emotional conflict that I felt over crafting it, are precisely an example of what I mean when I tell students that most of the time the cultural values, interests and orders that make up our senses of the world as 'common sense' are so deeply embedded that we do not notice them as such. They just 'are'. Despite my well-read feminist vocabulary, there I was, actively reconstituting hegemonic patriarchal structures of power through a deeply internalised sense of self-consciousness doubt in the possibility of being both an anthropologist 'in the field' and a woman-mother.

At this point in the story it is important to mention that I was not sending this email to a scary group. My PhD committee was made up of three of the kindest, most supportive and inspiring people that I have ever had the honour of knowing – Margaret Critchlow (formerly Rodman), Teresa Holmes and Kenneth Little. Three anthropologists, two mothers and one father. My trepidation in telling them about being pregnant was entirely a product of my own conditioning. I admire all three very much and wanted them to take me seriously as an anthropologist. Somehow in my mind, even though all three were themselves parents, I was hung up on the notion that I could not be taken seriously as an ethnographer 'in the field' if I was also a pregnant and then nursing mother with babe in arms.

I heard back from Margaret first. She made no mention of my (ridiculous) well-organised work-plan that would not be interrupted by childbirth or rearing. Instead she simply wrote – 'Wonderful news Lisa! Babies come when they come. The rest is details.'

The Rest is Details …

Despite Margaret's supportive words, I remained deeply self-conscious that being pregnant, having a baby and then being a mother 'in the field' would fundamentally alter people's perceptions of my abilities to also simultaneously be an academic and anthropologist. The reality was that on the ground, day-to-day, I was just doing what I always did. I conducted interviews and read articles. I transcribed interviews and tagged along on guided tours of various sites. I paid bills, visited with friends, made dinner and did the dishes. In the same way that 'the field' was the site of my daily life, and 'fieldwork' a process of living my life which happened to include gathering information about something that I was interested in, the 'doing' of being a researching anthropologist and a pregnant and then new mother was just what I did. Margaret was right; the rest really was all details.

Yet still, in practice, I worked hard to keep my mothering and ethnographer selves separate. Norry was born on 23 April 2007. A lovely baby boy. By May, he and I were out and about talking with visitors about their travels. I had a complex pillow system that I set up on my lap whereby I could type at the computer with two hands while aiming my nipple into his mouth on demand, uttering the occasional, 'see, I totally got this' to myself (high fiving both myself and the lone-male ethnographer, Malinowski-esk mythic ancestor of my discipline). Out and about, I really did try to pretend that my son was not there. I would walk up to people with Norry in his stroller and then step in front of it as I pulled out informed consent forms and starting asking questions. The reality, however, was that not only was he entirely there, he was an asset. The majority of the tourists that I was talking to were retired people on extended road trips from distant parts of Canada or the United States. They had been travelling in their motor homes for months and had months to go. They were far from home and missed their families, especially their grandchildren. As quickly as I would try to step in front of the stroller with my clipboard and informed consent forms, many would reach in and scoop him out, delighted to snuggle a baby. I came to appreciate his being with me for these moments. (What I did not realise yet was just how profoundly his being would serve my becoming an anthropologist, a point that I will return to shortly.)

The doing seemed to matter less to me than the perception of my ability to do, or rather than my perception of the perception of my abilities. I was so deeply hung up on the idea that my being 'in the field' as a female, mothering body was incompatible with my training that 'doing' fieldwork meant 'doing it like a man'. Despite Margaret's encouraging words, or the fact that my own lineage of academic influences was made up of mothering field-working women. My MA supervisor, Susan Frohlick, also a student of Margaret's as lineages go, had also had a baby during her PhD. With babe in arms and family at her side, she headed 'to the field' in Nepal. Partner and children in tow, Susan interviewed climbers at Mount Everest Basecamp. By all accounts, like mine, Susan's field site met the narrative requirements of being extreme, exotic and masculine. Like me, she too struggled with how to perform the 'lone-male ethnographer'/serious anthropologist as an attached nursing mother (Frohlick, 2002).

Like Frohlick, in 'the field', I was neither male nor lone. I had a baby son, a community of incredibly supportive friends, and often the help of my mother (Nana). My three most important 'field instruments' were my stroller, camper van and my mother. On several occasions over the first two summers of Norry's life my mother came to stay. Nana, Norry and I would head out 'into the field'. Nana and baby would wander about while I conducted interviews or joined tours. We met up on Norry's feeding schedule. I would nurse and debrief my experiences while my mother patiently took care of both of us.

When I look at this picture (Figure 10.1) now, I think about lineages. This was the actual lineage, as structure of relations, roles and responsibilities that got me to and through 'the field'. I am a product of this lineage of women – Margaret, Susan, Teresa and Judy (Nana). It is to them that I owe thanks. Not Malinowski or the mythic lone-male ancestor-figure that dominated my anthropological imagination to the point where I could not even fully grasp the importance of the actual women in my life. One of the gifts of this collection is that it offers me an opportunity to reflect on, acknowledge and give thanks. It grants a moment of pause to think about how profoundly my experiences as a woman, mother, researcher, teacher and Canadian were all shaped by the specific configurations of circumstances that came together to put me 'in the field' when, where and how I was there.

Figure 10.1 Nana, Norry, the stroller and the van (Photo by author July 2007)

Subjectivities Implode: When 'The Lone Male' Ethnographer is Actually a Nursing Mother …

I mentioned that Norry was born in the spring of 2007 and that he, I and often my mother spent our days touring about the Yukon looking for people to chat with about their travels. This took us to campgrounds and museums. We visited National Historic sites and marked 'points of interest' at the side of the road. We spent time in Whitehorse and Dawson City, making stops in between.

The summer in 2007 that Norry was born, my travelling field crew and I spent a lot of time in Dawson City. Dawson City is situated on the traditional territories of the Tr'ondëck Hwëch'in, a self-governing First Nation in central Yukon. Dänojà Zho is the Tr'ondëck Hwëch'in's cultural centre. Perched on the banks of the Klondike River, the Dänojà Zho Cultural Centre is a stunning structure merging contemporary and traditional architectural features (Figure 10.2). It stands as a beautiful expression and assertion of Tr'ondëck Hwëch'in presence in the present. The building itself stands in stark contrast to the dominant aesthetic in the rest of Dawson City that aims to recreate the historical period of the Klondike Gold Rush. Tourism is Dawson City's primary economic industry and the Klondike Gold Rush, as nationally significant to the story of Canadian nation building, its main attraction. The very architecture of the Dänojà Zho Cultural Centre is an act of resistance against the dominant settler colonial narrative of 'taming the wild frontier' as national–cultural achievement in Canada (Cooke, 2013, 2016).

That summer in 2007, the Tr'ondëck Hwëch'in hosted an incredibly powerful and brave exhibit at Dänojà Zho. The exhibit was called 'Where

Figure 10.2 The Dänojà Zho Cultural Centre, Dawson City, Yukon (Photo by author, August 2008)

are the Children? Healing the Legacy of the Residential Schools: Finding Our Way Home'. The exhibit consisted of several pieces. The first was a series of black and white photographs taken at residential schools all over Canada. These images were part of the national travelling exhibit, 'Where are the Children? Healing the Legacy of the Residential Schools'. (For more information about this exhibit, to see some of the images, or learn more about the residential school system in Canada please visit the Legacy of Hope interactive website, http://wherearethechildren.ca/en). The residential school system in Canada was in operation from the 1870s to 1996. There were a total of about 130 schools in virtually every part of the country, all serving the settler colonial mandate of aggressively assimilating Indigenous children into settler society. Generations of Indigenous children were forcibly taken from their families and communities and incarcerated in these schools (Truth and Reconciliation Commission of Canada, 2016).

The haunting images in the exhibit were of children lined up outside of schools, packed into the backs of trucks for transport to the schools, and kneeling to pray beside rows of tiny metal cots. I spent hours staring at these images that summer. I looked into the eyes of the children in these pictures – sad, lonely, scared, sweet, beautiful eyes – with infant Norry strapped to my body in his carrier. I remember breathing in the smell of the top of his head thinking about the mothers of the children in the pictures and feeling a pain in my heart and lump in my throat that I did not have words for.

In addition to these images, the Tr'ondëck Hwëch'in community curated two more components. These parts of the exhibit were called 'Finding Our Way Home' and reflected the efforts of the community over a year and a half as members came together to tell the stories of these schools and their legacies. One was a stunning scrapbook collection of first-hand accounts from Tr'ondëck Hwëch'in survivors of the schools. This collection, titled *Tr'ëhuhch'in Näwtr'udäh'a* has been published as a stunning book (a copy of which sits on my desk as a reminder of everything that I write about here). I spent as many hours poring through these pages as I did looking at the pictures that summer. The courage and generosity offered through this book is overwhelming. Survivors speak of their time at school and the impacts that their leaving had on their families. There are stories of abuse, pain, fear, alcoholism, loss, suffering and survival.

With the images and scrapbook on display, the voices of Tr'ondëck Hwëch'in community members of all ages filled the exhibit hall as a video played continuously. Young people reflected on what learning about their relatives' time at residential school had meant to them and how the legacies of pain and trauma left on the community impacted them. Survivors spoke of their experiences. Youth spoke of understanding their families better after learning about the schools.

There was no escaping the impact of this exhibit. 'Where are the Children? Healing the Legacy of Residential Schools – Finding our way Home' was set out in the main exhibit room of Dänojà Zho. Once through the entrance and small gift-shop space there was no escaping it – and this was by design. In the words of manager Glenda Bolt:

> Some of the residential school survivors that have spoken to me expressed the feeling of being trapped. They were alone with no way out, confused by all the new and strange things and consumed by feelings of being overwhelmed and scared to the core. I wanted to find a way to incorporate those intense emotions in the exhibition to make sure that people realized that we are speaking about children ... powerless, confused little kids that were far from home and help. I purchased free standing blackboards and created a maze of sorts to hang the framed black and white photographs on ... all hung with industrial looking wire and hooks fashioned from metal brackets. I wanted it to have the feel of an old style classroom but designed in such a way that almost by accident you realize that you are stuck in a corner, surrounded by the images and words, with the sound of children on the sound system overhead and not able to see a clear path to the exit. Trapped. (Cited with permission, personal communication with author in Dawson City, Yukon, July 2008)

Norry and I returned over and over – every time I noticed something new. One day my mom was with us. As we moved through the display of images in silence I looked over at her. Tears were pouring down her face. She was holding Norry and stroking his head. In that moment, I was both mother and daughter. I imagined first having my baby taken from me and then the pain of watching my mother's unspeakable grief as pain compounded from generation to generation. There were/are no words for the way that this exhibit registered in my body and on my nervous system. In this moment, I felt 'the field', as anthropological site of research, cave in. Caught in a knot of affective complexity entangling me, my son, my mother, our settler colonial privilege and my research to the past, present and future, this 'field' was not a place but a complex field of relations of which I was intricately a part. My body hurt under the weight of history and the lump that I felt in my throat was settler colonial privilege. I had known about residential schools for a long time. I had felt outrage at their genocidal impacts before. But I had never felt them in my body. Not really. Not like this. Not as mother and daughter.

The Child in the Poster

One day, a few weeks later, as Norry and I left the Dänojà Zho, we landed on the porch of the building. He was hungry and I needed a moment to collect myself. The impact of the exhibit never lessened. A few minutes later a woman that I had noticed inside the exhibit joined us. She stopped to chat as I nursed Norry. Without thinking, I launched into my ethnographer-in-the-field set of questions about what brought her North? How was she enjoying her trip? What things where standing out to her? Was it what she expected?

I'll call her Janice. Janice, a single woman from Ontario in her 50s who loved to travel, was delighted to share with me tales of her adventures. She told me about how she was on a flying tour of several northern communities. She told me about how much fun she was having. She talked about how neat it was to see this place called 'North' in real life after having heard, read and imagined it for so long. And then, with her hand on her chest and tears in her eyes, she told me about how profoundly proud she was to be Canadian. She said that she has always been proud, but being North and seeing the land and experiencing it for herself, her heart was filled with a new kind of pride for this nation.

As she spoke, over her shoulder, was a poster for the exhibit inside (Figure 10.3).

What Janice was offering me was a near perfect ethnographic narrative of travel, place and the national-cultural significance of ideas of North to her sense of Canadian self-hood. She spoke to my research question exactly. Her words matched precisely what I had set out to examine in my research proposal. And yet, in that moment, looking up at Janice, Norry nestled into my breast, my heart still pounding from the impact of the exhibit inside, listening to her words, all I could think was that the deeply

Figure 10.3 The Child in the Poster, taken at the Dänojà Zho Cultural Centre by the author, August 2007

felt love and pride that she was expressing about Canada was only possible by turning her back on the Child in the Poster behind her.

If Janice turned around and looked at her – really looked her in the eyes – the sense of pride in Canada that she felt would have been disrupted. The residential school system in Canada is a key chapter in the story of Canadian nation building. Settler colonialism requires the dispossession of Indigenous peoples from land and the elimination of Indigenous peoples from being, through cultural or full-scale genocide (Wolfe, 2006). The residential school system was an effective technology of settler colonial establishment. It decimated communities, families, languages, relationships and individuals. It is estimated that as many as 50% of children that entered the schools did not survive to, in the words of long-time head of Indian Affairs Canada, Duncan Campbell Scott, 'benefit from the education, which they had received therein' (cited in Truth and Reconciliation Commission of Canada, 2016). Many who did survive their incarceration at school faced lifelong struggles as a result (see Bussidor & Bilgen-Reinart, 1997; Grant, 1996; Merasty, 2015 for first-hand accounts of the experience and impacts of residential schools on survivors). The Dänojà Zho was filled with images and voices of the horrors of these schools. Janice had just seen and heard them. The stories of these children and what they endured, and continue to endure, are as much a part of the tale of Canadian nation building as the Klondike Gold Rush. One is not possible without the other. And yet, Janice, like so many settler Canadians, was able to turn her back on the Child in the Poster and not only ignore her and the estimated 150,000 other Indigenous children incarcerated in Residential Schools in Canada, but dis-appear her from intruding on her sense of national–cultural pride. To be fair, this erasure is not Janice's alone, but rather a cultural requirement of settler colonial nation-making whereby our colonial roots and routes are obscured out of sight in the narrative production of a new national entity (Cooke, 2013, 2016; Wolfe, 2006).

Fields of Relations

I dedicated my PhD dissertation to the Child in the Poster. Looking at her with my light-skinned settler, privileged son nestled into my arms and her young, beautiful, brave eyes looking back at us, I thought about her mother. Her grannies and aunties. Her brothers and sisters. Her father and cousins. I thought about the hole that would be left behind if someone took my son from my arms and the pain that my mother, brother, father would endure if he were gone and I was broken from the loss.

This moment on the porch of the Dänojà Zho Cultural Centre changed the way that I saw everything else around me. In this moment, my subjective positionalities as woman, settler, anthropologist, mother, daughter and researcher imploded in a kind of supernova of affective complexity, the impacts of which continue to shape my how I work, teach, write and think about this territory now most dominantly called Canada. 'The field' was not a far-flung exotic other place, nor I a lone-male, disembodied, participant observer of it. As a nursing mother with an aching heart and tears in my eyes, there was no escaping the depth of this embodied experience. This is what Susan (Frohlick, 2002: 50) meant when she so beautifully writes of 'the embodied entanglements that play out between our selves or subjectivities and our research sites'.

It is precisely these embodied entanglements that create the networks of relations that *are* our fields of inquiry – 'the field'. It is in this field, situated by our specific subjective positions, that we experience the world that we seek to understand. I was a better anthropologist that day on the porch of the Dänojà Zho Cultural Centre because I was also an emotionally vulnerable mother. Not only was being a woman-mother-daughter not incompatible with being a fieldworking anthropologist, these subjective positionalities dialled me into a particular frequency that landed on, in and through me in a way that profoundly changed the way I saw the world. My heart was cracked open by Norry. Nerve endings that I did not know I had were exposed. This was my 'major transformation: a student of culture becomes an anthropologist' (Freilich, 1970: 16) – not as a test of manhood, as Freilich and Malinowski had taught me but rather of woman-mother-humanhood.

To the Child in the Poster, Norry, my mom, dad, brother, friends, Susan, Margaret, Theresa, Kenneth, Janice and every other person that shared time, energy, company, guidance and experiences with me – thank you. It is the fields of relations that we share that created 'the field', and you are the lineage that made me an anthropologist.

References

Bussidor, I. and Bilgen-Reinart, Ü. (1997) *Night Spirits: The Story of the Relocation of the Saysi Dene*. Winnipeg: University of Manitoba Press.
Cooke, L. (2013) North takes place in Canada's Yukon Territory. In D. Jørgensen and S. Sörlin (eds) *Northscapes: History, Technology, and the Making of Northern Environments* (pp. 223–246). Vancouver, Canada: University of British Columbia Press.
Cooke, L. (2016) 'North' in contemporary Canadian national-cultural imaginaries: A haunted phantasm. *Settler Colonial Studies* 6, 235–251. doi: 10.1080/2201473X.2014.1001307
Discover Anthropology (2016) *Fieldwork*. See https://www.discoveranthropology.org.uk/about-anthropology/fieldwork.html (accessed 26 November 2016).
Durrenberger, E.P. and Erem, S. (2007) *Anthropology Unbound: A Field Guide to the 21st Century*. Boulder, CO: Paradigm.
Freilich, M. (1970) Fieldwork: An introduction. In M. Freilich (ed.) *Marginal Natives: Anthropologists at Work* (pp. 1–37). New York, NY: Harper and Row.
Frohlick, S. (2002) 'You brought your baby to base camp?': Families and field sites. *The Great Lakes Geographer* 9, 49–58.
Grant, A. (1996) *No End of Grief: Indian Residential Schools in Canada*. Winnipeg: Pemmican Publications.
Malinowski, B. (1922) *Argonauts of the Western Pacific: An Account of Native Enterprise and Adventure in the Archipelagos of Melanesian New Guinea*. London: Routledge.
Merasty, J.A. (2015) *The Education of Augie Merasty: A Residential School Memoir*. Regina, Canada: University of Regina Press.
Robben, A.C.G.M. and Sluka, J.A. (2012) Fieldwork in anthropology: An introduction. In A.C.G.M. Robben and J.A. Sluka (eds) *Ethnographic Fieldwork: An Anthropological Reader* (2nd edn, pp. 1–48). Oxford: Blackwell.
Truth and Reconciliation Commission of Canada (2016) *Residential schools*. See http://www.trc.ca/websites/trcinstitution/index.php?p=3 (accessed 26 November 2016).
Wolfe, P. (2006) Settler colonialism and the elimination of the native. *Journal of Genocide Research* 8, 387–409.

11 Icebreaker: Experiences of Conducting Fieldwork in Arctic Canada with my Infant Son

Emma J. Stewart

Dr Emma J. Stewart is a Human Geographer in the Department of Tourism, Sport and Society, at Lincoln University, New Zealand. Emma is a mid-career researcher and her work takes her to the Polar Regions and the High Mountain Environment where she is interested in the human dimensions of climate change and the implications of change for communities, resources and key sectors such as the tourism industry. Originally from the UK, she completed her Master's Degree at Lincoln University and finally returned to the same department in 2009, where she remains. She is an Associate Professor in Parks and Tourism. Previously she held a lecturing position in Wales, completed her doctoral studies at the University of Calgary, and had two children, who are now teenagers.

> *Between the ages of nine and twenty-two months, my infant son accompanied me during my doctoral fieldwork in Arctic Canada. Almost immediately, and in unexpected ways, he accelerated my acceptance into the mainly Inuit communities where I was working. Perhaps due to the child-centred nature of the communities, or the shared common ground of parenthood, Benjamin had the effect of breaking down several of the barriers some researchers face when entering communities for the first time. Essentially he was an icebreaker. Drawing on journal entries, this chapter adopts a reflexive approach to explore: the influences my son had on my experiences in the field (access and building trust); the adaptations I made; and the lessons learned that may help other parents considering taking an infant into the field.*

Introduction: The First Meal

When my Inuit host unexpectedly regurgitated a mouthful of caribou stew into the obliging mouth of my nine-month-old son I was momentarily horrified. It was our first evening in an Inuit community and the first of many experiences of doing things 'Inuit style' during my two field seasons of doctoral research in Arctic Canada. At the dinner table that evening, health concerns were at the forefront of my mind, but I tried to remain calm. I took the lead from Benjamin who was not in the least bit phased. To the contrary, he was relishing this new feeding experience. The half-chewed food was the right temperature, the perfect consistency and the salty meat taste was clearly something he was enjoying. It was like watching a mother bird feed her chick. I was mildly irritated that he no longer had any interest in the meal I had lovingly prepared for him. I had spent the morning creating his supposedly favourite meal – a sloppy concoction of sweet potato, chicken and onion (ingredients that are not cheap in the Arctic) – and freezing it into small portions to see him through our stay. However, I knew intuitively that our experiences around the kitchen table that evening were telling: we had been initiated into the Inuit way of doing things, and were on our way to being accepted into the family, and by association into the community. Any reservations about bringing Benjamin into the field vanished and I got a sense that evening that he was going to be more of a help then a hindrance: he was going to break the ice. Excuse the pun.

'Snow Goose' Researchers

My doctoral research examined local resident perspectives on the burgeoning tourism sector in the Canadian Arctic, which necessitated creating relationships with three communities at different stages of tourism development (Stewart, 2009). However, it soon became clear to me that research in this part of the world had not always been equitable. Some social science research had been criticised in the past by indigenous groups for perpetuating deeply embedded inequalities of power (Smith, 1999). These inequalities were manifested in research that is 'done' to indigenous communities, whereby researchers visit communities (often without informing the community first), obtain data and subsequently fail to report back their findings (Freeman, 1993). Not surprisingly, lingering mistrust and suspicion of researchers in some indigenous communities was the legacy created by decades of this 'helicopter' style of research (Smith, 1999).

It became clear to me that residents of these communities were tired of researchers who arrived, sometimes unannounced, with questions that had been devised without the input of local people. Because there was often no effort to report back research findings, people indicated to me that research is just a 'one-way process', with the benefits only accruing to the researcher, not the community. In a playful way, there was an analogy between snow geese and researchers. Snow geese arrive in the summer, make a lot of noise and a lot of mess, then leave at the end of the summer, only to return again the following year to repeat the process. In other parts of the Canadian Arctic, for similar reasons, researchers have been referred to as *siksiks* ('ground squirrels' in Inuktitut). As Gearheard and Shirley (2007) point out, this analogy sometimes is used in a joking manner, but sometimes 'the nickname expresses negative feelings toward researchers; a mistrust that stems from a history of non-communication, miscommunication and misunderstanding' (2007: 63). I did not want to be labelled as just another 'snow goose' researcher and was resolved from this point forward to do things in a different way.

I adopted a participatory approach to my research which is distinguished from other approaches in that it specifically facilitates research 'by' and 'for' communities (Legat, 1994; Smith *et al.*, 1997; Stevenson, 1996). It is not something 'done' to people (Patton, 2002: 183). Participatory research is the antithesis of 'helicopter' research, and is an overarching term for research that aims to empower community members through active engagement in research processes (Taylor *et al.*, 2004). Given that interest in participatory research has 'exploded' in recent years (Patton, 2002: 183), it is not surprising that a wide range of research approaches are found and have been variously labelled: participatory action research (PAR), collaborative, cooperative, emancipatory, community-based and community-involved research. In all these cases, there is a commitment to involve people in research, though the nature of participation may vary to some degree (Patton, 2002) depending on the extent to which community members are active – or share power – in participatory research processes (Bloodworth *et al.*, 2004; Israel *et al.*, 1998).

Getting In

In the early days of my doctoral studies, establishing a case study site for my emerging research turned out to be a long and frustrating one. As a non-Canadian and first-time visitor to Canada, I was acutely aware of my 'otherness' as a researcher. To help overcome my sense of isolation I looked for advice, and in the absence of literature on this matter, my supervisors advised me to get 'yourself out there'. I met and talked to as many people as possible over a year or so. Despite advances made conceptually in my research I kept asking myself: 'How do I make contact and gain permission to work in northern communities?', 'Where do I start?' and 'Can I get in, being such an outsider?' These questions plagued me for some time but I continued talking to people, emailing, writing, meeting and conference-going. The key was to stay active and eventually important openings presented themselves.

The first opening came through a successful application for Northern Research Funding (NRF) from the Churchill Northern Studies Centre (CNSC). I remember feeling some relief that this might be a 'way in', at last. It was staff at CNSC who suggested a preliminary visit to Churchill, Manitoba. Working out what is and what isn't feasible in a research setting is almost impossible without direct field experience, so I am grateful to the CNSC for suggesting a cautious, 'stepped' approach to my fieldwork. Later, with the award of a Trudeau Foundation Doctoral Scholarship, I was able to broaden the scale and scope of my proposed research to include another two case study sites. The second opening came as a result of my attendance at the Inuit Studies Conference in Calgary in August, 2004. By chance, one lunch time I sat next to Gwen and Emily, a sister-duo from Cambridge Bay who were eager for me to visit their community to see if my study might work there. By that time, I was six months pregnant with our second child, Benjamin, and I am convinced that my pregnancy, and conversations we shared between us as mothers, in part facilitated this all-important invitation to the community. This had a snow-balling effect, and as a result of direct field experience in Cambridge Bay I was able to develop contacts in Pond Inlet, which became a third case study site. Without knowing it, Benjamin, even in-utero, was having an influence on my research.

Journalling

A reflexive field journal was kept throughout the research period, and it served three purposes: (a) to record appointments, daily activities and other practicalities; (b) to enter hand-written field notes from participant observation activities; and (c) to reflect on emerging patterns from data and sketch out evolving ideas and concepts. As I look back through that journal, it is rich in daily reflections, and certainly in the early stages of my fieldwork I reflect on my family situation a lot – having two young children while juggling my doctoral studies – and the impact this had on me, and on my research.

In this chapter, I draw on the text in my journal to give some direct perspective on how the experience of 'accompanied' fieldwork (Frohlick, 2002) affected the research process and the data; what adaptations were made as a result of my personal circumstances; and what the lessons might be to help other parents who are considering taking their own child(ren) into the field.

Help from the Literature

When we contemplated Benjamin accompanying me during my fieldwork, at least in the early stages of it, there was scant advice from the literature. Few researchers report on their preliminary research experiences, and if they do they are typically written in a whimsical style so as to cover up their often painful experiences (Wax, 1985). This may explain the scarcity in the literature as the difficult early stages of field research require a certain academic courage to publish (Caine *et al.*, 2009). However, there were passing references to remote ethnographic fieldwork where researchers were accompanied by family members, and where the outcomes had – in the main – been positive. For example, in the Sudan:

> In a society where the extended family is the norm and the value placed on family life is high, there is no question in my mind that being identified as part of a family, originally with my husband and later with our daughter Josina, was an asset, probably even a vital element in conducting successful field research in the areas we selected. (Fluehr-Lobban & Lobban, 1986: 188)

While having a child facilitated this 'husband-wife' research team to develop more intensive and extensive access into the family-centred world of the Sudan, this was not a decision they 'made lightly […] Josina twice contracted malaria and also developed a very serious case of bronchial pneumonia' (Fluehr-Lobban & Lobban, 1986: 191). They claim their family circumstances allowed them to build trust with the community and because 'we had more varied reasons to interact with the people we met in our research settings since now our daughter could play with their children' (Fluehr-Lobban & Lobban, 1986: 191) deeper connections were formed than might otherwise have been the case. Similarly, Oboler (1986), researching in western Kenya, reported a tangible difference in her relationship with the community after she became pregnant. Although the pregnancy had a draining influence on her physically, it had a positive effect on her field relationships:

> As the news of my pregnancy made the rounds, a remarkable thing happened: my rapport with the women, which I already thought was quite good, took a sudden dramatic turn for the better. In people's minds I had moved from the category of 'probably barren woman' to 'childbearing woman' […] [they] were suddenly much more at ease with me and began to treat me fully as one of them. Many more confidences and jokes were directed my way. (Oboler, 1986: 45)

As with the Lobban's (1986) experience, Oboler's (1986) pregnancy was a way of establishing common ground. However, a different experience was reported by Frohlick (2002) who worked in the Himalaya for her doctoral research while being the mother of two young children. While she initially planned on excluding her family from her fieldwork expeditions, she soon realised that families should not be erased from fieldwork practices (Frohlick, 2002). I felt reassured by these limited experiences reported in the literature, but I was acutely aware of the place-specific nature of my field location. However, I knew I was not alone in the Canadian context.

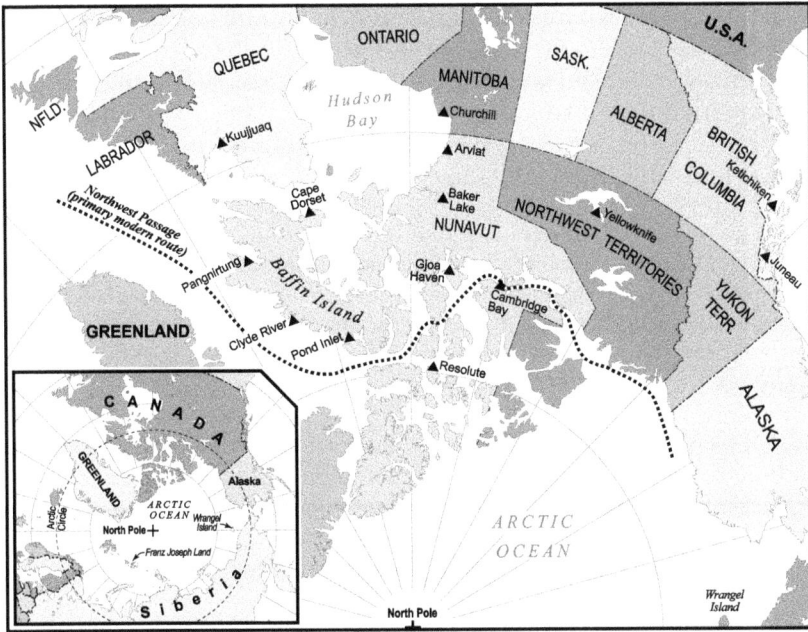

Figure 11.1 North Pole-projected map locating the case study sites of Churchill, Cambridge Bay and Pond Inlet (Cartography: Robin Potrias, University of Calgary)

Through my emerging academic networks (the Trudeau Foundation, the Canadian Association of Geographers, and the International Polar Tourism Research Network), I knew that other new parents were contemplating the same decision and I am forever grateful for the support from my fellow students. In the end, it was a pragmatic decision. While the decision to take a nine-month-old into an unknown community was not one we took lightly, there was little option. I was still feeding Benjamin at the time – so he needed me as much as I needed him. Our older daughter remained at home in Calgary with my husband and Benjamin and I went north. In total, he accompanied me to Cambridge Bay twice, and both Churchill and Pond Inlet once (four visits out of my 10) all before he turned two (see Figure 11.1). Serendipitously, those accompanied visits were all at the early stages of my fieldwork.

Cambridge Bay – a Research Assistant in Miniature

For me, it did not feel odd or abnormal having Benjamin alongside me during the very early days of my fieldwork. Quite the opposite. At home, I was used to having two pre-schoolers around while I was working on my doctoral studies, and I seemed to thrive on the chaos of balancing domestic and student life. I found I became more efficient in the small windows of time I did carve out in my day – like nap times and the hours the children were at day care or kindergarten. On the rare occasion when I did have extended time to think and write, I was useless! And it was no different in the field. When I went to Cambridge Bay for the first time I jotted in my journal that 'it seems so normal, in an abnormal sort of way!' (21 July 2005) to be travelling with Benjamin, although I do remember embarking on the travel with some trepidation:

> to my surprise Ben slept through the Calgary to Edmonton flight and after a long transit in Edmonton (including lots of crawling) he fell asleep again on the tarmac, and did not wake again until we had touched down, taken off, and then been in the air for almost an hour. I reckon I have a polar traveller at heart in Benjamin as he woke up as we passed over the Arctic Circle! (21 July 2005)

I took this as a good omen. To my surprise, and to my delight, I realised very early on in this first trip with Benjamin that I had a research assistant in miniature. The incident of the regurgitated caribou stew was just one of many signals. Benjamin's physical characteristics were so different to the dark skin and complexion of my Inuit hosts. '... She marvelled at his blue eyes and blond hair. His double crown continues to be a point of conversation. I was told that it meant that he had a dose of wisdom and a dose of humour!' (24 July 2005).

Other signals came when I was out in the wider community.

> Within moments Ben and I were surrounded by new faces; smiling. Benji (as he is already called here) is a real hit, a magnet and an *icebreaker*. I am introduced to folk [...] and before I know it I have an interview with the assistant Mayor and a dinner date with someone else. (21 July 2005)

I am convinced that access to key people such as these in the community would have been longer in coming if Benjamin had not been with me. He also, unknowingly, assisted me in difficult field situations, such as this first all-important meeting with the Elders from Cambridge Bay:

> I felt nervous about my meeting with the Elders [...] Ovie accompanied me so that she could mind Ben for me. It worked well. I wanted him there as it seemed right. I had twelve Elders looking at me. Conscious of being the white girl at the front, I shook hands with each of them, and smiled. None of them spoke English so I had help from Gwen who translated for me. As I introduced myself, I had Ben in my arms. It was rather nice as the last time I had seen Gwen was in Calgary when I was pregnant [at the Inuit Studies Conference referred to earlier]! It made for a nice connection; and a sense of me being connected in some way to the people here. (26 July 2005)

As alluded to in the above extract, in this early visit, I did make some informal day care arrangements. Ovilok (or Ovie) – my host's unassuming daughter – was paid to look after Benjamin while I attended my meetings.

This worked well and it gave me some clear thinking time, and being a sociable child he appeared to enjoy the company. 'They taught Ben how to rub noses and how to do the Indian call' (24 July 2005). My hosts were also keen to encourage me to adopt some Inuit-style parenting techniques. As Figure 11.2 depicts, 'I learned how to pack Ben in my coat and carry him Inuit-style, which eventually he seemed to quite like although I was very conscious that he might slip out at any moment' (24 July 2005).

It was not all fun of course. There were moments when things got tough, usually associated with a new routine, lack of sleep or health niggles. The 24 hours of daylight in the Arctic summer presented a challenge for sleep, for both of us. As I reveal in my journal, only a few days into our first trip together: 'A bad night. Awoken at 4.30 am by Ben who was struggling to sleep (it was bright outside). I'm putting him in the laundry tonight where there are no windows in the hope of a better night's sleep' (23 July 2005). Similarly, Benjamin was also struggling with teething at the time and I had forgotten to bring his teething ring with us. 'When quizzed how Inuit deal with a teething child they said a rubbery orange duck's foot was the answer [yes, a real one with bone-in and sealed at the ankle. Nothing wasted in this part of the world]. One was promptly produced and Ben gnawed happily away' (24 July 2005). I soon learnt that the ability to adapt to such challenges and come up with solutions – sometimes bizarre ones – was the key!

At the end of our first Arctic fieldtrip together I realised that standing out from the crowd through a deep connection with other parents in the community provided an opening that others may not have. These openings led to important turning points in my preliminary fieldwork and I realised that it was crucial to be aware of this positive bias in my work and take

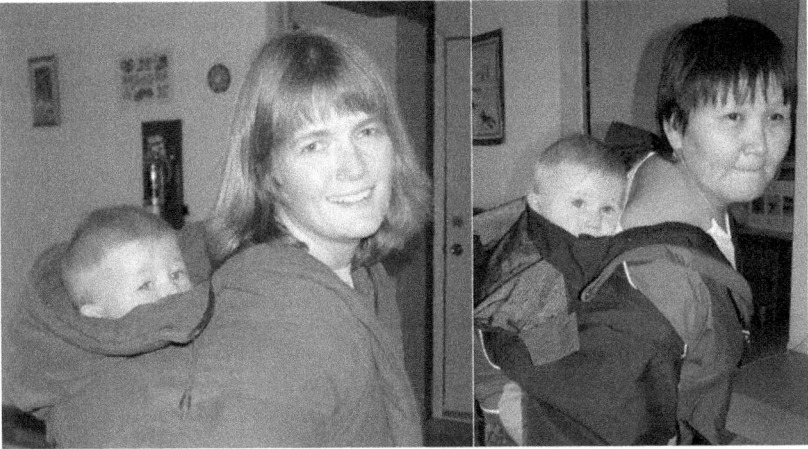

Figure 11.2 The look of fear in Benjamin's eyes while I attempt to pack him 'Inuit-style' in my parka contrasts with the expression of contentment when carried by our Inuit host! (May 2006)

advantage of the privileged access it facilitated. In some intangible way, I felt Benjamin had accelerated my acceptance into the community and that the mistrust that I had sensed prior to my arrival had evaporated. I realised that my personal circumstances, which initially I feared would be detrimental to my progress, were actually more of a help than a hindrance. 'Benjamin can come again' I thought.

Churchill – With and Without You

Later in the same year, and just before Benjamin turned one, we again departed for the North, but this time to Churchill, in northern Manitoba (see Figure 11.1). While I took some comfort from our largely positive trip to Cambridge Bay,

> ... I got the feeling that the journey was going to be a little stressful when Benjamin vomited just as the plane took off. My neighbouring passenger was not impressed (she was a fashion designer, apparently) but Ben worked his charm on her and got a few smiles. Things got worse on the second leg of the journey. It was just as well the plane was only a third full as Benjamin squawked through most of it. There was an exodus of passengers to the rear of the plane to save their ear drums. (30 August 2005)

This was my second visit to Churchill, but my first with Benjamin. 'I was welcomed back to the study centre which was nice and Ben was soon adopted by all despite his continuing noise' (30 August 2005). As in Cambridge Bay, I was able to arrange some day care and this meant I was able to get on with some of my pre-test interviews. I was grateful for this support because as Benjamin was getting older he was becoming more active and therefore more challenging to manage in unusual settings. I remember feeling exhausted after this trip, and began to doubt my earlier more glowing assessment of my research assistant.

In the April of the following year, I returned to Churchill, but this time without Benjamin.

> This time I am travelling alone and I hope it makes things less stressful. The fact that I might have time to sit down and reflect on my work speaks volumes. Mum and Dad have come over from the UK and they are looking after the children while I am away. (4 April 2006)

The respite from Benjamin was welcome in some respects, but while being physically separated, he (and his sister) were never far from my thoughts. As this diary entry reveals, his absence gave me time to reflect on his impact on my research:

> On my flight a child lets out an almighty shriek and I am reminded of my previous journey with Ben. Although sometimes a noisy companion he served an important role in establishing me in Churchill. I think folk saw

me as just a normal person getting on with life – juggling responsibilities and work. The common ground between me and many people I met was obvious. I think it made folk more relaxed knowing that I was just a mum, not just another white southern researcher asking questions. We had something in common. It also gave me a sense of normality. (4 April 2006)

Back to Cambridge Bay and Onwards to Resolute and Pond Inlet

In July of 2006, Benjamin accompanied me again to Cambridge Bay and then for the first time to Pond Inlet (my third case study community) via Resolute where we were in transit for 24 hours. It was a big trip with multiple flights, different locations with an ever-changing set of routines for Benjamin who was now 18 months. Our older child, Hannah, had just turned four.

> Goodbyes were hard this time firstly because Ben and I will be away for a month and secondly because Hannah now feels more 'raw' about the impact of our absence. But I know the very reason we are in Canada is for me to complete my PhD and inevitably this takes me away from home. So I just have to accept that and make the most of the time that I am away. It'll be good to have mother-son time and equally for father-daughter time for Richard and Hannah. (14 July 2006)

Clearly I was trying to convince myself, but it was painful leaving Hannah behind. A wise friend of mine reminded me that Hannah was unlikely to remember my absence, but instead would remember my return when I would be full of stories and reinvigorated by my travels. Not surprisingly, there were many times when I had to convince myself that this would be the case.

We were welcomed back into the community with open arms, and people seemed genuinely pleased that I had returned with Benjamin. However, he was now 18 months old and very active. Unlike the previous trip, I had to put more formalised child support measures in place. I booked him into the community childcare centre and thankfully he complied with the arrangement. 'I managed to get him into day care. He went in without any difficulty thank goodness. It's great to know he is having a different experience this time and perhaps making some Inuit friends for himself' (19 July 2006). I still have tucked away in his scrapbook some of the artwork he did there.

Leaving Cambridge Bay for Pond Inlet on Baffin Island, we had two flights on a small twin otter plane and an overnight stay in the remote northern hamlet of Resolute (see Figure 11.1). We struck some stunning Arctic conditions but our sense of adventure could easily have turned into misadventure.

> Ben and I ventured out along the bay. It was beautiful looking out over the ice – every shade of blue and white imaginable. Before long we were warned that given the ice and wind conditions that it would be wise to

turn back due to the increased risks of encountering a polar bear. Yikes! And I was happily taking photos oblivious to the risk! Consequently our Sunday morning stroll turned into a bit of a march back to the hotel. (30 July 2006)

I remember thinking that I had put our safety at risk and I felt stupid for doing so.

Pond Inlet – Skimming Stones

In Resolute, Benjamin started to run a temperature which I was able to quell with some standard off-the-shelf remedies, but when we arrived in Pond Inlet it wasn't long before things took a turn for the worse. As I reveal in my journal, 'Ben is suffering from a bad cold which has left both of us with 'sticky eyes'. As it turns out he has 'pink eye' which means a few days off day care' (2 August 2006). So my best laid plans to start my fieldwork were scuppered by a dose of highly infectious conjunctivitis. I ended up with it as well so we laid low for a few days: we were not a pretty sight! Fortunately, we both bounced back quickly and we fell into a routine of morning day care and afternoon naps; times when I could get on with my work without too much distraction. My journal is full of extracts along the lines of: 'I'd arranged to meet with one of the outfitters so I got Ben down in time for a nap […] I managed to get some transcription work done before Ben awoke' (5 August 2006). Not dissimilar to home life, I was making the most of those Ben-free times; but also enjoying our free time together. It was in Pond Inlet that Benjamin first learnt how to skim stones.

By this stage, we'd been away from home for almost a month and it was interesting to see how Benjamin had started to assimilate local customs. 'Ben exclaimed this morning that he wanted to put a baby down his jacket and carry him Inuit-style' (10 August 2006). As the pictures in Figure 11.3 reveal, he was clearly enjoying his new surrounds. 'It was picnic day at day care so I watched with delight as Ben was carried on a women's shoulders in addition to the other child she was carrying in her *amauti* [Inuit traditional dress]. These women are made of tough stuff!' (10 August 2006).

I was also aware that as a parent I was willing to take risks that I wouldn't back home. For example, in preparation for an important meeting at the Hamlet chamber I dropped Benjamin off at a baby-sitter.

> She was planning a trip out to the water lake [a favourite spot for teenagers to hang out] on the quad bike. I dubiously said it was OK so long as Ben was wearing a helmet. What was I thinking, but what could I do? I only had minutes to get to the Hamlet office. They ride around with their kids on the quads all the time, and even raising a concern seemed overly cautious. […] After my meeting I nervously awaited Ben's return which came around 8.45 pm, much to my relief. (10 August 2006)

Figure 11.3 Benjamin taking a ride at picnic day (left) and learning how to skim stones at the beach (right). (Pond Inlet, August 2006)

Looking back through my journal, I see a turning point at this stage. I am established in each of my three communities and my field notes become more fulsome with data as findings develop and observations and conversations fill the pages. Interestingly, less time is devoted to talking about Benjamin's impact on my research the deeper I go into the field. It is almost as if our routines have become normalised. However, toward the end of this month-long research expedition I did reflect on my wishes for Benjamin in the future, knowing this was likely his last trip north as an infant.

> I am hoping this won't be Ben's last trip to the Arctic, and hope that these early experiences might 'live-on' in him somehow [...] and one day he might be able to revisit those places we had visited together. (14 August 2006)

Reflecting on our visit, I stated quite clearly in my journal, that 'in unexpected and funny ways, I could not have done this fieldwork without Benjamin' (14 August 2006).

Missing Benjamin but I Find a Replacement

Once Benjamin turned two he was no longer a free seat on the plane and the cost of a full fare for him was prohibitively high. By this stage, I had completed about half of my fieldwork. In my later trips to the Canadian Arctic I make occasional references to him in my journal, and those references are indicative of the earlier impact he had made: 'First stop was with the Mayor. It went quite well and he remembered me and Ben. In fact he seemed quite disappointed that Ben was not with me on this trip' (28 May 2007). There were constant reminders of Benjamin in the communities and this did perpetuate my missing him. 'I read the local paper that evening and there was an article about kids as social catalysts and I could not help but compare Ben as being a community catalyst in my research. I was missing him'. However, for my penultimate trip to the Arctic my husband, Richard, joined me – my step-in research assistant.

> It's always hard to leave home and especially hard to leave the kids, but on this occasion its tempered by the fact Richard will be with me for five of those days. Mum and dad have come over from the UK to help out [...] I've told Hannah to count down the days on her fingers and toes and once they are all done, I'd be home. Twenty days later. (17 May 2007)

Last Days in the Field

Later in 2007, I journeyed back to Pond Inlet, alone this time. My data collection phase was over, and as my journal reveals, I became quite reflective of the impact my experiences had had on me as a mother:

> The strength of the women here continues to astound me; and it sometimes stops me in my tracks. I've shared stories and experiences with these women and we've trusted our tears to each other. It's the women folk who I am going to miss the most. They retain wonderful dignity and humour against a backdrop of pain and dislocation. I've loved my time with them, and learnt so much about tolerance and patience and the importance of family and children. The need – the overriding need – to give our children the best possible platform in life is what drives us, and we must all strive for that, even when times feel fraught [...] I simply can't wait to hold my children and husband again. (1 September 2007)

Just Another Mum

Through my early fieldwork experiences with Benjamin it quickly became obvious that he acted as a 'catalyst' and, in unexpected ways, he accelerated my 'acceptance' into my three case study communities, particularly Cambridge Bay and Pond Inlet. I am convinced that Benjamin's presence helped me build that all-important *trust* with these communities. I think this has to do with the child-centred nature of Inuit communities, but also this was because I was seen as just another mother juggling her responsibilities. In a way, we were on one level. Since we had something in common, I was seen as accessible and approachable; a 'person', not just another researcher. Perhaps with Benjamin alongside, I was less of a threat, and the shared connection of motherhood meant that I was less of an outsider. He certainly opened doors for me in the field. While I put measures in place during my fieldwork to ensure I was not regarded as a 'snow goose' researcher, such as reporting my findings in meaningful ways (see Stewart & Draper, 2009), Benjamin's presence certainly aligned well with my community-based participatory approach to my fieldwork. In this regard, he was a positive bias in my research. Since I don't have any way to compare those early days in the field without him, it is hard to gauge what adaptations I made to accommodate his presence in the field. I just got on with the routines of parenthood, but in another setting. I probably did do some things that I might not have done at home (the duck's foot as a teething ring comes to mind) but this was all part of the adventure.

In terms of lessons for other parents contemplating taking infants into the field, I would offer the following:

- Connect with other parent-researchers who might be contemplating similar decisions.
- Don't worry about leaving other children at home; they will only remember your return not your absence.
- Be prepared to adapt in the field and do things you might not do at home with your child(ren).
- Expect to have good days and bad days in the field and remember the same would happen if you didn't have children with you.
- Enjoy learning about and engaging in other cultural parenting practices.
- Have good support systems in place at home, and at least some childcare while you are in the field.
- Don't feel guilty about the privileged access your child might bring you in the field.
- Reflect on the impact your accompanied fieldwork has on your research process.
- Journal your experiences and share these with your child(ren) in later years.

Closing Words

While there were challenges, as every parent can probably appreciate (sleepless nights, long journeys, illness), to my surprise and delight and without any preconceived notion, Benjamin 'broke the ice' and he gave me a unique – and lasting – identity in the field. This seemed to have had the effect of breaking down several of the barriers some researchers face when entering communities for the first time, and perhaps gave me access to people that I may not have had without him (although there is no way of testing this). As my fieldwork progressed, I realised the strength of this 'researcher-mother-son' identity when people in the community remembered us from one visit to the next. When I made later visits without him, people seemed genuinely disappointed that he was not there; and I missed him in the field as well. He was my icebreaker after all.

Postscript

Benjamin never did finish that sweet potato meal I had lovingly prepared for him on that first day in Cambridge Bay. As a strapping 12 year old today – who will eat almost anything we put in front of him – he strangely refuses to eat sweet potato. But he is partial to venison: the closest meat we have in New Zealand to caribou! Clearly, his taste buds were altered for good that evening in Cambridge Bay. But just to clarify, he prefers to eat with a knife and fork these days!

Acknowledgements

In addition to all the amazing parents I met in the Canadian Arctic, a special mention goes to my family because on so many occasions I had to put you second behind my fieldwork, even though in my heart, you were first. To Hannah: I hope the pain of our separation during my fieldwork is forgotten, and that all you remember is a mother who returned (as I promised I would each time I left you) inspired and invigorated. Benjamin: I know you won't remember your visits to Arctic Canada but I hope through the stories I tell, the words written here and the pictures we share, that your experiences in the North will remain with you for a lifetime. One day we *will* return north again. Richard: a simple thank you for being you and for being there.

References

Bloodworth, M., Kapungu, C., Majer, J., McDonald, K., Sharma, A., Viola, J. and Wilson, B. (2004) Student reflections on community research practices and their implications. In L.A. Jason, C.B. Keys, Y. Suarez-Balcazar, R.R. Taylor and M.I. Davis (eds) *Participatory Community Research: Theories and Methods in Action* (pp. 227–232). Washington, DC: American Psychological Association.

Caine, K.J., Davison, C.M. and Stewart, E.J. (2009) Preliminary field-work: Methodological reflections from northern Canadian research. *Qualitative Research* 9, 489–513.

Fluehr-Lobban, C. and Lobban, R.A. (1986) Families, gender and methodology in the Sudan. In T.L. Whitehead and M.E. Conaway (eds) *Self, Sex and Gender in Cross-cultural Fieldwork* (pp. 152–195). Urbana, IL: University of Illinois Press.

Freeman, W.L. (1993) Research in rural native communities. In M.J. Bass, E.V. Dunn, P.G. Norton, M. Stewart and F. Tudiver (eds) *Conducting Research in the Practice Setting* (pp. 179–196). London: Sage Publications.

Frohlick, S.E. (2002) 'You brought your baby to base camp?': Families and field sites. *The Great Lakes Geographer* 9, 49–58.

Gearheard, S. and Shirley, J. (2007) Challenges in community-research relationships: Learning from natural science in Nunavut. *Arctic* 60, 62–74.

Israel, B.A., Schulz, A.J., Parker, E.A. and Becker, A.B. (1998) Review of community-based research: Assessing partnership approaches to improve public health. *Annual Review of Public Health* 19, 173–202.

Legat, A. (1994) Participatory action research in Rae Lakes, N.W.T.: The traditional government project. *Information North* 20 (2), 1–4.

Oboler, R.S. (1986) For better or worse: Anthropologists and husbands in the field. In T.L. Whitehead and M.E. Conaway (eds) *Self, Sex and Gender in Cross-cultural Fieldwork* (pp. 28–51). Urbana, IL: University of Illinois Press.

Patton, M.Q. (2002) *Qualitative Research and Evaluation Methods* (3rd edn). London: Sage.

Smith, L.T. (1999) *Decolonizing Methodologies: Research and Indigenous Peoples*. London: Zed Books.
Smith, S.E., Willms, D.G. and Johnson, N.A. (eds) (1997) *Nurtured by Knowledge: Learning to Do Participatory Action-research*. New York, NY: The Apex Press.
Stevenson, M.G. (1996) Indigenous knowledge in environmental assessment. *Arctic* 49, 278–291.
Stewart, E.J. (2009) *Comparing Resident Attitudes Toward Tourism: Community-based Cases from Arctic Canada*. Unpublished PhD dissertation. University of Calgary, Alberta, Canada.
Stewart, E.J. and Draper, D. (2009) Reporting back research findings: A case study of community-based tourism research in northern Canada. *Journal of Ecotourism* 8, 128–143.
Taylor, R.R., Jason, L.A., Keys, C.B., Suarez-Balcazar, Y., Davis, M., Durlak, J.A. and Holtz Isenberg, D. (2004) Capturing theory and methodology in participatory research. In L.A. Jason, C.B. Keys, Y. Suarez-Balcazar, R.R. Taylor and M.I. Davis (eds) *Participatory Community Research: Theories and Methods in Action* (pp. 3–14). Washington, DC: American Psychological Association.
Wax, R. (1985) *Doing Fieldwork: Warnings and Advice*. Chicago, IL: University of Chicago Press (Midway Reprint).

12 Researching in a Men's Paradise: The Emotional Negotiations of Drunken Tourism Fieldwork

Ana María Munar

Ana María Munar is an Associate Professor at Copenhagen Business School, Denmark. She decided to pursue an academic career in her early 30s and had her third child while pursuing a doctoral degree and working part time. With research interests in digital technologies, epistemology, higher education and gender, her latest publications focus on postdisciplinarity, social media and gender in academia. Ana is an experienced scholar and has served on several national and international boards and networks. Nowadays, she holds positions at the Diversity and Inclusion Council at Copenhagen Business School, the Critical Tourism Studies Network, Women Academics in Tourism and several tourism journals. She has extensive experience in curriculum and education development, and coordinates the tourism and hospitality concentration at the Bachelor of Service Management and Business Administration. Ana has delivered numerous conference presentations and keynote addresses in her research areas.

Introduction

How does my gender impact upon the field experience? This study addresses this question by analysing a challenging personal experience. It examines the personal and emotional negotiations of conducting fieldwork in the *Bierstrasse* (German for 'Beer Street'). The Bierstrasse is an iconic drunken/alcohol mass tourism destination in the seaside city of Palma de Majorca, Spain. The popularity and success of the experience of the Bierstrasse are rooted in high alcohol consumption, staged nationalism, touristic rituals of camaraderie, hegemonic masculinity, heteronormativity, sex and borderline behaviours (Munar, 2013). This study is an exercise in self-reflectivity, which aims at revealing the role that gender plays in some aspects of my research life. In this chapter, I apply the theoretical frameworks of positionality and the situatedness of knowledge to critically examine my research practices and emotional negotiations in the landscape of extreme drinking cultures. This chapter is also an attempt to better understand the importance of subjectivity and biography in our seemingly 'objective' academic endeavours.

Mary Poppins in the Bierstrasse

A major contribution of feminist philosophy has been the idea of the situatedness of knowledge (Grasswick, 2011, 2013). This notion advances that knowers are 'situated in particular relations to what is known and to other knowers' (para. 1); 'people may understand the same object/phenomenon in different ways that reflect their distinct relations in which they stand to it' (Anderson, 2015, 'Section heading,' para. 2). Situatedness is relevant to this case because I am interested in examining how my biographical gender identity interacts with gendered structures and cultures in academia and in fieldwork settings, and how this relationship affects my possibilities for knowledge production and my agency as a researcher.

The reason why gender matters for the possibilities of creating knowledge is not only because it is a feature or an attribute of individuals, but because it is a key aspect of social relations and societies are structured around the axis of gender (Grasswick, 2013: xiv). 'Situatedness' refers to what is autobiographical, individual and subjective and also to what is communal, social and collective. It is me in the context and the context in me. Research contexts have, however, two very different natures. One is the academic context. When I embark on a research project I do that as part of a collective; as a representative of a specific institution (my university), and of scholarly norms and disciplinary traditions in anthropology or cultural studies, for example, that have for decades structured what fieldwork means, its methods and tools and even a collection of possible mindsets that one is supposed to choose among when embarking on a fieldwork project. As a researcher in the field, I am a representative of an abstract yet real global academy.

The second context is the field itself with its specific gendered cultures. A fanciful way to imagine this is to recall the famous Disney film, *Mary Poppins*. There is a moment in this film where Mary and the children meet Bert (Mary's friend) who has been painting some chalk drawings in the park. They are admiring the drawings and then, thanks to Mary's magic, they jump inside one of them. The actors enter a beautiful world where they are able to interact with animated characters until eventually it begins to rain. The drawings in the real world begin to dissolve and Mary Poppins and her friends return to reality (an image from this sequence can be seen in Figure 12.1).

In fieldwork, Mary's magic is similar to adopting a specific form of reflexivity, a 'mode' of knowing and of being conscious that is different to our usual way of being in the world. If we look at this jump from a philosophical perspective, this 'magic' happens because we increase the level of consciousness about ourselves (as knowers) and change our gaze and the way we are interacting with people, spaces and materials. Like Mary, I did not jump into my fieldwork alone but accompanied by a multifaceted, wonderful friend like Bert, who also happens to be my husband. As in Mary's story, there is always a moment where it rains and the magic of the scene created by the reflective gaze dissolves and we get back to being our more ordinary selves. We are us, but yet transformed by what we experienced in the different chalk world, which is the field. The comparison to the scene of Mary Poppins is not applicable to all forms of fieldwork. For researchers who travel to faraway places and station themselves in a foreign community for months or years (what is often considered the more traditional way of conducting anthropological fieldwork), this may not feel like an appropriate metaphor for what happens. However, the image is highly accurate for the type of fieldwork that results in studying a very

Figure 12.1 Mary Poppins jumping into the chalk drawing. Art by Brooke A. Porter

specific leisure space with clear spatial and temporary borders like the Bierstrasse. This street resembles entering a theatrical scene, a theme park or a cultural event such as a festival, where the researcher will stay for a few days or hours every time. It is fair to say that the 'chalk world' of the Bierstrasse (which is introduced in the next section) is a much more challenging and risky version than the summer walk in a park of the Disney movie, and yet the Bierstrasse experience also presents a world that appeals to desires for fantasy and escape.

The following sections are a reflection of my fieldwork experiences in this drunken tourism destination in the Mediterranean. To conduct this analysis, I rely on memories, the many fieldwork notes, photographs, advertisement pamphlets and other objects (such as paper napkins) that I transcribed and collected during three different periods of fieldwork in the summers of 2012, 2013 and 2014.

Situating the context

Bierstrasse is an iconic destination located at the centre of Palma Beach (Majorca, Spain). It was created and developed by Mallorquin entrepreneurs during the 1970s. Bierstrasse comprises both a single street and a larger geographical area that stretches for one kilometre along the seaside. The destination has four main attractions and several touristic and spatial markers. The attractions are: Schinkenstrasse, which includes the Bierkönig, a large and very popular beer venue; the surroundings and facilities of a large open-air discotheque, 'Mega Park'; the iconic beer street; and the beach promenade where the *balnearios* – open-air bars situated on the beach – are located. The Bierstrasse area comprises the space between *balnearios* five and seven; the most iconic and symbolic of the *balnearios* being the one at the centre of the area: 'Balneario Six'. The number, pronounced as 'sex' in German, gives this Balneario a very specific connotation. 'Balneario six' is also the name of a controversial German TV documentary, which describes extreme forms of tourist behaviour in the Bierstrasse area.

The Bierstrasse is similar to other tourist attractions, which have been developed to cater for gender-specific desires, such as the sexual needs of male tourists (Wearing *et al.*, 2010). Some examples in Europe include Sunny Beach in Bulgaria, Magaluf in Majorca, Playa del Inglés in Gran Canaria and Lloret de Mar and Calella in Catalonia. Bierstrasse in Majorca shares many similarities with these destinations, such as attracting young holidaymakers, being located on the seaside and offering drunken circuits. In the Spanish media, this form of tourism has been described as *drunken tourism*. Drunken tourism is often associated with erotic or sexual experiences (Andrews *et al.*, 2007). Studies of drinking destinations show alcohol-related behaviour resulting in exaggerated camaraderie, sexuality and house-party-like familiarity (Stringer & McAllister, 2012) and a strong link between identity, gender and beer consumption (Duarte Alonso, 2011; Gee & Jackson, 2012; Larsen, 1997).

Larsen (1997) suggests how drinking spaces are frames of reference for the making of rituals, traditions, symbols and specific aesthetics. Tourists on Bierstrasse go through a touristic socialisation and education. They learn to codify and make sense of new norms and rituals of alcohol consumption. In this touristified environment, taken-for-granted societal values are suspended and exchanged for a novel set of rules. The alcoholic offering, pricing and service provision of the Bierstrasse area are adapted to extreme forms of drinking and combined with a hypersexual and heteronormative nightlife environment where sex is constantly present in advertising, shows (lap-dancers and strippers), availability of sex workers, t-shirts with sexualised slogans and images, and sexual toys in the souvenir shops surrounding the venues (Figure 12.2).

My fieldwork consisted of repeat visits to the Bierstrasse area, visual data collection in the form of photographs and videos, brief interviews with service providers and tourists, and extensive note taking. I collected visual data of the spatial and functional use of the attractions and different sites at the destination. These included photos of venues, alcohol providers, tourism provision (hotels, shops and so on), recreational spaces, signs and tourists. Short videos were recorded to document the soundscapes in the area and specific behavioural patterns of drinking tourists, such as loud singing/shouting, and to gain a general overview of the atmosphere at the most important attractions. Before beginning this fieldwork, I had often been in Playa de Palma and experienced the behaviour of groups of drunken tourists, seen the t-shirts with demeaning sexualised texts, heard the stories of vandalism, prostitution and balconing (i.e. tourists trying to jump between hotel balconies or from the balconies to the swimming pool, which has resulted in the death of several tourists in Majorca) and was aware of the increase in criminality and the many

Figure 12.2 The Bierkönig venue and a souvenir shop at the Bierstrasse

health problems related to alcohol and drug consumption. It took many visits and a committed effort to be able to see the lighter and less obvious side of the Bierstrasse experience. Drunken tourism is also an exercise in joint affirmation, social enjoyment and trust, a place to engage in performative experiences of lost masculinity and friendship and, in some cases, coming-of-age rituals (Munar, 2013).

Situating me

Gender studies differentiate between sex and gender. Sex corresponds to the biological differences between male and female; gender to what societies and cultures make of those differences. I was born a woman, with a female body, and have always felt that my gender identity coincides with my sex identity. Intersectionality makes us aware of our situatedness as researchers by expanding and complementing the singular feature of gender with other equally relevant characteristics that play a role in how we are perceived by others and ourselves. It allows us to see how 'certain structures collaborate and collude to produce positions' (Falcón & Nash, 2015: 3). Besides being a woman, I am also white, Spanish and born on Majorca into an upper-middle-class family. For this specific case, the reference to social class is an important one. The type of tourism experience offered by the Bierstrasse or similar destinations in the Mediterranean has, in my social environment, always been considered an example of 'bad taste'. My cultural identity is complex and mixed after having lived in Denmark for 17 years (in my daily life I communicate in three different languages). Although living abroad, my family and I spend all our summers in Majorca. I have a strong emotional attachment to Mallorquin identity and to the island, and besides Spanish I also speak the local language, Catalan.

As mentioned previously, the Bierstrasse is a hypersexualised environment and sexuality is an important aspect of this research experience. I am a heterosexual woman in my 40s. Gender studies often stress the importance of the body. However, it is seldom, if ever, that researchers reflect on their relationships to their own body, how we see our bodies and how we believe they are perceived by others. I can feel that I am entering a taboo area of academic communication in the discomfort and shame that I feel in having to disclose this information as part of a book chapter. In order to do this, I must silence an internal voice that says that this is actually not appropriate for an academic manuscript. While writing this, there is also the fear of being seen as ridiculous or vain. Interestingly enough, it is precisely that voice and that feeling that make it even more relevant to bring into scrutiny and awareness my own perception of how femininity and my gender become alive and performed in my body.

My challenge when doing fieldwork in the Bierstrasse is directly linked to how I have experienced my body being seen or perceived by others during my nightlife experiences. I can be considered tall for Spanish standards, but otherwise my physical traits match the Spanish stereotype – brown curly hair, brown eyes and a lean, yet curvy, body shape. I am athletic and my dressing style conforms to what could be considered middle-class with traditional feminine traits (e.g. use of make-up, skirts, jewellery). The femininity of my dress code is part of my psychological wellbeing and being at ease with myself. I recall many occasions during my life where I have received attention, invitations or comments of an aesthetic, romantic or sexualised nature by strangers or people that I barely knew in public settings of different types, such as parties, public transport, night life spaces or social gatherings at work, due to my physical appearance. Sexualised or erotic encounters are not easily put into a binary of good and bad; while some of these experiences were nice, respectful, witty or lovely, there were also many examples of everyday sexism and a few much more unpleasant ones of sexual harassment. These accumulated experiences are important to understanding my own reservations and fears in engaging with a highly sexualised environment such as the Bierstrasse. Jennifer Fleetwood (2014) reflects on her own experience of being grabbed at the bar while getting a drink at a pub in a short auto ethnographic piece entitled, 'A feminist, narrative analysis of drinking stories', and, like her, I have often felt that our learned cultural scripts of how to react after an unpleasant sexist advance does leave women with little room for action. It is often a choice between getting angry and spoiling the 'fun' or letting go and feeling passively objectified. Nobody is interested in performing victimhood during what was supposed to be an enjoyable night out.

> Cultural scripts of masculinity, and 'drinking stories' converge and facilitate problematic behaviours whilst cultural scripts of femininity offer women different possibilities. The groped woman has little to gain from either passivity, or retaliation. Neither makes a story, far less a good story. This is not to fall into binaries of male/female but rather to state that gender is relational and an inevitable part of drinking cultures. (Fleetwood, 2014: 351)

Doing Fieldwork and Reinventing Gender Roles

The Bierstrasse appeared to me as an unknown, risky and strange territory, very different to what had constituted the environments of my daily, working and personal life or my usual holiday or leisure experiences. Looking back at how I was preparing for this fieldwork, I had two imaginings of the role of the researcher in such a setting: (1) the adventurer-explorer academic; and (2) the risk-taking mass leisure tourist. In both visualisations, the researcher was male and the gender roles were dominated by masculine traits detached from what my own role as a researcher or as a tourist had been. These two options were not much of a choice for someone who can imagine herself more as an independent Mary Poppins jumping into art.

Societies tend to assign men and women different social roles and often this can be seen in occupations. For example, the fieldwork method is traditionally related to ethnography – a tradition in anthropology related to travel and adventures in unknown territories. The imaginaries of the traveller, the adventurer and the pioneer have masculine connotations and have traditionally been perceived as roles that are more appropriate for men than for women. The roles have a halo of risk and courage. I did not feel comfortable in identifying with the adventurer-explorer researcher. My academic background is in sociology and political science and my research is mostly conceptual writings and qualitative research. None of my previous fieldwork experiences had been in an environment that I would consider 'unsafe' or risky.

If I did not feel comfortable adopting the adventurer-anthropologist role, I felt even less attracted to the risk-taking mass-tourist role. In retrospection, I can see that my imagination of this second role was highly influenced by how the media and my social environment had portrayed these kinds of tourists – as brainless, loud and rowdy, immature and careless towards the local culture and the residents. Becoming acquainted with the literature of alcohol and tourism did not provide much help either. Studies of drinking destinations show alcohol-related behaviour resulting in exaggerated camaraderie, sexuality and house-party-like familiarity (Stringer & McAllister, 2012) and mass tourism is often linked to alimentary and alcoholic excess (Andrews *et al.*, 2007).

Part of my difficulty in preparing this fieldwork experience was how to reinvent these gendered roles to fit my own identity. A possible way to create and play a role is by dressing up to that role. This idea appears often in liberal feminist discourses that recommend to 'dress up to succeed' or the importance of 'suits' or dressing like a man for being accepted in corporate or organisational cultures. In this case, I tried to accommodate a self-adapted version of the mass-tourist role by dressing to blend into the Bierstrasse partying population. I took inspiration from the many tourists that I had seen walking by the seaside during the evenings with their casual summer evening outfit, a t-shirt and a short jeans skirt, sandals and a summer bag (see Figure 12.3), but I tried to maintain a form of personal integrity and still feel comfortable in my usual self. I avoided, on purpose, the grotesque – like dressing in the highly popular t-shirts given by nightclubs in the area that have obscene images, slogans or acronyms, such as 'MILF' ('Mother I'd Love to Fuck') and 'YOLO' ('You Only Live Once'), or the 'sexy' mini-dresses that are so popular among tourists at this kind of destination.

The Bierstrasse is specially designed for tourists who come in groups, and part of the partying culture of the destination is achieved by group members all wearing the same t-shirt. I recall a bittersweet feeling when

Figure 12.3 A photo of the author writing field notes in the Bierstrasse area

looking at these outfits. A form of research thrill by observing such clear signs of the culture that I was there to examine, and a feeling of disgust at the way the word 'Majorca' (my home) was used in many of these slogans (e.g. 'Majorca triathlon: Drinking, eating, fucking') and by the clear objectification of women in the wet t-shirts events at some of the venues (an example of such an event in Megapark can be seen below). One of the groups I interviewed during my fieldwork consisted of five German girls in their early 20s, all of them dressed with the same t-shirt with the slogan 'Life is a show and we are the show'. They, among many others I also talked to, confirmed what was obvious by looking at the composition of the crowd in this area: that tourists come to the Bierstrassse in groups as either single boys or girls and never with your formal 'boyfriend' or 'girlfriend' because 'What happens in Majorca stays in Majorca'. In the words of one of the taxi chauffeurs who was waiting to pick up the next group of drunk tourists, the atmosphere of the night life there resembled a contemporary beach version of 'Sodom and Gomorrah'.

Due to the reputation of the Bierstrasse, I did not feel comfortable going there on my own or adopting a form of adventurer role, which I could only visualise either as the female stereotype of a 'vamp' (Fiske *et al.*, 2002) (i.e. a woman who feels comfortable in highly sexualised environments) or a ridiculous female version of Crocodile Dundee (i.e. a strong, athletic woman who could manage any attack in the middle of a massive jungle of drunken people). Although now, while sharing this story, I can feel the embarrassment of having to reveal that I am not up to meeting those adventurous risk standards because I do admire the willingness to risk in other women adventurers, *a la* Amelia Earhart. I have to recognise that I am simply not one of them and that my personality puts some limitations and some frame to the research that I conduct. For example, I visited all the main venues and spent time there with many tourists and service providers, but I did not enter the prostitution or striptease venues situated in obscure basements of narrow streets that announce their offering with photos of naked women and with slogans such as 'Lick my pussy' in neon letters.

This was a conscious choice; several times I stood in front of an entrance deciding whether to enter or not. I have never understood the lure of prostitution; the reality of sex workers in these touristic areas resembles a modern form of slavery and it is miles away from Buñuel's artistic 'Belle du Jour' (the story of a high-class prostitute by choice). Most of the sex workers who are visible in the streets are black immigrants and many are victims of trafficking. The prostitutes are not the only victims here. Several of the medical professionals I talked to reported stories of violent assaults allegedly perpetrated by sex workers and their pimps, who took intoxicated tourists to isolated areas to have oral sex and instead robbed and assaulted them. I had already collected plenty of empirical material for my research piece, which was on beer cultures and not sexual practices, but, most importantly, prostitution venues marked my 'safety' frontier. Entering prostitution venues was not a risk I was willing to take while pursuing my fieldwork. Looking back at this decision, I can understand why, as pointed out by Radcliffe and Measham (2014), much of our drunken tourism research neglects the voices of Southern Europe's sex workers.

Besides the prostitution venues, I recall strong feelings of shame and disgust while looking at both the gendered and sexualised photos and the advertising slogans of many of the nightclubs. Take a look at Figure 12.4 and what do you feel? Maybe you will also recognise such feelings. I found the language and aesthetics aggressive (as if these imaginaries corresponded to the groping or pushing of drunken men) and objectifying in relation to women's bodies – a form of collective insult. I believe that my reaction was not as much due to the display of half-naked women but mostly due to the absence of men being portrayed in a similar way, as sexual objects. The ads were also completely heteronormative in their propaganda with no mention of erotic or sexual performances addressing LGTBQIA tourists.

While female tourists could be seen in the beer venues, they were a minority. Doing fieldwork in the Bierstrasse is witnessing a staged hegemonic masculinity which reproduces specific gender stereotypes, and forms of tourism that present women as sex objects and maintain attractions as male-dominated ghettos. A characteristic view of the Bierstrasse venues are the table-dancing girls dressed in 'sexy' underwear displayed on top of big beer barrels in front of enormous TV screen that show sporting events (Figure 12.5). This specific display sets the stage for one of the

Figure 12.4 Bierstrasse advertisements from the venues Megapark, Paradies and Bierkönig

Figure 12.5 Male tourists and go-go girls in the Bierkönig

social practices of beer tourism. Young male tourists, often only dressed in swim shorts, drinking and singing around these barrels will take turns climbing on top of the barrel to be photographed by the rest of their peers while touching or hugging the dancer.

The tourists' act of hugging half-naked young women appears as a display of masculinity and 'manhood', resembling the imaginary and fantasies of the last bastions of masculinity described by Gee and Jackson (2012) in their study of Australian beer or the use of beer promotion girls in Hong Kong venues (Pettigrew & Charters, 2010). Beer tourists do not only 'enact' masculinity, they memorialise it. Beer tourists' photographing of masculinity is a social act. Tourists stand and pose for an audience.

Research shows that there are two common cultural presumptions about female gender roles and drinking (Månsson & Bogren, 2014) and both are part of my cultural baggage. One is that women do not drink as hard as men, that they 'by nature' do not consume the same amount of alcohol, and that, if drunk, they are better behaved. This view has been criticised by studies that show that this ideal may have some strong, class connotations (Rúdólfsdóttir & Morgan, 2009). Through my life I have experienced women (and also female academics) being heavily drunk; however, the idea that women, in general, do not drink as hard was pervasive in my family and through my formative years. The second one is that, in the few cases when women drink as heavily as men, they are perceived as being 'worse' than them. Women, who indulge in binge drinking, risk being heavily criticised and stigmatised by media and society (Jackson & Tinkler, 2007). A change in women's drinking habits has been considered to be the product of increased equality among genders but also to represent a troublesome form of femininity and disgraceful hedonism. However, there is a clear intersectional dimension to this view. How we perceive drinking cultures is also divided on lines of race and class. High-class female professionals enjoying fancy cocktails in New York (i.e. the kind of drinking portrayed in the famous TV series, *Sex and the City*) are seldom stigmatised in the same ways as working-class binge-drinkers in Sunny Beach or the Bierstrasse. I doubt I would have had the same concerns if the drinking environment of my fieldwork corresponded to an upper- or middle-class setting, such as drinking cultures at academic conferences, for example.

Thanking my bodyguard

The strategy that I adopted to cope with my insecurities was to invite my husband to accompany me during my visits to the Bierstrasse area. It was when reflecting on the call for papers for this book that I first realised that the invitation to my husband responded to my personal need to have a bodyguard with me, and that this was due to me being a woman entering an environment characterised by hegemonic masculinity. I needed someone that could protect me in a situation that I imagined as hostile, so that instead of feeling intimidated by the sexualised atmosphere and the heavy drinking, I could relax, and free my mind and my senses to observe and to appreciate what I was experiencing, unrestricted. By having the company of my husband, I had gone from being a woman alone at a boys' binge-drinking party, to being part of a couple enjoying a summer night out. I expected that we would be approached by waiters and other tourists in a non-threatening way and differently than had I been there on my own.

Although I was aware that anthropology had a long tradition of wives accompanying their academic husbands and facilitating their fieldwork by taking care of translations and transcriptions, I had never personally encountered the opposite – a man accompanying his wife to facilitate her fieldwork. The Bierstrasse was for me (and for us) an experiment in how my husband could support me in my research. However, this experiment was not free of the dominant gender roles of our culture either. It never crossed my mind that the help that my husband could provide might resemble the kind of support that wives had usually provided researchers in the field (such as note taking or typing transcripts). Actually, I did not make the link between my husband's role as fieldwork facilitator and these 'wives' until I started to read literature for this chapter (years after I had finished my fieldwork in the Bierstrasse). The role that I imagined for him and that he eventually played was that of a bodyguard providing physical safety and intellectual companionship, someone with whom to share my impressions and ideas but, most importantly, someone who will protect me from being sexually harassed by drunken tourists.

I had planned a route and a series of venues (the most important ones) that I wanted to visit. In the evening, we would start with a walk, observing, exploring and interviewing. We would stop here and there and I would be taking plenty of notes on a notebook that I carried in my bag and we would both be recording images and videos with our iPhones. As the evening went on and we moved from one venue to the other, I would tell my husband some of my impressions, while he (who is a journalist by training) would point out to me things that he believed were worth noticing. We would act as a couple of tourists and buy a beer or a gin and tonic and by the end of the night, around 2am, we would abandon our researcher roles then sit somewhere, order some of the traditional German food that it is sold in that area and laugh together at some of the weird experiences of the night. Eventually, I published some of the insights from that fieldwork in a chapter entitled 'Sun, Alcohol and Sex: Enacting Beer Tourism' (Munar, 2013) and gave different presentations at academic conferences. However, while writing the methodological section of that chapter, I did not think of including a reflection on the role of my husband as my 'safety' keeper and playful intellectual partner. This omission was not due to a sense of embarrassment or lack of appreciation for his help, but merely to a lack of awareness about how much my own self-perception of being a woman in a highly sexualised, heavy-drinking environment mattered for the knowledge that I was able to produce.

Conclusion

This chapter began with the question of how my gender impacts my fieldwork and these are some of the most important lessons that I have learnt while trying to answer this. I am far from having a gender-neutral view of the world. I have a gendered gaze on drinking cultures and sexualised environments, which is due to a complex set of factors such as the prejudices of Western cultures in relation to women and alcohol, and aesthetic and ethical values related to my social class, status and upbringing. This does not mean that my gaze is fixed; it is not. The engagement with the field and extensive reading were transformative both of how I presented knowledge about the Bierstrasse to the world and also of my understanding of self.

The second learning is that we need to make an effort to question and to expand common imaginings of researcher roles and of our 'objects' of research. Stereotypes act as iron cages for our imaginations and as blinders to our possibilities for discovery. Additionally, we should have the courage to talk more openly about the anxieties related to conducting research, including identifying one's needs for safety. As researchers, it should be fine to recognise that due to our personalities or biographical experiences we have some limitations, and that sometimes teaming up with a colleague (male or female) or asking a friend for a favour, so that there would be 'two of us', is all what it takes. The presence of a trusted person can make the whole difference when entering a 'risky' environment.

While my husband's help was the solution to my problem, this may not be an optimal or possible option for others. Some scholars may achieve a feeling of safety and a sense of empowerment in the field by adopting and playing with specific attitudes, aesthetics and bodily postures which correspond to different characters, such as a cool female police detective, an adventurous reporter or an undercover agent. Also, and this is as important, for others the excitement of the fieldwork may be closely related to a perception of risk and adventure. A deeply challenging environment could be what they are looking for, maybe as a compensation for the safe but often boring spaces of the academic buildings and campuses where most of our working lives take place. The feeling of overcoming fear is closely linked to the intensity of feeling alive and present in the moment. In this sense, any challenging fieldwork experience can be turned into a possibility for growth and courage.

I wonder how many times in our research methodologies we tend to omit the key roles played by our gendered identities and by the support provided by colleagues, partners or friends. Who we are, our biographical histories and our gendered perceptions about ourselves and others matter for how we interpret the world around us, and that, despite our academic culture's fascination with performance metrics, individual rankings and the myth of the 'genius', we are seldom able to achieve anything without the love and the encouragement of those around us. Mary Poppins would never have ventured to jump into the painting if she had not been urged by her good friend Bert, and I would not have conducted my research on alcohol tourism without my husband. Here is a grateful recognition with several years delay: thank you Bjarke!

References

Anderson, E. (2015) Feminist epistemology and philosophy of science. In N. Zalta (ed.) *The Stanford Encyclopedia of Philosophy*. See http://plato.stanford.edu/entries/feminism-epistemology/

Andrews, H., Roberts, L. and Selwyn, T. (2007) Hospitality and eroticism. *International Journal of Culture, Tourism and Hospitality Research* 1, 247–262.

Duarte Alonso, A. (2011) Opportunities and challenges in the development of microbrewing and beer tourism: A preliminary study from Alabama. *Tourism Planning and Development* 8, 415–431.

Falcón, S.M. and Nash, J. (2015) Shifting analytics and linking theories: A conversation about the meaning-making of intersectionality and transnational feminism. *Women's Studies International Forum*, 50, 1–10.

Fiske, S.T., Cuddy, A.J.C., Glick, P. and Xu, J. (2002) A model of (often mixed) stereotype content: Competence and warmth respectively follow from perceived status and competition. *Journal of Personality and Social Psychology* 82, 878–902. doi: 10.1037/0022-3514.82.6.878

Fleetwood, J. (2014) A feminist, narrative analysis of drinking stories. *The International Journal of Drug Policy* 25, 351–352.

Gee, S. and Jackson, S.J. (2012) Leisure corporations, beer brand culture, and the crisis of masculinity: The Speight's 'Southern man' advertising campaign. *Leisure Studies* 31, 83–102.

Grasswick, H.E. (2011) Introduction: Feminist epistemology and philosophy of science in the twenty-first century. In H.E. Grasswick (ed.) *Feminist Epistemology and Philosophy of Science* (pp. xiii–xxx). London: Springer.

Grasswick, H.E. (2013) Feminist social epistemology. In N. Zalta (ed.) *The Stanford Encyclopedia of Philosophy*. See http://plato.stanford.edu/archives/spr2013/entries/feminist-social-epistemology/

Jackson, C. and Tinkler, P. (2007) 'Ladettes' and 'Modern Girls': 'Troublesome' young femininities. *The Sociological Review* 55, 251–272.

Larsen, C. K. (1997) Relax and have a homebrew: Beer, the public sphere, and (re)invented traditions. *Food and Foodways: Explorations in the History and Culture of Human Nourishment* 7, 265–288.

Månsson, E. and Bogren, A. (2014) Health, risk, and pleasure: The formation of gendered discourses on women's alcohol consumption. *Addiction Research and Theory* 22, 27–36.

Munar, A.M. (2013) Chapter 12: Sun, alcohol and sex: Enacting beer tourism. In J. Gammelgaard and C. Dörrenbächer (eds) *The Global Brewery Industry: Markets, Strategies, and Rivalries* (pp. 310–333). Cheltenham: Edward Elgar Publishing Incorporated (New Horizons in International Business).

Pettigrew, S. and Charters, S. (2010) Alcohol consumption motivations and behaviours in Hong Kong. *Asia Pacific Journal of Marketing and Logistics* 22, 210–221.

Radcliffe, P. and Measham, F. (2014) Repositioning the cultural: Intoxicating stories in social context. *International Journal of Drug Policy* 25, 346–347.

Rúdólfsdóttir, A.G. and Morgan, P. (2009) 'Alcohol is my friend': Young middle class women discuss their relationship with alcohol. *Journal of Community and Applied Social Psychology* 19, 492–505.

Stringer, B. and McAllister, J. (2012) *Fluorescent Heart of Magaluf*. See upcommons.upc.edu/revistes/bitstream/2099/12248/1/C_195_3.pdf

Wearing, S., Stevenson, D. and Young, T. (2010) *Tourist Cultures: Identity, Place and the Traveller*. London: Sage.

13 Motherhood within Family Tourism Research: Case Studies in New Zealand and Samoa

Heike A. Schänzel

Dr Heike Schänzel is a Senior Lecturer and programme leader postgraduate in International Tourism Management at Auckland University of Technology in New Zealand. It had taken her 20 years in between having three children to finish studying and enter academia. She considers herself as a mid-career researcher with a particular focus on families, children and adolescents in tourism who draws on her own experiences as a mother travelling and researching. Her other research interests include: tourist behaviour and experiences; sociality in tourism; femininities and paternal masculinities in tourism research; innovative and qualitative research methodologies; and critical theory development in tourism. She is passionate about better understanding family fun (along with the avoidance of conflict) and the facilitation of sociality and meaningful experiences from the perspectives of diverse families within the context of leisure, tourism and hospitality.

Introduction

All around the world mothers are usually considered the gatekeepers of the family, but how does this apply when it comes to academic research? Based on my own experiences, this chapter discusses the notion of motherhood within family tourism research in two ways: firstly, the influence motherhood had on the nature of the field site itself; and, secondly, the role of motherhood in gaining access to family participants and their children. It tackles the question, through acknowledging my own subjectivities, of how scientific or academic knowledge is produced when it comes to family tourism. To this end, this chapter is about how gender may influence our research topics, our contributions of knowledge, and our practices of enquiry. Rather than treating academic research as objective and dispassionate, my own experience and other research experiences discussed in this book are about embracing our emotional and passionate selves when it comes to our research interests. It is about revealing the integration and entanglements of our personal and professional selves (Bell, 1993). In this case, it is about including my being a mother and my subjective experiences with my children in New Zealand and Samoa (see Figure 13.1) into my research story. Here, I openly discuss the advantages and disadvantages (or biases) of such an approach.

Like many other academics, I stumbled onto my doctoral research project through observations – in my case when travelling with my children in

Figure 13.1 Map of Oceania with New Zealand and Samoa. Map copyright Enrico Andreini

New Zealand and through past research experiences. For example, as part of my master's thesis on 'The effectiveness of environmental interpretation' at the Marine Education Centre in Wellington, New Zealand (Schänzel, 2001), I interviewed a visiting group of high school students. What struck me the most when interviewing these adolescents were their passionate and thoughtful responses and the real effect these educational visits had on them compared with adults older than them. This research experience alerted me to the missing voices of adolescents and children in tourism research (Small, 2008), and I vowed that in future I would actively involve children in my research projects. Years later, when attending a PhD workshop at an Australasian conference, a comment from a fellow doctoral student stayed with me: 'Teenagers – no way!' Teenagers or adolescents often get a bad name for their supposedly uncooperative or unruly behaviour, but that has never been my experience. So easily can the insights gained from these young people on the cusp of adulthood be dismissed when there is much to be gained for our understanding on matters concerning tourism from listening to what they have to say. My perspective concerning the inclusion of research participants has certainly been helped by being a mother of teenagers myself. I would argue that having an affinity and emotional connection to research participants with similar life circumstances can only aid in the research process when it comes to family studies.

The other part of my research journey involved going on regular family holidays with my three children in New Zealand. Enjoyment of New Zealand's outdoors, and particularly its extensive coastal areas, is considered an essential part of the Kiwi lifestyle (Barnett & Wolfe, 1993). For New Zealanders, or 'Kiwis', the annual summer holiday is a much-loved tradition and a symbol of Kiwi identity. Camping holidays have featured strongly for Kiwi families over the years and are appreciated for their back-to-basics approach and ability to strengthen social relationships between family members and friends. New Zealand is an island nation with a small population (4.71 million in January 2017), varied natural resources and relative distance from other countries. Families, including children, then represent a large domestic market for the tourism industry in New Zealand. However, I increasingly came to realise, families get little recognition in tourism research or government attention, largely because family holidays are perceived as less economically valuable than the international tourists who bring foreign exchange earnings (Schänzel, 2010a). Instead of being captured in research, the social significance of these Kiwi family holidays was largely left to telling stories and memory building. My personal and professional journey then became entwined, and my doctoral research project on the social experiences and meanings of family holidays in New Zealand was born. As I delved deeper into the family tourism literature, it emerged that, despite the significant size of the family market globally (accounting for about 30% of the leisure travel market), there is little academic research on understanding the tourism experiences of children and families (Schänzel & Yeoman, 2014). With my PhD study and other later family studies, I set out to change the course of tourism research to fill some of those gaps. I had found my academic niche largely through acknowledging my personal story and embracing my motherhood discourse.

Family Tourism Research

I have argued before that children and families form the closest and most important emotional bond in humans. This relationship is what drives humanity and society, and positions the family at the centre of human activity. Family holidays are all about spending 'quality family time', bonding to ensure the happiness and togetherness of the family, away from the distractions or busyness of everyday life. In most societies around the world, an increasing importance is placed on families spending time together because of the perception that parents are too busy and have less time to relax, play, communicate and share meals with their children. In fact, holidays are often the only time the whole family spends together for an extended period without the distractions of work, school or other commitments. Family travel is predicted to grow at a faster rate than all other forms of leisure, mainly because it represents a way to reunite the family, especially if family members live geographically apart (Schänzel & Yeoman, 2014). It then seems surprising to me that tourism research has rarely taken notice of families' holiday experiences (Obrador, 2012). Putting the economic benefit of family tourism aside, why is there so little interest in the significant psychological and social contributions of families coming together through travel?

From the dawn of modern psychology, psychological theorists have emphasised the importance of positive human social connection for health and well-being. The aim of bringing families together through travelling is to enable such connections. However, in a climate of performance measures encouraging the dominance of positivist approaches, voices in tourism have been muted on family connections because of their perception as being mundane, economically insignificant and associated with female concerns. In a recent editorial on 'illuminating the blind spots', some colleagues and I argued that tourism researchers tend to tinker with the perceived exotic and sexy, such as dolphin-watching tours and adventure tourism in far-flung places, while the real meanings of tourism experiences and encounters remain neglected (Mooney *et al.*, 2017). The tourism academy generally ignores the presence of ordinary life and people, yet by doing so, it fails to see magic in the mundane, including in the contributions of families with young and older children. Children are usually relegated to the sidelines, as if unworthy of being in full view, because their purchasing power relies on influencing their parents and their voices are considered as banal. However, markets, such as the sweets at the supermarket checkout line, are built on the purchasing power, or pester power, of children. There is also the issue that family tourism may be considered a female research site and, as such, less prestigious (Schänzel & Carr, 2016). Traditionally, research on family holiday experiences has been largely informed by feminist perspectives and thus focused on mothers (e.g. Davidson, 1996; Deem, 1996; Small, 2005). These studies highlight the never-ending physical and emotional work of motherhood both at home and when travelling, which I have found to be true from my own experience. The more feminist gender representations also highlight that little is known about fatherhood on holiday and that tourism is lagging behind other social research when it comes to family leisure life, representing diversity, and gender scholarship.

This leads me to raise the matter of whether children and families in tourism are identifiable as more of a women's research topic (see Schänzel & Carr, 2016). If this is true, questions need to be asked about why this is the case and if it is a healthy situation. On the surface, a research field dominated by women may appear to be a good thing; something that exists in the face of historical (and regrettably still current in too many areas) discrimination. However, scratch beneath this surface and questions of the gendered and discriminatory construction of 'appropriate' or 'acceptable' research fields for men and women raise their ugly heads, potentially undermining the positive surface image. The underlying image may be one of continued gender-based discrimination where women should research children and families in tourism due to the continuing pervasiveness of the notion of women as 'carers' leaving men who examine children in tourism to be constructed as deviant, reflecting wider social constructions of the relation between men and children. Further, there are issues regarding gaining access to families and it is possible that women or mothers have an automatic advantage over men. My field experience is quite different to that of a middle-aged man (see Hay, 2017), who as a solitary male researcher working in family and childhood studies may face particular challenges because of his gender, such as difficulty in gaining permission to interview children due to child protection issues. The gendered construction of family research is also linked to ongoing concerns in education regarding the existence and persistence of gender divisions and stereotypes that, for example, construct science as masculine (Kelly, 1985), and the perception of qualitative family tourism research as not being scientific. I will now illustrate these ideas with my own field research experiences in New Zealand and Samoa, which are shaped strongly by my motherhood and shared travel narratives.

Family Holiday Research in New Zealand

Once I had the main topic identified for my doctoral research, I turned to designing the data collection and selecting the field site. The focus was on family holidays in New Zealand, yet it was not considered practically feasible for me to chase participants at family holiday spots around the country, especially given that I had three children of various ages myself (12, 10 and 4 years old when I started my doctoral thesis). Instead, I initially accessed families through my children's local primary school and once I had their permission granted, I could approach other schools in the area to conduct a parental survey. I considered that gaining access through the school system was the best way to contact a broad range of families across socioeconomic lines, and such an approach has been commonly used in previous studies (e.g. Carr, 2006; Shaw *et al.*, 2008). I need to acknowledge here that personally knowing the principal of my children's primary school helped me with getting that initial access to a school for conducting research. I am unsure if access would have been that easy for a family researcher who did not have an established network of educational facilities in which their children were enrolled.

The parental responses from the survey conducted through the five primary schools that agreed to my family study then formed the voluntary pool (option of ticking a box to participate in family interviews later) that resulted in 10 families volunteering for three rounds of whole-family interviews over the course of one year. I have previously published on the methodology used for this study and the finer details of the data collection (see Schänzel, 2010b), but what is missing from this and other academic journal articles is my own gendered perspective. There is no doubt that being a mother with primary-school-aged children helped in securing access for data collection and also had an influence on my choice of field research site. The primary schools chosen were deliberately from the Wellington region and close to my place of residence to ensure that the families could be interviewed in their homes during later phases of the research. This allowed me to structure and organise my doctoral research around running a household with three children rather than taking off for several months to conduct research at some exotic location.

The second stage of my doctoral research involved whole-family interviews with the 10 families (20 parents and 20 children) in their own homes. Qualitative family research is almost always conducted in the home (LaRossa *et al.*, 1994) because it ensures that the family members are in their natural environment and thus more willing to participate. This is particularly important when including children in the research process, as is the case for whole-family methodology which involves first a group interview (like a focus group) and then individual interviews with all the family members. The family group interviews capture shared meanings while the individual interviews guard against one family member dominating the conversation, and give individual family members the opportunity to describe their own experiences without the scrutiny of the rest of the family. However, first I had to find a way to make my research participants feel comfortable and build up trust with me, especially with the children who I planned to interview both with their parents and separately.

Gaining access to families through a school is one thing but the dynamics shift when entering someone else's house to conduct interviews with all the family members. Scheduling the interviews proved extremely difficult as many families today are busy and there was hardly any time available when every family member was at home at the same time. I had to be extremely flexible with my own family arrangements and, during that time, my research had to come first, which was particularly difficult to negotiate on weekends. Invariably, almost all the family interviews were conducted on weekends, as this seemed to be the only time available despite it clashing with my own family commitments.

In order to break the ice and gain the trust of the participating families, I brought photos of my children with me. Even though my children were physically absent for this study, they had a presence, which was important in legitimising my identity as a mother and breaking down barriers. Because of them, I could introduce myself as a fellow mother with children of similar ages and straight away take on a non-threatening persona and an insider perspective. I would argue here that being a mother myself helped significantly in firstly, finding families to volunteer for my research (as I stated this fact in my information letter) and secondly, gaining access to families and their children in their homes. The open-plan design of modern homes alleviated most safety issues and women are rarely considered sexual predators. Even when I conducted the individual interviews with the children, their parents were still nearby rather than behind closed doors. Families also had the option of having a parent present during the individual interviews with the children and three families requested this. This meant that confidentiality of the individual interviews with the children was hard to achieve but made the process more transparent and safe for the children and myself as researcher. There was, however, one family who lived in an older-style house and the parents were happy for me to conduct the individual interviews with their two children in a separate room.

Conducting research in family homes allows for a level of intimacy and privacy that more public spaces are not able to provide, especially when it comes to involving younger children. However, the intimate spaces of the participants' homes also proved difficult at times to extricate myself from. Invariably once the interviews were completed, I ended up talking mainly with the mothers about matters relating to children in general. As Levey (2009) pointed out, having children in common gives people a familiar subject to talk about which enhances rapport and, to some degree, increases trust. However, it also meant that finding the right time to leave without appearing rude was not always easy. After all, I had been welcomed into their homes, but remained aware that I was taking up their valuable time. Despite the time pressures for modern families, many parents were more than happy to keep on entertaining me, introducing a constraint associated with private spaces. I am certain that the ease with which I was allowed access and welcomed into these families would look quite different compared to, for example, a single male conducting a similar research study. In the next section, I continue to discuss the role of gender in family research through a comparative reflection on family research in public spaces at resorts and beach *fales* in Samoa.

Family Holiday Research in Samoa

Considering that my doctoral research field site was based around Wellington, where we lived at the time, I vowed that my next research study would involve a more exotic location to prove that family tourism research can be alluring, too. We had never been to Samoa but the islands always held a special fascination and I wanted to gain research experience involving the family tourism market in the South Pacific. For this reason, I applied for a university research grant to conduct research in Samoa and for my daughters to join me at my own expense. The purpose of this study was to explore the holiday experiences in Samoa of families (mainly New Zealand and Australian families) travelling with their children. I learnt through my doctoral research that the popularity of overseas holidays for families increases with the age of their children, as more exotic experiences are sought compared to domestic holidays. A better understanding was then needed about what is perceived as exotic about Pacific Island holidays for families. The lack of research into family holidays (Carr, 2011) is particularly surprising when considering the importance of the family tourism market for the Pacific Islands, with Samoa specifically marketing towards families (see http://www.samoa.travel/about/a18/Families). In order to examine differences in family hospitality experiences, two accommodation sites were chosen: a beach resort; and beach *fale,* or bungalows, which Samoa is renowned for. This allowed further insight into the hospitality offered to families by commercial resorts compared to the hospitality found in commercial homes owned by Samoan families. My aim was to employ again a whole-family methodology with New Zealand and Australian families holidaying in Samoa in April and July of 2014, which is inclusive of the group and individual perspectives of all family members. However, conducting research with families while on holiday proved quite different from researching families in the privacy of their homes.

In April 2014, I set out with my two daughters (aged 11 and 17 at the time) in tow to Apia, the capital of Samoa, to conduct research with families who stayed at commercial beach resorts. A major constraint with family tourism research is that most travelling is dictated by the school holidays, at least when including school-aged children. For this reason, we only had two windows of opportunity, one during the Easter school holidays and the other during the two-week mid-winter break when many families seek to escape from the New Zealand winter weather and fly to South Pacific Islands. April is still considered the shoulder season and we learnt quickly that there were not many families holidaying at this time of year. Since it was our first visit to Samoa, or any South Pacific island, it was hard for me to judge the number of family tourists I would be able to approach as potential research participants. I had to be flexible in my method and approach any families that I encountered (including families with babies), and also cast my research field wider than Apia by travelling to some beach resorts around Upolu (the main island of Samoa, see Figure 13.2 for a map). For the travelling, I employed a local taxi driver (pictured in Figure 13.3 with my daughters at the hotel where we were staying), which proved cheaper and less stressful than driving myself on unfamiliar roads where there are often stray dogs and pigs to be found. This might have been different for a sole male researcher wanting to explore the island, but I had to consider the safety of my children. At the hotel where we were staying or at any beach resort we visited, having my daughters with me instantly gave me the identity of a mother and made research access to the few families holidaying there easier. In this sense, 'accompanied research' was a real bonus for doing family tourism research overseas but the presence of my children also provided me with additional insights through observing and questioning them about their own travel experiences in Samoa.

Frohlick (2002) has previously written about bringing family to field sites (in her case, a baby to Mount Everest base camp in Nepal) and the challenges and advantages of accompanied research. In my case, having my daughters (largely independent with my 17-year-old looking after her sister) come along presented only advantages for my field research and myself. Not only did they keep me company in the down time and allowed us to spend a desirable family holiday together in Samoa but they provided

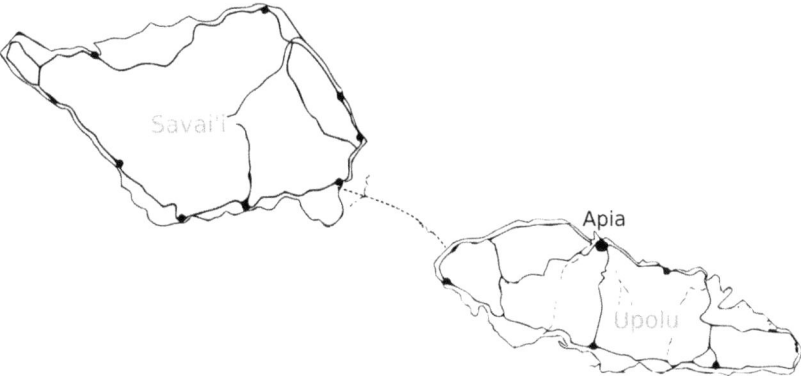

Figure 13.2 Map of Samoa

Figure 13.3 My daughters and the local taxi driver at a hotel field research site in Apia, Samoa in 2014

me with valuable theoretical insights into their own experiential dimensions. The presence of my children also smoothed the way in terms of field access to participants: a mother with her children doing research on other holidaying families. In this way, my children normalised my presence and acted as 'wedges', or as instrumentally important in helping me gain access in various ways (Levey, 2009). Still, I was hesitant to announce to anyone at the university that my children would come along when I was conducting 'serious research' in Samoa. So much does the conventional and masculinist mode of the lone, male, detached researcher prevail that having accompanying family at field research sites is considered a hindrance rather than an asset. I take up Susan Frohlick's (2002) argument here that we should not erase our family from fieldwork practices but instead embrace their presence and blur the boundaries of our field sites with visible traces of our personal lives and relationships that enable us to better understand the phenomenon we are studying. When it comes to family research, and arguably other research, the field is never detached from social relations and personal commitments, for field sites are embodied spaces. I found accompanied fieldwork to be extremely rewarding for my children, and myself, even more so when we returned for the second stage of my research study to conduct family interviews at beach *fales* on Savaii in July 2014.

My youngest daughter had always wanted to stay at a fancy resort and, since my research budget allowed it, we had the first night booked at one of the top commercial beach resorts on Upolu in Samoa. While my children frolicked at the pool and enjoyed the novelty of having a drink at the pool bar, I managed to conduct two more interviews with families staying there. I am always amazed by how generous people are when it comes to giving up their time to take part in research, even on their holidays. Nevertheless, conducting interviews at resorts in public spaces (usually in the restaurant or café area) takes on a different dynamic from private spaces at home and it emerged quickly that a family group interview and individual interviews with all the family members would not work. Separating the family out and taking up more of their time while on holiday was just not a feasible option. Instead, I resorted to always conducting family group interviews and only the occasional individual interview when the opportunity presented itself, as a supplement. The important lesson here was to adopt a flexible approach and abandon the rigidity of the whole-family methodology, with group and individual interviews, which did not work in on-holiday environments and public spaces. Maybe another lesson was that women could be more flexible when it comes to adopting research methods according to the field situation.

In Samoa, most of its tourism accommodation is locally-owned and operated. As an alternative livelihood strategy to increasingly foreign-owned large hotels and resorts, local families have built low-cost beach *fale* accommodation in prime beachfront locations. These traditional *fale* range from basic, open-sided huts with thatched roofs and woven blinds in the place of walls, to walled bungalows with small verandas. Bathroom and dining facilities are shared with other guests, and the relations between guests and those catering to their needs are more friendly than servile, providing tourists with 'genuine Samoan hospitality' (Scheyvens, 2005: 197). These beach *fale* are proving popular with visiting families from overseas as offering cultural immersion into the Samoan way of life or *fa'a Samoa*. Many families are no longer satisfied with traditional sun and sea resort holidays but want to expose their children to more holistic living with a slower pace and a deeper connection to place and people, or what has become known as 'slow tourism' (Fullagar *et al.*, 2012). After our stay at the upmarket resort, we travelled by ferry to the island of

Savaii to stay at a beach *fale* on the Northern coast (see Figure 13.4) for a week, while I continued my research there with families who were seeking an alternative or slower holiday experience. Samoa is generally perceived as a safe destination and safety for my children was not a concern.

What emerged from our stay at the beach *fale* and through talking to other tourists and the wonderful women hosting us was how much we enjoyed the simplicity and genuineness of the place. There was a cycling family with five children staying for two nights with whom I managed to conduct a long and insightful family group interview. A mother and her teenage daughter were staying at the same *fale* for several days and we ended up spending time together as well as them taking part in my research project. The shared living space and commensality (the act of eating together) at the beach *fale* we stayed in allowed for relationships that were more intimate, with the fellow travellers and the host family making us feel completely at home. I also managed to approach other families staying at different beach *fale* nearby and interview them but generally, even in the high season, there were not many tourists around. In our spare time, we went for swims in the warm sea (our *fale* was right at the waterfront), read books, relaxed and ate the food that had been prepared locally by our Samoan hosts. We absolutely fell in love with the place and its people and ruefully thought back to our stay at the resort and swimming in its chlorinated pool. As a family, including my youngest

Figure 13.4 My daughters at beach *fale* field research site in Savaii, Samoa in 2014

daughter, we all agreed that we much preferred staying at these simple beach *fale* than any fancy resort.

My children's personal sentiments about their travel experiences were reflected and confirmed by the research findings and it was our own transformative experience that deepened my understanding of the research project. We got to experience, ourselves, the benefits reported by these visiting families, of living with locals and immersion in warm water and sea air – or thalasso tourism which is part of the body–mind–spirit spectrum of health tourism (Smith & Puczkó, 2009) – and the families reported feeling particularly relaxed staying there. Our embodied entanglements played out between ourselves or subjectivities and the field research sites provided me with deeper insights. I would not have gained the same level of insights and transformative experience without the presence of my children. A child can let the researcher know if the findings correspond to her or his understanding of the social world and this is particularly significant when a researcher is studying the children's world (Levey, 2009) on their holiday. My children's embodied social beings lived out the beach *fale* hospitality, which provides family wellness benefits through promoting a sense of affinity between culture and nature in Samoan society, a vital finding of my study. Writing my children into my research story acknowledges those entanglements, autobiographical origins and the reflexive knowledge production.

Conclusions and Reflections

My own research journey, choice of field research sites and access to family participants have all been shaped and influenced by my motherhood. I would argue that motherhood for family tourism research presents an advantage that needs to be acknowledged but like anything there is a darker side to it. Family studies, particularly in tourism, deserve more attention and must be embraced as serious research by everyone in academia, including actively involving children and adolescents as participants. There is an absence of research on fatherhood in tourism and, unless we consider matters of parenthood and childhood as integral to our societal fabric and academic enquiries, there will be little change regarding gender inequalities and gendered research interests. From my own perspective, there is nothing mundane about researching the experiences of families coming together on holiday, for the true meaning of life has always been about enabling and maintaining social connections. My research interest in family tourism should then not be solely determined by my motherhood or gendered influence but by my wish to contribute to knowledge that is fundamental to human understanding. Below are a few of my research lessons gained:

- It is important that, before entering the field, researchers consider the ways in which their families and their own status as mother (or father)

may influence the types of information they gather and the relationships they may form.
- It is important to acknowledge our embodied and highly visible identities as a mother (or father) in our field research as a form of deviance that challenges scientific taboos and arbitrary notions of research boundaries. Accompanied field research should be considered as the norm rather than the exception, for the theoretical insights it can provide.
- It is important to acknowledge that research involves embodied social beings and subjectivities, along with deeper thinking about whether being a mother in the field affects the research process differently compared to being a father, because the generation of knowledge happens at the interface of self, family and others – where life is lived.

References

Barnett, S. and Wolfe, R. (1993) *At the Beach: The Great New Zealand Holiday*. Auckland, New Zealand: Hodder and Stoughton.
Bell, D. (1993) Introduction: The context. In D. Bell, P. Caplan and W.J. Karim (eds) *Gendered Fields: Women, Men and Ethnography* (pp. 1–18). London: Routledge.
Carr, N. (2006) A comparison of adolescents' and parents' holiday motivations and desires. *Tourism and Hospitality Research* 6, 129–142.
Carr, N. (2011) *Children's and Families' Holiday Experiences*. London: Routledge.
Davidson, P. (1996) The holiday and work experiences of women with young children. *Leisure Studies* 15 (2), 89–103.
Deem, R. (1996) Women, the city and holidays. *Leisure Studies* 15, 105–119.
Frohlick, S. (2002) 'You brought your baby to base camp?': Families and field sites. *The Great Lakes Geographer* 9, 49–58.
Fullagar, S., Markwell, K. and Wilson, E. (2012) *Slow Tourism: Experiences and Mobilities*. Bristol: Channel View Publications.
Hay, B. (2017) Missing voices: Australian children's insights and perceptions of family holidays. *Hospitality and Society* 7 (2), 133–155.
Kelly, A. 1985. 'The construction of masculine science'. *British Journal of Sociology of Education* 6 (2), 133–154. doi: 10.1080/0142569850060201.
LaRossa, R., Bennett, L.A. and Gelles, R.J. (1994) Ethical dilemmas in qualitative family research. In G. Handel and G.G. Whitchurch (eds) *The Psychosocial Interior of the Family* (4th edn). New York, NY: Aldine de Gruyter.
Levey, H. (2009) 'Which one is yours?': Children and ethnography. *Qualitative Sociology* 32, 311–331.
Mooney, S., Schänzel, H. and Poulston, J. (2017) Editorial to the special issue: Illuminating the blind spots: Challenging dominant thinking about hospitality work and encounters. *Hospitality and Society* 7 (2), 105–201.
Obrador, P. (2012) The place of the family in tourism research: Domesticity and thick sociality by the pool. *Annals of Tourism Research* 39, 401–420.
Schänzel, H.A. (2001) Meaningful experiences: Understanding the values gained from wildlife-visitor interaction. Unpublished master's thesis. Victoria University of Wellington, New Zealand.
Schänzel, H. (2010a) Domestic tourism in New Zealand: The Kiwi family holiday. *Pacific News* 33, 24–26.

Schänzel, H.A. (2010b) Whole-family research: Towards a methodology in tourism for encompassing generation, gender, and group dynamic perspectives. *Tourism Analysis* 15, 555–569.

Schänzel, H. and Carr, N. (2016) Introduction: Special issue on children, families and leisure – part three. *Annals of Leisure Research* 19, 381–385. doi: 10.1080/11745398.2016.1201241.

Schänzel, H.A. and Yeoman, I. (2014) The future of family tourism. *Tourism Recreation Research* 39, 343–360.

Scheyvens, R. (2005) Growth of beach fale tourism in Samoa: The high value of low-cost tourism. In C.M. Hall and S. Boyd (eds) *Nature-based Tourism in Peripheral Areas: Development or Disaster?* (pp. 188–202). Clevedon: Channel View Publications.

Shaw, S.M., Havitz, M.E. and Delamere, F.M. (2008) I decided to invest in my kids' memories: Family vacations, memories, and the social construction of the family. *Tourism Culture and Communication* 8, 13–26.

Small, J. (2005) Women's holidays: Disruption of the motherhood myth. *Tourism Review International* 9, 139–154.

Small, J. (2008) The absence of childhood in tourism studies. *Annals of Tourism Research* 35, 772–789.

Smith, M. and Puczkó, L. (2009) *Health and Wellness Tourism*. Oxford: Butterworth-Heinemann.

Conclusion – Gender: A Variable and a Practice

Brooke A. Porter and Heike A. Schänzel

Introduction

In brief, the intent of this volume was to expose the influences of gender on women conducting tourism research. While there was similar attention given to the role of gender on fieldwork in the 1980s and 90s in anthropology and ethnography, this movement seemingly lost momentum and never expanded to include tourism studies. Despite evolving our disciplines, a space for gender as a variable in tourism research is still lacking. The field experiences presented in this book compilation offer a first for women tourism researchers and the biases and challenges we encounter. More importantly, they offer lessons learned for all researchers (whether early career or experienced), supervisors and ethics committees, regardless of gender.

Revisiting data sets is a standard practice in academia; however, once published, revisiting and reanalysing field experience is a more exceptional exercise. The devotion to practice and discipline is evident in all the experiences shared. Characteristic of any field experience, the authors invested their passions and made personal sacrifices. Additionally, in an academy where the field generally remains envisioned as a masculine space, all confronted gendered stereotypes in the name of science. While for some contributors writing these experiences was more of a challenge evoking feelings of anxiety or unsettling memories, others described writing these chapters as cathartic, an adjective seldom used in conjunction with academic writing. For other contributors, these chapters were an extension of their gendered-focus approach. Perhaps these varied emotions came from places of oppression, or alternatively from the achievement of going against the norms (i.e. bringing family to the field). In her autobiographic novel that details her academic career in the natural sciences, including the many gendered challenges she faced, Jahren (2016) poignantly acknowledged that there is 'still no journal where [she] can tell the story of how [her] science is done with both the heart and the hands' (2016: 20). This begs the question, where is the place for 'heart' or emotion in science? 'Heart' in this context may be more palpable in the female field experience, as we lug our little ones around, cover our bodies to deter sexism, or literally flee from dangerous situations. The emotions and subjectivities attached to every piece of research become apparent through a gendered lens. Conceivably, male researchers are just as eager to share their emotions, yet, like us, have not been given an acceptable space to do so (see also Caplan, 1993). Alternatively, heart may be more of a function of gender – one that is more commonly female. More importantly, these 'emotions' and 'subjectivities' might bias the fieldwork but addressing them brings transparency and reflexivity to the research. Thus, struggling towards androgyny or suggesting the need for objectivity in the field is just sloppy science.

Femininities are dynamic, changing over time and adapting to places, and so is gender *per se*, with increasing debates happening in societies about gender fluidity and gender diversity. In the future, there is a need for acknowledgment of this gender revolution through moving away from binary understandings of gender. However, as this edited book signifies a first on gender in tourism research, the contributions offer examples of how femininities contextualise us as researchers within the field experience. We are all insiders and outsiders at times when it comes to fieldwork. The insider/outsider association is also an effect of gender. This shifting of place can be, at times, beneficial and at others an inconvenience, but this fluidity is a reflection of life in general. Take for example, Usher (Chapter 4) who described the norms and etiquette of the surf line up and how gendered influences were at play. If we are to replace the ocean with offices and swap catching a wave with writing publications, surfing quite mirrors corporate life or academic institutions.

The contributions to this volume are as diverse as they are similar. In every experience, the influences of gender on the fieldwork and research processes are obvious. For some, gender was advantageous, for others it created additional risks, challenges or even monetary expenses, and for nearly all, a combination of positive and negative biases. Repetitive issues or themes throughout the chapters include:

(1) access;
(2) attire and conduct;
(3) sexual harassment;
(4) personal safety; and
(5) accompanied research and well-being.

These are practically identical to the themes suggested by Warren's (1988) look at gender in anthropological research nearly three decades ago: (1) entree; (2) finding a place within the culture; (3) sexuality and the body; and (4) sexual politics. However, we have the added notion of 'accompanied research and well-being' raised by seven of the contributors, which is connected to motherhood and bringing their child(ren) or husband along to the field. The themes from this collection, though entwined with one another, are discussed individually in the following sections.

Access

Access was a notable theme. Being female was largely an asset in terms of accessing the participants. This idea has been well supported in the literature (Douglas, 1985; Levry, 2009; Mead, 1986; Nader, 1986; Warren, 1988). For some it was a 'friendly face' that increased access (Hamilton and Fielding; Martinez and Peters); for others, it positioned them as a non-threat to their participants (Carvalho; Godfrey and Wearing; Munar; Swanson; Usher); for those with children, the shared connection of motherhood proved to be a considerable advantage in gaining access (Canosa; Cooke; Khoo-Lattimore; Porter; Stewart; Schänzel). For Cooke, Porter and Stewart, their infant sons' presence helped in building that all-important trust with communities by enabling them to be considered an approachable person and not just another researcher. While this amounted to a privileged access and positive bias in the field, an important lesson was not to feel guilty about merging motherhood and academia but instead to openly reflect on this as part of the research process. It is worth noting that although being female can often be advantageous in terms of access this benefit may have its limitations. For example, some cultures, mainly those abiding by Sharia Law, still limit a woman's ability to approach men. Such gendered limitations make a male assistant a requirement (see Alkhalaf, 2015) at perhaps extra financial cost to the female wishing to conduct research in these locales. Many of our contributors' accounts suggest that females may have an advantage in accessing participants; however, it could be that women are accustomed to 'getting on with it', brushing over any hardships that may hinder their research.

Attire and Conduct

Slightly variant from Warren's (1988) 'finding entry into the culture', this theme emphasises field attire and personal conduct. While we will never achieve insider status, technology (e.g. Google Street View) has allowed us to virtually place ourselves into many locations before visiting. Additionally, the expansion of the internet has made it possible to instantly connect with people in different cultures and learn voyeuristically through social media outlets. Despite seeing and learning about cultures, appropriateness of attire and proper conduct was a repetitive concern for many contributors. For example, Martinez and Peters adopted a 'gender-neutral' attire and required the same of their female team members. Despite these efforts at de-sexing themselves, they still dealt with sexual harassment from men. Swanson described being chastised for wearing a 'sexy' shirt, while Usher chose board shorts and a rash guard over a bikini to keep sexist comments at bay. Godfrey reverted to jeans after dealing with sexist remarks from wearing a conservative skirt. Concerns with attire are common with female travellers. Participants in Yang et al.'s (2017) study on Asian-female solo travellers found that women were attempting to look poorer (i.e. like a beggar) and dressing 'butch' to avoid sexual harassment. These examples are quite different from the male field experience where dress is seldom of concern. In Bell *et al*.'s (1993) edited volume on gendered fields, dress/attire was not mentioned by any of the male contributors.

Unfortunately, victimisation or the fear of victimisation when it comes to sexism and sexual assault is still present. The female body remains objectified by many and thus the need for conservative dress and restrained conduct in fieldwork remains, such as not going out to pubs alone drinking. In many ways, female researchers, like any field researcher, are engaging in a form of voluntary risk-taking similar to that of solo female travellers (see Yang *et al*., 2017). While this idea of conforming to dress codes seemingly goes against the feminist movement (Wilson *et al*., 2009), for the purposes of fieldwork and personal safety, it seems that modest Western-type attire is a better choice for many field locations. Keeping a consistent dress, rather than attempting to become an 'insider' via the wardrobe may have benefits beyond personal safety. For residents in lesser-developed regions and/or remote locations, a foreign friend/acquaintance may be a mark of social status (Cole, 2004; Kerstetter & Bricker, 2009; Porter & Orams, 2014). Overall, as Martinez and Peters stated, as researchers we should behave and act with confidence, professionalism, and rise above gender bias.

Sexual Harassment

Given remarkable societal advances and increased levels of global education, it is a shame that we find this theme valid nearly three decades after Warren's (1988) observations of the themes 'sexual politics' and 'sexuality and the body'. We have chosen to combine the ideas of sexual-based gender discrimination into a single theme: sexism and sexual harassment. Together these words identify chauvinistic actions towards the female researcher (for example, Martinez and Peters being belittled for skippering marine vessels) or unwanted sexualised comments, advances, or actions (see Godfrey and Wearing). The appropriate response to this type of treatment has not been adequately addressed in the literature (Warren, 1988), even today. Caplan (1993) explored the taboo effect of gender on sexuality noting that confessing sexual activity in the field has 'very different consequences than for men' (1993: 23), harking back to the theme of proper conduct for women researchers.

In the chapter by Godfrey and Wearing, Godfrey noted that a friend thwarted street harassment by shouting and threatening. This type of behaviour may serve to successfully stop unwanted harassment; however, there are very real personal risks in this approach. Given the diversity in experiences detailed by our contributors, the appropriate response to sexism and sexual harassment remains culturally and situationally dependent. These chapters have documented different field experiences, and in many cases included the authors' responses to sexism and sexual harassment in the field. By advancing the literature to include these responses to such situations we are attempting to transform them from field 'myths' into applicable strategies (refer to Warren, 1988). One strategy, as outlined by Godfrey and Wearing, is that when planning data collection in a male-dominated culture overseas, female researchers should consider the possibility of sexual harassment/assault in the field and have a plan in place to ensure both their physical safety and their emotional wellbeing. More importantly, any encounter with physical or sexual harassment should not be framed as the reflection of poor research skills or victim blaming but rather raise awareness of the heightened risk in the field. Another strategy, as outlined by Hamilton and Fielding, is the provision of additional training opportunities and additional funding for women conducting research in order to keep themselves safe.

Personal Safety

Reflecting on the field experiences of our contributors, here we examine biases of gender and precautions in the field. As noted in Chapter 1 by co-author Fielding, women do not have the luxury of sleeping on the beach alone as a measure to cut research costs. Additionally, as argued by Hamilton and Fielding, women's heightened sense of risk, the precautionary measures they take stemming from gendered lessons of safety taught from a young age, and the inherent nature of conducting research in unfamiliar locations, may prevent them from expanding their local connections in favour of personal safety. While male researchers are by no means outside of harm's way, there are more obvious threats to the personal safety of female researchers. In the case of Munar, she brought her husband along for her research on masculine-dominated spaces and for the first time openly talked about her anxieties relating to keeping herself safe. The presence of a trusted person then can make the difference when entering a 'risky' environment, supporting the argument for accompanied research. Additionally, for many mother-researchers (e.g. Cooke; Khoo-Lattimore; Porter; Schänzel; Stewart), it is in both the researcher's and their child-dependent's best interests to go together into the field. However, this embodied entanglement (Frohlick, 2002) means that there is at least one more person to keep safe. So how do we increase our personal safety in the field? Does it require additional funding? Fielding's and Munar's examples suggest situations where financial links may be attached to gender, meaning supplementary gender research budgets for some fieldwork may be necessary to avoid compromising personal safety. It is important to consider the biases that gender and precaution may contribute to a study, acknowledging the positives and negatives of these biases and exploring together the ways that these biases could be lessened in the future.

Accompanied Research and Wellbeing

There were two cases that included spousal accompaniment. Munar brought her husband along for safety while doing research and Porter brought her husband along on some trips to help with childcare, but there were several other women in this book (Canosa; Cooke; Khoo-Lattimore; Porter; Schänzel; Stewart) bringing their children along to the field or research destination. These stories illustrated the real benefits of accompanied research, which are deeper theoretical insights and even transformations brought about by the embodied entanglements through which we experience the world that we seek to understand. Being a woman, then, is intrinsically bound up with who we are and is integral to our field research. Any generation of knowledge for these women happened not in isolation or through objectivity, but through the connections of self, family and others where life is lived. Additionally, bringing family along while doing research made these women more comfortable and ensured their emotional wellbeing, just as it did for Frohlick (2002) who famously wrote about her field experiences of bringing her baby to Everest base camp. Considering that personal safety and emotional comfort should be at the forefront for any researcher – male or female or gender-diverse – then maybe the most important argument for accompanied research is the general sense of well-being it can provide.

Limitations

The experiences detailed in this book have been limited to the field of tourism for consistency. While it is likely that parts of the experiences are transferable to other discourses within and even outside of the social sciences, there are other parts that will remain unique to the authors. There are also experiences which have been overlooked by this volume. In particular, lesbian, bisexual, gay, transgender, and queer (LBGTQ) perspectives are entirely absent. With more research emerging on the gendered biases faced by the LBGTQ community, future work focusing on these field experiences will be crucial. Our contributors identify as cisgender with 14 women and two men. Heterosexual-type experiences were discussed (largely in the form of sexism); however, sexual orientations were not emphasised, nor claimed by the contributors. Male researchers have written about their sexual experiences in the field (see Abramson, 1993), yet it appears this is still an unconventional topic for female researchers to detail (Caplan, 1993). Additional limitations of this project were the lack of ethnicities represented. Khoo-Lattimore (Malaysian) and Carvahlo (Brazilian) are the only contributors of non-European decent. Interestingly, however, these are the two authors whose contributions discussed research experiences conducted either in or with participants from their home countries. This is remarkably similar to the demographics in Bell *et al.* (1993) where all three non-European authors did their fieldwork in their own countries (Caplan, 1993). Despite the largely Eurocentric nature of the contributors for this book, the diversity that is represented by their Italian, Spanish, German, Malaysian, French and Portuguese first languages is, nevertheless, encouraging. The limitations of ethnicities and different sexual orientations were not deliberate, but simply a combined result of personal networks and responses to a general call for contributors. A final limitation is that of reflexivity. Though this entire volume was built on reflexive case study, Rose (1997) states that achieving transparent reflexivity is impossible. Rather, she suggests that what is of value is the disclosure and the exploration of the relationships between the researcher and the researched. It is the messiness and the hybrid spaces that are created in the entanglements between the researcher and the researched that are of value. These uncertainties deserve acknowledgement and visibility which is what we were seeking with this volume. Despite such limitations, this book provides the first in-depth insights into how femininities play out in the field of tourism research.

Moving Ahead

If we continue to suppress the role of gender, be it female, male or non-binary, in field experiences, we are lessening the transparency of our research. As described by our female contributors, the field can be a place of power, fear, achievement or some tangled combination of these emotions. For many, field anxieties resulted from concerns about personal safety and sexual harassment. The lessons learned from the contributors' accounts reveal the significance of simply ignoring sexism or sexual harassment in the field. The power of non-action is an important part of Buddhist or Taoist teachings. In these spiritual contexts, non-action is described to as *Wu Wei* (literally 'not doing'). For example, Buddhist master Phap Dung states, 'Sometimes we underestimate someone sitting very calm, very solid and not reacting and that they can touch a place of peace, a place of love, a place of non-discrimination. That is not inaction' (Confino, 2017: n.p.). Dung's spiritual advice was in reference to the current political conflicts in the United States; however, it is as relevant to sexual harassment or sexism received by female researchers in the field. Many contributors unknowingly applied concepts of *Wu Wei*. For example, Martinez and Peters as well as Porter, chose inaction when faced with inappropriate comments in the field. Similarly, in response to a physical incident, Godfrey responded with inaction. Swanson, though unaccompanied, was content to have a husband who, as she described, gave her a cloak of neutrality in the field. Likewise, Munar used her husband to 'shield' her from sexual harassment. All the women who contributed to this book found a way to keep themselves safe and shield themselves or respond to emotional or physical attacks or criticisms:

> Everybody was *Wu Wei* Fighting
> Documenting every sighting
> In fact, it was a little bit enlightening
> Fighting sexism with poignant timing

As demonstrated by the experiences presented in this volume, gender is a most influential variable and one that significantly shapes the research design, process and data. By ignoring the gendered influences on research, we will only reduce the reliability and validity of the social sciences, which drive us all. What remains necessary, is accepting gender, in every form, as a discernible variable, noteworthy of attention in every piece of research. It is time to normalise the 'awkward relationship between anthropology and feminism' (Bell, 1993: 29) and, by extension, tourism and feminism. Therefore, as stated by Shannon Swanson in Chapter 3, 'women field researchers must remain committed to keep on acknowledging and engaging with their femininities in order to continue conducting relevant research with meaningful outcomes'.

We also have to remember the words of Freya Stark, the explorer and adventurer: 'To be treated with consideration is, in the case of female travellers [researchers], too often synonymous with being prevented from doing what one wants'. Well-meaning advice and guidance can also help to keep women in their place. Just because women have always been taught to keep themselves safe, this should not prevent them from breaking new grounds in research. All it means is that women should continue to follow their passions, but use their instincts and common sense wisely when doing so.

References

Abramson, A. (1993) Between autobiography and method: Being male, seeing myth and the analysis of structures of gender and sexuality in the eastern interior of Fiji. In D. Bell, P. Caplan and W. J. Karim (eds) *Gendered Fields: Women, Men & Ethnography* (pp. 63–77). London: Routledge.

Alkhalaf, F. (2015) The characteristics, motivations and activities of visitors to Half Moon Beach, Saudi Arabia. Unpublished doctoral dissertation. Auckland University of Technology, Auckland, New Zealand.

Bell, D. (1993) Yes Virginia, there is a feminist ethnography. In D. Bell, P. Caplan and W.J. Karim (eds) *Gendered Fields: Women, Men & Ethnography* (pp. 28–43). London: Routledge.

Bell, D., Caplan, P. and Karim, W.J. (eds) (1993) *Gendered Fields: Women, Men & Ethnography*. London: Routledge.

Caplan, P. (1993) Introduction 2: The volume. In D. Bell, P. Caplan and W.J. Karim (eds) *Gendered Fields: Women, Men & Ethnography* (pp. 19–27). London: Routledge.

Cole, S. (2004) Shared benefits: Longitudinal research in eastern Indonesia. In J. Phillimore and L. Goodson (eds) *Qualitative Research in Tourism: Ontologies, Epistemologies and Methodologies*. New York, NY: Routledge.

Confino, J. (2017, 17 February) A Zen Master's advice on coping with Trump: It involves a lot more than meditating. *Huffington Post*. See http://www.huffingtonpost.com/entry/zen-and-the-art-of-activism_us_58a118b6e4b094a129ec59af

Douglas, J.D. (1985) *Creative Interviewing*. Newbury Park, CA: Sage.

Frohlick, S. (2002) 'You brought your baby to Base Camp?': Families and field sites. *The Great Lakes Geographer* 9, 49–58.

Jahren, H. (2016) *Lab Girl*. London: Fleet.

Kerstetter, D. and Bricker, K. (2009) Exploring Fijian's sense of place after exposure to tourism development. *Journal of Sustainable Tourism* 17, 691–708.

Levey, H. (2009) 'Which one is yours?': Children and ethnography. *Qualitative Sociology* 32 (3) 311–331.

Mead, M. (1986) Field work in Pacific Islands, 1925–1967. In P. Golde (ed.) *Women in the Field: Anthropological Experiences* (2nd edn, pp. 292–331). Los Angeles, CA: University of California Press.

Nader, L. (1986) From anguish to exultation. In P. Golde (ed) *Women in the Field: Anthropological Experiences* (2nd edn, pp. 67–96). Los Angeles, CA: University of California Press.

Porter, B.A. and Orams, M.B. (2014) Exploring tourism as a potential development strategy for an artisanal fishing community in the Philippines: The case of Barangay Victory in Bolinao. *Tourism in Marine Environments* 10, 49–70.

Rose, G. (1997) Situating knowledges: Positionality, reflexivities and other tactics. *Progress in Human Geography* 21 (3), 305–320.

Warren, C.A.B. (1988) *Gender Issues in Field Research* (Qualitative Research Methods Series 9). Newbury Park, CA: Sage Publications.

Wilson, E., Holdsworth, L. and Witsel, M. (2009) Gutsy women?: Conflicting discourses in women's travel guidebooks. *Tourism Recreation Research* 34, 3–11.

Yang, E.C.L., Khoo-Lattimore, C. and Arcodia, C. (2017) Constructing space and self through risk taking: A case of Asian solo female travelers. *Journal of Travel Research*. doi: 0047287517692447.

Index

[academic] supervisor(s), ix, 6, 75, 81, 103, 144, 146, 156, 200, *see also* supervisory, xiii, 69
accessible, 15, 20, 88, 92, 166
accommodation(s), 12, 128, 192, 195
accompanied fieldwork, 7, 92, 157, 167, 195, 198
accompanied research, x, xiv, 7, 193, 201, 204–205
accompanying family, 85–86, 88–89, 92, 194, *see also* 158
adventure(r), 18, 70, 143, 163, 167, 176–178, 183 *see also* risk
age, ix, xi, 2, 5, 6, 11, 13–16, 20, 21, 33, 38, 40, 44–46, 48, 113–114, 118, 204,
ambition(s), 43, 122, *see also ambitious*
ambitious, 118, *see also ambition*
androgynous, 2, 3, 69
androgyny, 3–5, 73, 201
anthropology, 3, 31, 38, 97, 141–143, 171, 177, 182, 200, 207
anthropological, 4, 70, 142, 146, 150, 172, 201
anthropologist(s), 2–4, 34, 38, 78, 85, 141–146, 152, 177
anxiety(ies), 115, 183, 200, 204, 206
apologise, 63
Asian, 127–128, 133, 135, 136, 203
assertive, 64, 132
attire, 46–47, 73, 119, 201–203, *see also dress*
authority, 15, 49, 85, 116–117, 133–134
autoethnography, 131–132
autonomy, 40, 97

bisexual, 205
blonde(r), 119–120
body language, 102, 115
bodyguard, 181–182

boy(s), 117, 178
boyfriend, 56, 178, 181
breastfed, 76, 78, *see also breastfeed, breastfeeding, nursing*
breastfeed, 80, *see also breastfed, breastfeeding, nursing*
breastfeeding, 75, 78, *see also breastfed, breastfeed, nursing*
budget(s), 20, 42–43, 112, 195, 204
buttock(s), 25, 27, 115

camaraderie, 33, 39, 43–44, 171, 173, 177
catalyst, 165–166
catcalled, 55, *see also catcalling, catcalls, hustling*
catcalling, 54, *see also catcalled, catcalls, hustling*
catcalls, 29, *see also catcalled, catcalling, hustling*
chaperone, 33
chauvinistic, 99, 203
child(ren), x, xiii, xiv, 7, 38, 40, 44–46, 59, 64, 70, 73, 75, 77–81, 85
childcare, 75, 163
childless, 70, 72, 74, 79, 85
cisgender, 205
co-construction, 102
construction, 74, 103, 119, 141–142, 189
constructionist, 34
colloquial names, 116
commensality, 196
competent, 4, 111, 116–117, 132,
community(ies), x, 4, 6–7, 12–13, 21, 24–26, 32–34, 40–46, 49, 50, 54, 57, 61, 65–66, 70, 77, 87–91, 117–118, 123, 133, 143, 146, 148–149, 150, 155–163, 165–167, 172, 202, 205
constraint(s), 4, 6, 46, 57, 97–98, 104–105, 127, 192

209

cosmetic use, 120
cross-cultural, 3, 28, 35, 54, 65–66
cross-disciplinary, 3, 93
cultural biases, 48
cultural duality, 128

deconstruction, 103, 106
demeaning, 115, 174
denigrates/denigrating/denigration, 4, 114–115, 122
derogatory [speech], 115–116
developing countries, 24, 54, *see also lesser-developed regions, third world*
disability, 85
disembodied, 85, 89, 152
domestic [duties/responsibilities], x, 72, 75, 129–130, 159
domesticity, 3
dominance, 29, 31, 35, 54, 58, 64
drift, 69, 79–81
drinking [alcohol], 16, 30, 62, 171, 173–174, 176–178, 180–183, 203

embodied, xiii, 5, 24, 85–86, 88–89, 91, 131, 152, 195, 197–198, 204–205
emotion(s), ix, xi, 5, 35, 122, 149, 200–201, 206
emotional, x, 7–8, 35, 50, 85, 88, 90–91, 104–105, 111, 122, 144, 171, 175, 186, 187–189, 204–205, 207
emotionally, 32, 48, 152
empower(ment), 39, 98–99, 106–108, 158, 185
entangled, 6, 92
entanglement(s), xiii, 85, 89, 142, 152, 186, 197, 204–206, *see also embodied entanglements*
epistemological(ly), 127, 134–136, *see also epistemology*
epistemology, 134, 136, *see also epistemological*
equality, x, 2, 3, 98, 181
erotic, 173, 176, 179
ethics, ix, 6, 33, 90, 132, 142, 200
ethical, 92–93, 103, 107, 127, 132, 183
ethnicity(ies), xi, 5, 38, 113–114, 118, 205–206
ethnographer(s), 2, 7, 43, 46, 86, 90, 117, 143–147, 150
ethnographic, 2, 39, 56, 70, 85, 88–91, 93, 97, 142–143, 150, 158, 176

ethnography(ies), 3, 65, 89, 177, 200
Eurocentric, 206
expatriate(s), 54, 58–59, 62–66

familial status, 48
family(ies), x, 4, 13, 34, 40–41, 44, 47–48, 54–57, 59, 78, 82, 85–90, 92–93, 97, 127–131, 134, 146, 148–149, 151, 155, 157–158, 166, 168, 175, 181, 186–198, 200, 205
feeding [breast], 78, 146, 159
female gender, 2, 4, 69, 105, 107, 181
femaleness, 50
feminine, 4, 5, 72, 106–107, 119, 121, 176
femininity(ies), ix, x, 2, 7, 39, 44–46, 48, 50–51, 54, 70, 88–89, 91, 93, 114, 118–119, 175, 176, 181, 201, 206, 207
feminist(s), xiii, 2, 3, 31, 39, 54, 70, 85, 92–93, 97, 104–105, 123, 129, 143–144, 171, 176–177, 189, 203
field mother, 79, *see also mother-researcher*
first world, 55
flattery, 115
flirtation, 14, 21
flirtatious, 56, 115
flirted, 30, 56
flirting, 28
foreigner(s), 26, 32, 58, 62, 71, 88
fragile, 106, 121
funding, 21, 42, 142, 144, 204

gaining access, 81, 132–133, 136, 186, 189–191, 202
gatekeepers, 186
gender bias(ed)(es), 2–7, 70, 71, 79, 86, 89, 93, 114–116, 120–123, 203
gender inequity, 86, 113–114, 122
gender issue(s), 2–5, 70, 79, 99–100, 105, 107, 111, 123
gender role(s), xiii, 2, 4–5, 54–55, 57, 59, 65, 176, 181–182
gender-neutral, 119, 182, 202
gendered gaze, 183
gendered interaction(s), 14, 66
genderless, 46
girl(s), 3, 58, 64, 73, 111, 115–117, 160, 178–180

grief, 150
gringa/o(s), 57, 61 *see also white*
guilt(y), 73, 88, 90, 167, 202

harassment, x, xi, 6, 24, 26–35, 114–115, 122, 176, 201–204, 206–207
health concerns, 155, *see also medical*
heckling, 115, *see also catcalled, catcalling, catcalls, hustling*
hedonism, 181
hedonistic, 62
hegemonic masculinity, 115–117, 171, 179, 181
hegemonic patriarchal structures, 144
heteronormative
heteronormativity
heterosexism, 116
heterosexual, 39, 175, 205
hierarchy, 30, 31, 65, 115
hierarchical, 134
hitchhiking, 19, 21, 21
holiday(s), 129–131, 187, 189, 193, 197
hostile, 181
hostility, 113
humorous, 116
humour, 115, 160, 166
husband(s), 7, 39–40, 43, 46–47, 64, 69, 72–76, 78–80, 82, 128, 158–159, 166, 172, 181–183, 201, 204–206
hustled, 121, *see also hustling*
hustling, 115, 120, *see also hustled*
hypersexual(ised), 174, 175

incompetent, 117
indigenous, 30, 55, 141, 148, 151, 155
inequality(ies), x, 4, 55, 66, 120, 129, 155, 197, *see also* equality
insider(s), 65, 66, 127, 191, 201–203
intersectional(ity), 175, 181
isolation, 118, 156, 205

language skills, 20
less competent, 111, 116–117
less of a threat, 166, *see also less threatening, non-threat*
less threatening, 115, 117
lesser-developed regions, 78, 203, *see also developing countries, third world*
LGBTQ (lesbian, gay, bisexual, transgender, queer), 179, 205

liminal construct, 4
lineages, 141–143, 146
localism, 54, 60, 62–63
logistics, 44, 61, 73, 76, 79, 81, 142
lone male, 7, 143–147, 152, 194

machismo, xi, 28–30, 55–56, 58–60
male-dominated, ix, 35, 54, 59, 64–65, 106, 114–115, 119–122, 179, 204
maleness, 20
manhood, 141, 143, 152, 180
marginalisation, 111
marital status, 2, 5, 40, 44–45, 48, 74, 79
masculine 2, 4, 64, 70, 72, 82, 111, 119, 123, 141, 143, 146, 176–177, 189, 200, 204, *see also masculinist, masculinity*
masculinist 194, *see also masculine, masculinity*
masculinity, 51, 58, 60, 74–75, 79, 114–117, 122, 143, 171, 175–176, 179–181, *see also* masculine, masculinist, 194
matron, 121
minority(ies), 104, 122, 179
miscommunication, 156
mistrust, 155, 156, 162
medical (concerns), 75–77, 81, *see also health concerns*
mother-researcher, 127, 131, 133–136, 204, *see also field mother*
motherhood, x, 7, 69–70, 74, 79–82, 86, 88, 92, 127–136, 143, 166, 186, 188–189, 197, 201–202
multidisciplinary, 7, 134, 141

name-calling, 115–116, *see also heckling, catcalling, catcalled, catcalls*
neutrality, 39, 206
non-binary, x, 2
non-threat(ing), 39, 45, 49, 181, 191, 202 *see also less-threatening, non-threat*
normality, 163
nursing, 141, 145–147, 152, *see also breastfeeding, feeding*

objectification, 24, 34, 40, 46, 66, 79, 80, 121, 178
objectified, 30, 33, 176, 203

objection(s), 28, 81
objectivity, 39, 201, 205
omission, 182
oppression, 64, 200
otherness, 156
outsider, 47, 49, 65–66, 127, 156, 166, 201

parent(s), 40, 132–133, 135, 142, 145, 157, 159, 161, 164, 167–168, 188, 192
parental 132, 135
parenthood, 74, 167, 197
parenting, 70, 75, 78–79, 82, 128, 132, 161, 167
participatory approach, 156, 166
paternal squeeze, 115, *see also body language*
physical contact, 115, *see also harassment*
positionality(ies), ix, 39–40, 42, 45, 48, 50, 51, 143, 152, 171
positivist(ic), 34, 136, 188
postfeminist, 27, 142
postmodern, 2, 85, 142
power, 29, 30, 39, 45, 66, 88, 92, 115, 117, 120–121, 133–134, 144, 155–156, 188–189, 206, *see also powerful*
powerful, 21, 93, 98, 141, 147
powerless, 149
pragmatic, 159
pragmatism, 81
precautionary, 13–14, 16, 20, 204
pregnancy, 69–70, 73–76, 80–81, 157–158
pregnant, 6, 73–74, 141, 144–145, 157–158, 160
prejudice(s), 6, 98, 104–106, 114, 116, 120, 183
privilege(d), 20, 58, 65–66, 150, 152, 162, 167, 202
professional(ly), 19, 40, 43–44, 57, 69, 86, 92, 105, 114, 118–121, 142, 179, 181, 186, 187
professionalism, 118, 120–121, 123, 203
reciprocity, 73, 81
reflexive (engagement), 6, 65, 70, 86, 92–93, 127, 131, 135, 157, 197, 206
reflexivity, 2, 39, 93, 128, 134, 172, 201, 206
remote(ness)(ly), 7, 60, 70, 78, 118, 158, 163, 203, *see also accessibility*

resistance, 97–98, 101, 105–106, 130, 147
risk-taking, 176, 177, 203
risky, 173, 176, 177, 183, 204

safety, xi-xiii, 6, 11, 13–14, 16, 20–21, 33, 35, 71, 75–78, 81, 98, 114, 121, 164, 179, 182–183, 191, 193, 196, 201, 203–206
self-analysis, 105
self-confidence, 116
self-conscious(ness), 141, 144, 145
self-doubt, 59, 64
self-examine, 131
self-perception, 182
self-reflection(s), 6, 114
self-reflective, ix, 2, 5–6
self-reflectivity, 171
self-worth, 97
sex (copulation), 29, 30, 171, 173, 174, 179, 182,
see also sexual
sex(es)(ed), xi, 3–4, 6, 48, 97, 117, 175
sexism, x, 32, 55, 65, 74, 79, 104, 120–121, 123, 176, 201, 203–207
sexist, 55, 65–66, 74, 106, 115–117, 176, 202
sex(ual) object(s), 31, 40, 115, 179
sexual (advances, desire, power), 29, 115, 121
sexualisation, 46
sexually, 30, 33, 56–57, 115, 182
sexy, 46–47, 177, 179, 188, 202
situatedness, 171, 175
social connection, 188, 197
solo, 85–86, 99, 203
stay-at-home mum, 87
stereotype(d)(s), 7, 51, 55–57, 60, 66, 111, 115, 122–123, 176, 178–179, 183, 189, 200
student(s) ix, xi, xiv, 11, 13, 15, 17, 18, 20–21, 141–142, 144, 152, 159, 187
subjectivities, xiii, 2, 6, 93, 147, 152, 186, 198, 201
subordination, 116

third world, 55, *see also lesser-developed, developing countries*
threat(s), 15, 121, 123, 134, 166, 204
threatened, 55, 66

threatening, 33, 203
tourist area, 24, 26
tourist destination, 32, 86, 87
touristic, 143, 171, 173, 174, 179
touristified, 174
transdiciplinary, 103
transformative, 141, 183, 197
transnational community, *see also* expatriate, 61, 65
trust(worthy), 7, 11, 21, 66, 101, 104, 121, 133, 134, 158, 166, 175, 191, 191, 202
trusted, 12, 78, 168, 183, 204
unprofessional, 120
unsexed, 3
untrustworthy, 106
verbal (attacks or confrontation), 15–16, 26, 58
victimhood, 176
vulnerability, 16, 19, 41, 43, 91, 97–99, 106, 107
weakness, x, 34
well-being, 50, 103, 129, 188, 201, 205
Western [culture or society], 4, 27, 30, 115, 128, 143, 145, 183, 203, *see also first world*
white [skin colour], 29–30, 38, 57, 73, 128, 143, 160, 163, 175
whiteness, 14, 18, 20

For Product Safety Concerns and Information please contact our EU Authorised Representative:

Easy Access System Europe

Mustamäe tee 50

10621 Tallinn

Estonia

gpsr.requests@easproject.com

www.ingramcontent.com/pod-product-compliance
Ingram Content Group UK Ltd.
Pitfield, Milton Keynes, MK11 3LW, UK
UKHW021823220426
5349IPUK00003B/53